Godwin and the Book

Edinburgh Critical Studies in Romanticism
Series Editors: Ian Duncan and Penny Fielding

Available Titles
A Feminine Enlightenment: British Women Writers and the Philosophy of Progress, 1759–1820
JoEllen DeLucia
Reinventing Liberty: Nation, Commerce and the Historical Novel from Walpole to Scott
Fiona Price
The Politics of Romanticism: The Social Contract and Literature
Zoe Beenstock
Radical Romantics: Prophets, Pirates, and the Space Beyond Nation
Talissa J. Ford
Literature and Medicine in the Nineteenth-Century Periodical Press: Blackwood's Edinburgh Magazine, 1817–1858
Megan Coyer
Discovering the Footsteps of Time: Geological Travel Writing in Scotland, 1700–1820
Tom Furniss
The Dissolution of Character in Late Romanticism
Jonas Cope
Commemorating Peterloo: Violence, Resilience, and Claim-making during the Romantic Era
Michael Demson and Regina Hewitt
Dialectics of Improvement: Scottish Romanticism, 1786–1831
Gerard Lee McKeever
Literary Manuscript Culture in Romantic Britain
Michelle Levy
Scottish Romanticism and Collective Memory in the British Atlantic
Kenneth McNeil
Romantic Periodicals in the Twenty-First Century: Eleven Case Studies from Blackwood's Edinburgh Magazine
Nicholas Mason and Tom Mole
Godwin and the Book: Imagining Media, 1783–1836
J. Louise McCray

Forthcoming Titles
Romantic Environmental Sensibility: Nature, Class and Empire
Ve-Yin Tee
Romantic Pasts: History, Fiction and Feeling in Britain and Ireland, 1790–1850
Porscha Fermanis
Romantic Networks in Europe: Transnational Encounters, 1786–1850
Carmen Casaliggi
Thomas De Quincey, Dark Interpreter: Romanticism in Translation
Brecht de Groote
Romanticism and Consciousness
Richard Sha and Joel Faflak
Death, Blackwood's Edinburgh Magazine and Authoring Romantic Scotland
Sarah Sharp

Visit our website at: www.edinburghuniversitypress.com/series/ECSR

Godwin and the Book

Imagining Media, 1783–1836

J. Louise McCray

EDINBURGH
University Press

Edinburgh University Press is one of the leading university presses in the UK. We publish academic books and journals in our selected subject areas across the humanities and social sciences, combining cutting-edge scholarship with high editorial and production values to produce academic works of lasting importance. For more information visit our website: edinburghuniversitypress.com

© J. Louise McCray, 2021, 2023

Edinburgh University Press Ltd
The Tun – Holyrood Road, 12(2f) Jackson's Entry, Edinburgh EH8 8PJ

First published in hardback by Edinburgh University Press 2021

Typeset in 11/14 Adobe Sabon by
IDSUK (DataConnection) Ltd

A CIP record for this book is available from the British Library

ISBN 978 1 4744 7576 1 (hardback)
ISBN9781474475778(paperback)
ISBN 978 1 4744 7578 5 (webready PDF)
ISBN 978 1 4744 7579 2 (epub)

The right of J. Louise McCray to be identified as the author of this work has been asserted in accordance with the Copyright, Designs and Patents Act 1988, and the Copyright and Related Rights Regulations 2003 (SI No. 2498).

Contents

Acknowledgements	vi
Abbreviations	vii
Introduction	1
1. The Matter of the Reader: Materialism and Private Judgement	25
2. The Ethics of Novel-Reading: Fiction and Moral Law	58
3. The Discipline of Reading: 'Enquiry' and Religious Dissent	84
4. Truth and Social Media: Books and Intellectual Regulation	119
5. Books, Bodies and Monuments: Print and Perfectibility	148
Bibliography	182
Index	199

Acknowledgements

Without Penny Fielding's encouragement and counsel, this book would not have been written. Many thanks are due to Penny and to the supportive Department of English Literature at the University of Edinburgh. For thoughtful reading, feedback and guidance on specific points I am indebted to Tom Mole, Pamela Clemit, Timothy Milnes, Christopher Tilmouth, Isabel Rivers, Charles Rzepka, Philip Connell, Robert Irvine, Charlotte Saul, Jon W. Thompson, Hetty Saunders, Tess Goodman and Michael Adams. The team at Edinburgh University Press have been highly professional and diligent throughout the process of editing and producing this book: thank you.

I am grateful for the support of the Arts and Humanities Research Council, which provided the funding that enabled this book to be researched. Thanks are also due to the staff at the Bodleian Library in Oxford, who granted me access to the Abinger archive and offered guidance as I explored Godwin's manuscripts.

Elements of Chapter 2 originally appeared in *Studies in Romanticism* 59.2 (2020): 209–30. Elements of Chapter 4 originally appeared in *Journal of the History of Ideas* 81.1 (2020): 67–84. I am grateful to the Johns Hopkins University Press and University of Pennsylvania Press for permission to reproduce those materials here.

Above all, I am thankful for the intellectual companionship and loving support of my husband, Alden C. McCray.

Abbreviations

CNM   *Collected Novels and Memoirs of William Godwin*, ed. Mark Philp, Pamela Clemit and Maurice Hindle, 8 vols (London: Pickering & Chatto, 1992)

DWG   *The Diary of William Godwin*, ed. Victoria Myers, David O'Shaughnessy and Mark Philp (Oxford: Oxford Digital Library, 2010) <http://godwindiary.bodleian.ox.ac.uk> (last accessed 15 October 2020)

LWG   *The Letters of William Godwin*, ed. Pamela Clemit, 2 vols (Oxford: Oxford University Press, 2011–15)

PPW   *Political and Philosophical Writings of William Godwin*, ed. Mark Philp, Pamela Clemit and Martin Fitzpatrick, 7 vols (London: Pickering & Chatto, 1993)

Introduction

> Books are the depository of every thing that is most honourable to man. Literature, taken in all its bearings, forms the grand line of demarcation between the human and the animal kingdoms. He that loves reading, has every thing within his reach. He has but to desire; and he may possess himself of every species of wisdom to judge, and power to perform.[1]

Book-reading has a powerful and peculiar presence in the writings of William Godwin, the notorious British philosopher, novelist and social critic. As the extract above from *The Enquirer* (1797) shows, he invested it with the authority to categorise living things. Its practice operates as a 'grand line of demarcation' not only between 'the human and the animal kingdoms' but also between different human persons: 'He that loves reading' is implicitly set against he that does not, endowed with superiority of mind ('wisdom to judge') and body ('power to perform'). The contrast is explicit in the essay from which these comments are taken and functions as a way of interrogating the forces that condition human life. As he distinguishes the 'man of talent' from the 'dull man' Godwin outlines multiple ways in which temperament, education and social environment may threaten one's potential to assume the former's bookish mode of being. The activity of book-reading becomes a locus of both anxiety and hope for Godwin, something that troubles his aspirations for human life as much as it defines them.

Such tensions are not unique to this essay. Godwin repeatedly interrogated, theorised and symbolised both the activity of reading in general and the printed codex as a specific medium, and this preoccupation cuts across the generic variety of his fifty-year corpus. Books are as integral to his discussion of human nature in later works such as *Thoughts on Man* (1831) and *The Genius of Christianity Unveiled* (1836) as they are to his better-known writings of the 1790s. Media-centricity is essential to Godwin's oeuvre. This has been largely neglected by his readers, despite increasing recognition of his seminal position in the history of literature and education. It matters because its importance reaches far beyond the scope of a single author: Godwin hit a cultural nerve. When he wrote about media technology he was tapping into a network of live debates that animated and helped to define British society as the nineteenth century dawned. This book starts from the conviction that we won't fully understand Romantic cultural history unless we confront the way that Godwin – and his interlocutors – imagined media.

The aim of this book is twofold: to present William Godwin in his overlooked capacity as media critic, and to expose through that presentation a network of wider controversies concerning the relationship of media to social change. It focuses on how Godwin figured books with an eye to what this figuration tells us about the place of printed media – and the concept of mediation more generally – in the cultural imagination of Romantic-period Britain. Godwin wrote increasingly about the material properties of printed books as his career progressed, and 'the book' became a conceptual tool by which he expressed and defended his progressivist convictions about epistemology and sociopolitical organisation (hence the abstraction in my title). This strategy underpinned his poetics of the novel: he evaluated and designed fiction with regard to the mediatory potential of the printed codex as he understood it. Most startling, perhaps, is that Godwin came to view books themselves as essential to the human mind's existence, objects that enabled its development and structured its future.

Godwin wrote at a time during which media such as print and speech played important roles in competing narratives about the trajectory of the British nation. His work thus provides a potent example of how communications technologies were recruited in order to encourage belief in particular stories about the nature and ends of human life. Examining this phenomenon is a gateway to a unique period of cultural history, which has long been considered 'a most exceptional and grandiose phase for the arts as a theatre for public discussion and intellectual war'.[2] It also draws our attention to aspects of that culture which still resonate today. Our digital age has fostered an unprecedented number of research projects, university courses and textbooks centred upon communications technology. Godwin's bookish vision can help to expose and contextualise the ways in which writers and other cultural influencers continue to use media history to make arguments about human societies and where they are headed.

Mediation and Romantic-Period Literature

Godwin pursued his career as a writer during a time in which books were objects of special interest within literary culture. Several recent studies identify 'a proliferation of representations of the book in visual and linguistic media' in the British Romantic period; its literary culture was, as Ina Ferris puts it, 'forged in tandem with an intensified response to the physical book'.[3] This interest in writing about communications technology was certainly not new in itself. Readers of earlier eighteenth-century literature, for example, will call to mind works by Defoe, Swift and Pope that emphasise, satirise and mythologise the printed media of their day in order to make arguments about their historical moment. Christina Lupton has shown that mid-eighteenth-century texts were particularly self-conscious about the material conditions of mediation and used them to make claims about literary authority and purpose; Paula McDowell argues that the concept of oral culture was 'invented' in eighteenth-century writing as a response to the expansion of the print industry and the spectre of mass literacy.[4] A range of responses to media technology and its uses thus laid the imaginative foundations upon which writers of the Romantic period built. As the eighteenth century drew to a close, however, 'a new awareness of the "presence" of books and printed matter [...] took increasing hold in the culture'.[5] Intensified media consciousness marked out published works across the generic spectrum, including novels, essays, poems and political treatises.

The distinctive nature of the Romantic period's literary investment in print media could be – and has been – described and explained in relation to several dimensions of its history and culture. Perhaps the most obvious of these is its book trade: new copyright laws in the later eighteenth century enabled cheap reprints of older works and encouraged the production of new collections and anthologies; libraries proliferated and diversified, facilitating widespread access to reading matter throughout the country and across social strata; new technologies developed in the early nineteenth century, including mechanised paper manufacture, stereotyping and the steam-powered press, which would revolutionise book production. During this period the term *book* could signify a variety of written and printed forms, not necessarily bound, ranging from ephemeral works to weighty encyclopaedias. The annual number of printed titles in Britain increased dramatically, as did the overall number of readers (although literacy rates were relatively low and the average price of new books remained high until at least the 1840s).[6] Although prior to the era of 'mass print' proper, there was certainly a strong perception that printed matter was dominating all aspects of society. Clifford Siskin and William Warner have identified the Romantic period with a new sense that society was becoming 'saturated' with print, in distinction from the tropes of 'circulation' and 'increase' that characterised earlier eighteenth-century writing.[7] As writer and critic Maria Jane Jewsbury exclaimed in 1825, 'Surely no one will deny the propriety of distinguishing the present age as an age of books! of book making! book reading! book reviewing! and book forgetting!'[8] New cultural images of 'bookish' figures gained currency in this context, both positive and negative, including the notorious bibliomaniac of the Regency period.[9] The activity of reading – long a controversial topic – continued to inflect and intensify debates about morality, health, politics, social class and gender roles (among other things), while assumptions about good reading practice underwrote authorial strategies and aspirations.[10]

It wasn't only print media that sparked such interest and controversy. Attention to print and its social effects went hand in hand with attention to orality – including elocution, conversation, popular song and public speaking – and especially its relation to literacy as a mode of communication: did they compete with each other, supplement each other, modify each other? Ideas about sound, song, speech and their relations to manuscript and typographic culture have informed a number of important studies of Romantic-period literature, including histories of the novel, lyric poetry and political writing.[11] Godwin was himself a persistent theorist of relations between literate and oral modes of transmission, writing about them from the early 1790s until the end of his life in the 1830s.

One consistent structural element of this cultural interest in media form, however – and one that Godwin's writing helps us to expose – is attention to the more fundamental concept of mediation. This has been explored by scholars including Kevis Goodman and John Guillroy, whose work underscores that the common equation of 'media' and 'technology' (such as printed books) is reductive – *mediation* names an ancient and more basic concern with the means of perception or apprehension across space and time. Mediation as such had become particularly prominent in writings from the late seventeenth century onwards, as developments in the natural sciences and epistemology brought it to the fore: these included new instruments of scientific perception (such as the microscope), new linguistic studies (including universal language theory), and new accounts of knowledge in relation to tradition, rationality and empirical evidence. In Goodman's account the concept of mediation became an unprecedented means of anxiety and disturbance as the eighteenth century progressed, in part because it was bound up with new ways of perceiving time and new means of spatial connectivity and expansion. This concern manifested itself variously, including in the development of literary form and attitudes towards reading.[12]

Godwin should be understood as a media critic in this capacious sense, for his writing about book-reading was bound up with the various – and sometimes conflicting – models of mediation entailed by salient accounts of mind, body and history. In particular, Godwin represented a set of inherited tensions surrounding the concept of mediation in the philosophy, theology and social cultures of religious dissent, which became particularly explicit in dissenting-educated authors of the Romantic period. This book's chapter sequence reflects this concern: Chapter 1 explores relations between mind, body and world, focusing on how debates about materialism shaped Godwin's account of the genesis of independent thought or 'private judgement' through reading; the next two chapters discuss Godwin's theory of literary form and practical reading advice in light of this view of the mind and its mediatory qualities; the final two chapters examine Godwin's writings about books as mediatory objects, especially in relation to the competing ideas about 'truth' and its apprehension which energised them. These writings unearth some of the complex issues of mediation that underlay seemingly straightforward debates about the social implications of books and book-reading.

Godwin's work also exposes the narrative shape of these interrelated interests in mediation and media technology that characterised the Romantic period. It exemplifies the way in which media forms – especially print and speech – were employed to tell stories and make claims about human nature and its history. Godwin lived in the heyday of conjectural stadial histories, many of which made communications technologies fundamental to the development, and often 'improvement', of societies across the globe.[13] It was the age of millenarianism, which shaped the way that futurity was imagined and anticipated in a variety of cultural forms, both overtly religious and otherwise.[14] It was the age that spawned catastrophising narratives by cultural critics and political economists such as Robert Thomas Malthus and Thomas Carlyle, whose work often co-opted mass print production into stories of national decline. Negative images of the printing press as a cipher of degeneracy (Carlyle's 'huge subterranean, puffing bellows') sat uneasily alongside utopian images of the printing press as harbinger of political and social emancipation (Godwin's 'glorious instrument for advancing the march of human improvement') – the latter most notorious in writings of the 1790s but which continued well on into the nineteenth century.[15] Romantic-period culture was thus driven by competing and often contradictory narratives about print media and social history. Adrian Johns has emphasised that modern conceptions of 'print culture' had to be made; in Godwin's lifetime this process occurred in a climate of new temporal consciousness, in which the future was obsessively narrated, predicted, invoked and anticipated.[16]

Godwin, then, was representative of a distinctly Romantic-period imaginative investment in media form and deserves a more prominent place in accounts of its operation in British culture. His writing enables us to excavate the conversations of a society for which media forms were integral to stories about the purpose and future of human life – writing about print technology became, among other things, a way to intervene in debates about the 'spirit of the age'. Drawing from a tradition of religious and intellectual dissent, Godwin came to imagine 'the book' as a remedy that regulated the pace of mediation in a world thrown off tempo and ensured its continuation in the face of death; for him, it was the form most successful at negotiating the apprehension of truth across space and time.

This study's attention to the cultural figuration of books and reading is indebted to a growing body of scholarship that recognises symbiotic relations between materially oriented media histories (such as those that document aspects of book production, distribution and use) and their artistic, literary and intellectual contexts. These works challenge a common assumption that representations of books and reading are inferior to – or even obfuscatory of – their 'actual' history, underscoring the real power of the figurative.[17] Andrew Piper, for example, sets out to show in a study of Romantic writing that 'Literature makes books as much as books make literature.' The self-reflexive angle of this critical approach sometimes courts short-sightedness, however; media consciousness within literature can illuminate much more than simply the history of media culture.[18] The figuration of books is an arresting subject for readers of Godwin's work precisely because he exploited the book's metonymic potential – its ability to signify and distil the diverse areas of social, historical and political life that he believed were ripe for debate. His writing shows that book-reading, as something discussed, conceptualised and symbolised in the literature of Romantic-period Britain, participated in crucial debates about knowledge and human nature. It was not simply a reflection of these debates in the sense of bearing witness to them as secondary receptacles, but was integral to them. Indeed, Godwin developed the conviction that books were an essential part of the human mind itself, objects that induced – or had the potential to induce – fundamental changes in the way individuals and (by extension) societies conceived of themselves.

Godwin and the Book thus draws from the methodologies of historicist literary critics and intellectual historians in order to explore what Godwin's work reveals about the cultural significance of book-reading in Romantic-period Britain. It responds in part to Jonathan Israel's call for 'controversialist' intellectual history, a 'reformed intellectual history presiding over a two-way traffic, or dialectic of ideas and social reality, [. . .] focusing less on finished theories [. . .] than on "thinking" and debates'.[19] Godwin particularly lends himself to such a controversialist approach because his life and work were bound up overtly in the unresolved arguments of his day. His writing dramatically foregrounds the competing narratives of social progress and corruption that marked out this period, showing that they were rooted in urgent and practical debates such as those about population growth, industrialisation and social unrest. In short, Godwin wrote about books and reading in order to navigate the intellectual and social turbulence of his time. Book-reading became a locus through which he formulated, expressed and defended his convictions about knowledge, ethics and history. When we explore the media consciousness of his work, we uncover his place within a nexus of debates about what gives meaning and value to human existence.

Godwin, Media and Perfectibility

William Godwin began his literary career in London in the early 1780s, following several unsuccessful attempts to work as a dissenting minister. Given the breadth and variety of his output he is best approached as a 'man of letters' rather than simply a novelist or a philosopher. As the unimpressed *Critical Review* put it in 1804:

> The literary raiment of Mr. Godwin is variegated. He wears a grotesque suit, chequered with patches, laboriously selected from political, moral, and philosophical romances, dramas, novels, and 'light memorials of the frail and fair.' Distinguished by this panoply, his characteristic energy enlivens the masquerade of modern learning.[20]

Cynicism aside, this reviewer is not alone in identifying a 'characteristic energy' behind Godwin's diverse literary output. Throughout fluctuating personal circumstances and forays across the generic landscape, Godwin explored and defended several foundational convictions across nearly fifty years of literary work. Foremost among these was his belief that human minds were innately perfectible and would ultimately – and necessarily – undergo a process of improvement as history ran its course. This belief was bound up with a particular concept of mediation, and entailed complex and sometimes unstable commitments concerning the nature and acquirement of knowledge, the composition of the human mind, social organisation, and political authority.[21]

Perhaps the most formative influence upon Godwin's career was his upbringing in the cultural environment of religious dissent. His father and grandfather were dissenting ministers, he was educated at Hoxton dissenting academy, and when he moved to London in the 1780s he became involved in a predominantly dissenting literary network. Godwin inherited a cluster of basic commitments from the theology, philosophy and social practices of so-called rational dissenters, and these remained foundational to his work: most prominently, commitments to 'private judgement' and to 'frank' public discussion, which were understood within a framework of necessity and perfectibility.[22] *An Enquiry Concerning Political Justice* (1793) gave these principles their most systematic and well-known expression, but evidence suggests that they preceded the treatise. Godwin himself, in an attempt to chart the development of his philosophical principles before the composition of *Political Justice*, dated his commitments to the necessity and perfectibility of human lives, the centrality of intellect to ethics, and the immutability of truth (among other things) to the 1770s and 80s.[23] Careful attention to Godwin's subsequent work reveals that these commitments continued well beyond the 1790s. They undergirded his political pamphlets and his essays; his educational writings and books for children; his biographies; his novels; his plays; his writings on religion.

To argue for such continuity is not to deny that Godwin's writing developed or that some of his views changed. As his earliest biographer William Hazlitt noted with approval, 'he changes his opinions, and changes them for the better'. In fact, as Godwin himself attested, his high view of individual judgement meant that he considered it a moral duty to keep one's opinions open to revision.[24] Most famously he adapted his work to accommodate the shifting concerns and terminology of philosophical debate in the 1790s, becoming more alert to the power of feeling and sentiment in the formation of judgement. These changes inflected his work of the later 1790s with a more sceptical tone, including revised editions of *Political Justice*.[25] Yet as his essay 'Of Scepticism' (1797) shows, he saw such caution (what he termed 'rational scepticism') to be compatible with his basic belief in the reality and accessibility of truth, rather than a threat to it: '[t]he sceptic makes bare his own bosom to receive the beams of truth'.[26] The apprehension of truth through private judgement was still the cornerstone of his ethical and social theory, and Godwin was at pains to communicate this throughout the 1790s. '[T]he spirit and great outlines of [my] work [. . .] remain untouched', he insisted; the alterations made were 'not of a fundamental nature'.[27]

Godwin adapted and developed many other ideas through his literary career, a process which included the introduction of apparent qualifications to his confidence in the omnipotence of educational environment. Yet not even this cautionary note obscured his overarching conviction that all human persons had the innate potential to develop true judgement – that is, his belief in intellectual perfectibility. This is nowhere more evident than in Godwin's final words to his 1831 essay collection *Thoughts on Man*, which echo those of his 1801 pamphlet 'Reply to the attacks of Dr. Parr'. Both present a view of perfected human nature which is as unashamedly idealistic as that of the much-ridiculed first edition of *Political Justice*: 'human understanding and human virtue will hereafter accomplish such things as the heart of man has never yet been daring enough to conceive'.[28]

Above all else, Godwin's work is characterised by an interest in the life of the mind. His fictions, essays and histories alike are fuelled by a sense that the intellectual conditions of national life are the most important things to be investigated, critiqued and challenged. Whether discussing political structures, childhood education or literary form, one basic question remains the same: how active – or how alive – is the mind in this situation? To put it another way, what possibilities for the mind does this mode of education, this political structure or this literary form allow? When it came to history, the story of an individual mind at a certain point in time could be understood as a direct window into the story of his or her nation, because it demonstrated the extent to which that nation allowed the mind to flourish. Godwin certainly appreciated the body; at times he even troubled the distinction between body and mind. Yet he consistently described the mind as the thing that made people truly human: 'Be it however where or what it may, [the mind] constitutes the great essence of, and gives value to, our existence.'[29]

This enduring interest in intellectual vitality stemmed from the centrality of private judgement to Godwin's ethical, social and political commitments. Like many eighteenth-century dissenters, he believed that individual judgement was a perfectible faculty – that it had an innate capacity to apprehend truth and that it would improve necessarily given the free and 'frank' dissemination of ideas. 'Man is in a state of perpetual progress', he argued in *Political Justice*. 'If we would arrive at truth, each man must be taught to enquire and think for himself.'[30] This process went hand in hand with social reform, because for Godwin, people necessarily live out their opinions and beliefs: 'to reform a man is to change the sentiments of his mind'.[31] He consistently described private judgement as 'a doctrine [. . .] unspeakably beautiful',[32] the key to a future of increasing intellectual – and thus necessarily social and political – improvement towards a state of perfection.

Godwin was full of caution, however, when it came to discussing the conditions required for such mental development to occur in the present day. He found threats to the vitality of private judgement in political structures, educational environments, social practices – even in the substance and nature of the mind itself. *Political Justice* is perhaps more explicit about threats to private judgement than it is about the potential of private judgement to bring about good. The work explores the many ways in which 'By its very nature political institution has a tendency to suspend the elasticity, and put an end to the advancement of mind.' It considers how religious traditions, social customs and even politically radical organisations pose a similar threat, observing that '*Every* scheme for embodying imperfection must be injurious.'[33] Godwin believed that reformation of the mind would bring about reformation of society, but it often appeared as a chicken-and-egg situation: which came first, and how?

While many critics have noted this tension surrounding Godwin's conception of social reform, it is not always recognised that the problem lay not primarily in his theory of transition from one state to another, but in his theory of mediation.[34] He repeatedly posited truth as an objective entity with independent force; he consistently stated that once apprehended, truth was irresistible to every mind; but the means of its apprehension was the sticking point. How was truth conveyed to the mind, if not through potentially corrupt human channels? Textual and aural media, historical customs, individual cognition – all were vital means of knowledge, yet all aroused suspicion. Godwin's obsession with this mediatory conundrum was informed and enflamed by his materialist leanings, his literary environment, his educational background, and even his understanding of death. It was ultimately the reason why book-reading became such a locus of hope and anxiety in his work.

Godwin's search for the means of intellectual perfectibility should not be understood solely as a response to internal philosophical tensions. He was engaging with debates about the future of the human mind which were neither private nor abstract, even when he articulated himself in such terms. He wrote in a historical moment in which the theory of ideas and their transmission was highly politicised, and this environment deeply affected his arguments in the 1790s and early 1800s. The pamphlet war sparked by Edmund Burke's *Reflections on the Revolution* (1790) and Thomas Paine's *Rights of Man* (1791) testified to the ways in which the intellectual foundations of the British political system, including the proper role and scope of public opinion in its formation, were being intensely debated. *Political Justice* was published weeks after the execution of Louis XVI and days after war with France was announced. The timing was in this respect unfortunate, for Godwin's critique of social institutions was inevitably associated with revolutionary uprising. He was portrayed by the conservative press as dangerous, discreditable and disloyal until the end of his life – and indeed far beyond.[35] This hostile context heightened Godwin's ambivalence concerning the means of intellectual advance, for in propounding his belief in necessary perfectibility he was anxious to stress that the political implications of this process were both real and powerful (providing hope for the future), yet also peaceful and gradualist (providing safety in the present). His 1795 pamphlet 'Considerations on Lord Grenville's and Mr Pitt's Bills' exemplifies this dual inflection. It can be seen in the very title, for in purporting to be written 'by a lover of order' it simultaneously advertises the author's gradualist credentials and establishes the central, unsettling question of the pamphlet: whose order?[36] Godwin's rather conflicted answer is the necessary order of truth.

Godwin's progressivist framework was also prominently attacked by the political economist Thomas Robert Malthus, symbolising how emerging debates about Britain's rapidly growing population were placing cultural narratives of linear social progress under strain.[37] Malthus set out to refute Godwin in his *Essay on the Principle of Population* (first published in 1798) by demonstrating that social improvement had known limits: misery and vice were necessary forces that brought population size and food supply into equilibrium. Godwin responded briefly to Malthus in his 'Reply to the attacks of Dr. Parr' (1801), and then at length in his *Of Population* in 1820. He spent many pages disputing Malthus's statistics, but his most powerful line of argument was that Malthus's focus upon bodily desire led him to misunderstand and underestimate the mind. He contended that logic, philosophy and historical observation justified the conclusion that the human mind was progressive by nature, including its ability to exercise judgement (e.g. in refraining from reproduction), foresight (e.g. in planning ahead for crises) and innovation (e.g. in creating solutions to new problems): 'the progressive power of increase in the numbers of mankind, will never outrun the progressive power of improvement which human intellect is enabled to develop in the means of subsistence'. He was echoing an argument made by his late wife Mary Wollstonecraft, who had proposed in her *Letters Written in Sweden, Norway, and Denmark* (1796) – a work Godwin much admired – that 'The increasing population of the earth must necessarily tend to its improvement, as the means of existence are multiplied by invention.'[38] Godwin was anxious to make this point in part because he was convinced that understanding the progressive process was essential to its smooth trajectory. Humankind, he believed, would advance in mind only insofar as they summoned the courage to conceive of themselves advancing, to imagine its possibility. This key role played by the imagination exposes one important link in Godwin's work between intellectual perfectibility and book-reading. The interrelation of literature, mind and history became a topic of increasing interest to him in the 1820s, as shown by his essays 'Of the Durability of Human Achievements and Productions' and 'Of Imitation and Invention' in *Thoughts on Man*.

It was in this context that Godwin became a narrator of media history. Throughout his career he developed and defended a conviction that print technology was a beneficent force that steered humankind towards their future. When he first published an explicit argument for belief in intellectual progressivism in 1793, he used the global development of speech, writing and reading as his foremost piece of evidence: 'in the invention of printing', he argued, 'is contained the embryo, which in its maturity and vigour is destined to annihilate the slavery of the human race'.[39] He expanded upon this in a political pamphlet of 1795, describing the printing press as 'that great engine for raising men to the dignity of gods, for expanding and impregnating the human understanding, for annihilating, by the most gentle and salubrious methods, all the arts of oppression'.[40] Millennialist eschatology was just one source of inspiration for this construction of printing history; he also built upon dissenting ideals of free communication that reached back at least as far as Milton's *Areopagitica* (1644). Godwin overtly acknowledged a further debt to the Marquis de Condorcet, whose *Sketch for a Historical Picture of the Progress of the Human Mind* (1795) made printing integral to the 'eighth stage' of civilisational history and eulogised the press as a saviour that would 'unmask and dethrone' corrupt authorities, accelerating 'the forward march of the human mind'.[41] In Scotland, Dugald Stewart was publishing versions of a 'conjectural' history in which the invention of printing was 'sufficient to change the whole course of human affairs', and this change was again specifically conceived in terms of intellectual development: 'the means of communication afforded by the press, have, in the course of two centuries, accelerated the progress of the human mind, far beyond what the most sanguine hopes of our predecessors could have imagined'.[42]

Godwin continued to draw from these accounts as he defended his belief in perfectibility against its critics in the nineteenth century. In 1801 he refuted the idea that 'vice and misery, as my antagonists so earnestly maintain, [are] entailed on us for ever', by describing the power of literary works to prefigure and elicit the highest capacities of human nature.[43] In 1831 he described the printing press as 'that glorious instrument for advancing the march of human improvement'.[44] Godwin employed the narrative until the very end of his life in 1836: as he anticipated the diminishing hold of Christian religion over the life of the mind, he noted that 'Writing and reading are becoming almost universal. [. . .] Natural knowledge has made a perpetual progress. Arts of every kind have been eternally improving.'[45] He told a familiar story about the printing press as an agent of change, as these quotations make clear. His account had a dark side, however, which has been often overlooked. Godwin's characteristic ambivalence about the practical nature and means of intellectual advance cast a shadow over his hymns to print, rendering them complex and arguably even more interesting through the ensuing tension.

Many more personal circumstances, of course, gave Godwin reason and opportunity to reflect upon his media environment. As he was beginning to seek his living by the pen he produced *The Herald of Literature* (1784), a convincing spoof of the contemporary reviewing scene that indicates his familiarity with the social and material conditions of literary craft from an early date. He experienced all the highs and lows of literary fame, becoming a celebrity almost overnight with the renown of *Political Justice* and *Caleb Williams* and experiencing a fall from social grace almost as sudden following his *Memoirs* of Mary Wollstonecraft in 1798, which was exacerbated by his stubborn adherence to radical views at a time when others were changing camp. He increasingly reflected upon his life in terms of his books, often self-identifying with their public reception ('I may be a martyr of this work' he wrote of *Political Justice* in 1824).[46] He also clashed with his publishers over the economic constraints of book production: his letters show him disputing the material form his works would take, including 'that space between the paragraphs which distinguishes all elegantly printed books'.[47] In 1805 he started a publishing imprint and bookshop with his second wife Mary Jane Clairmont, which proved a lengthy and complex commercial failure. The Godwins were forced to declare bankruptcy in 1825 – a disastrous time for the British book trade more generally following a national banking crisis – and were dogged by poverty for the rest of their lives.[48] Godwin's volatile experience of the book trade once again prompted him to reflect upon the media environment in which he was emotionally and financially invested, including the disparity, in his experience, between literary labour and the commercial world of print. As his essay 'Of the Length of the Life of Man' (1822) makes clear, he continued to place his hope in the future of his books, which he believed would continue speaking long after he had become 'a clod in the valley'.[49]

The following chapters examine in detail William Godwin's life-long role as media critic, and in doing so they expose some of the Romantic period's key controversies concerning the relationship between print media and the mind. Readers interested in Godwin's ideas and career as a whole will find that this book builds a cumulative argument that repays being read in its entirety. Those more concerned with particular debates in which Godwin participated may wish to turn directly to the individual chapters that address them: Chapter 1 for philosophy of mind, epistemology and the concept of private judgement; Chapter 2 for the novel as a literary form and its relation to law and ethics; Chapter 3 for pedagogy, reading advice and dissenting academies; Chapter 4 for comparative evaluations of media forms, temporality and the concept of truth; Chapter 5 for 'the book' as a material object and an ideal, especially in relation to death and the afterlife.

Chapter 1 uses Godwin's representations of reading in *Political Justice* (1793), *Caleb Williams* (1794) and *Mandeville* (1817) to uncover late eighteenth-century debates about the relationship between matter and thought. Like many with a background in religious dissent,

Godwin believed that only independent thinking or 'private judgement' could give rise to beneficial social reform, and he considered reading a vital means of achieving this independence. Yet in his fiction and philosophy he increasingly described the reading mind in material terms, apparently reducing thought to matter's mechanical realm. He wasn't alone in doing so, as evidenced by the writings of many in the so-called Jacobin circle – most prominently Mary Hays's *Memoirs of Emma Courtney* (1796). Godwin drew from an ambivalent or 'double' reading of mind that was integral to philosophical and physiological writing in the eighteenth century, including works by John Locke, David Hume and Joseph Priestley. By exploiting the uncertain line between literal and metaphoric language in these texts, Godwin and his contemporaries could emphasise both the formative power of corrupt social environments and the ability of individuals to escape their confines and achieve intellectual agency. Godwin thus represents a literary culture that was attuned to the ways in which 'the matter of the reader' could be transformed through fiction from an intellectual problem into a space for imagining social possibility.

Godwin remained a champion of prose fiction to the end of his life. Chapter 2 attends to his writings of the 1830s in order to investigate his long-standing attempt to equate the value of the novel form with its potential to instigate ethical reform. Prefaces to *Cloudesley* (1830) and the 1832 *Fleetwood* theorise prose fiction as a special medium of moral knowledge; *Deloraine* (1833), his final novel, dramatises their specific suggestion that confessional narrative could germinate a reformatory concept of criminal law. Throughout, however, faith in reform is haunted by the spectre of a morally illiterate reading nation. Godwin's work sheds light on a growing, conflicted public discourse that allied fiction-reading to ethics, which included the writings of fellow dissenters Anna Barbauld and William Hazlitt. In the process it exposes key elements of the novel's social elevation in the nineteenth century, including its connection to the lingering dissenting concept of private judgement.

Godwin's ideas and expectations surrounding the practice of reading itself were deeply indebted to the conceptual legacies of eighteenth-century dissenting culture. Chapter 3 explores his instructions for reading in conversation with an educational subculture spearheaded by John Jennings, Philip Doddridge and Isaac Watts, in which the activity of reading became a new focus of study or 'discipline' in itself. These educators conceived of reading as a form of training, a 'discipline' in the sense that applied to military, medical and moral regimes. Godwin remediated and adapted this pedagogical tradition across forty years of practical reading advice, presenting reading as a form of rigorous training which should be undertaken in accordance with principles of exposure, routine and skill. His interest in the concept of reading discipline elucidates the conflicted view of the human mind that he had inherited and which he shared with many of his contemporaries. Great confidence in the mind's discriminating powers converges with great fear of its adverse principles, such as passivity, distraction and rebellion. Godwin also developed his key response to this tension, which represents a new point of interest in Romantic-period pedagogical theory: investment in textual production.

Chapter 4 uses Godwin's direct evaluations of different media forms to draw attention to an ambivalent concept of truth in Romantic-period writing, and to show that this ambivalence was bound up with long-standing debates about the social effects of particular means of communication. *Political Justice* (1793), *The Enquirer* (1797) and *Thoughts on Man* (1831) each compare the social roles of book-reading and conversation, and are united by a concern with temporal regulation. The more Godwin describes these roles, however, the more they become ambiguous and qualified, raising questions about sources of epistemic authority. He faced a problem that had perplexed writers for many decades: to what extent is truth dependent upon the activities, structures and mediation of social groups, and to what extent is it external to them? Throughout the eighteenth century a twofold conception of truth had resonated in texts as apparently disparate as Samuel Johnson's 'On Studies' (1753), Hume's 'Of Essay Writing' (1742) and Watts's *Improvement of the Mind* (1741, 1751). The conflicted ways in which the problem of truth's apprehension was navigated by dissenters such as Watts, in particular, left a conceptual legacy that fuelled Godwin's clashes with fellow political radicals later in the century, notably John Thelwall. Godwin's writing about media form highlights the alethic dialogue of his time, and indicates ways in which this shaped public disagreement about the book's role in British society.

The properties of the book as a medium were of increasing interest to Godwin. Chapter 5 contends that his literary investment in 'the book' as material object and ideal renders him one of history's most powerful apologists for the social importance of the printed codex. His public disagreement with Malthus epitomises the pressure that he faced throughout his career to justify his foundational belief in necessary intellectual perfectibility. In response he increasingly presented printed books as substitutes for human minds, initially through literary biography and subsequently through his *Essay on Sepulchres* (1809) and manuscript essay 'On Death' (1810). Godwin tapped into pressing debates about national identity, literary canon and cultural progress, rewriting Sir Thomas Browne's ideas about bodily resurrection in order to argue that the book embodied a mind, which functioned as an ongoing member of intellectual community and thus had the potential to instigate social change. 'On Death' is the climax to this argument, which claims that books do not simply perpetuate human minds but transform them into something that transcends mortal limitations and, ultimately, regenerates human nature.

In this way Godwin exploited the symbolic power of the book-object in order to cast death as the ultimate means of intellectual advance. His literary figuration of the book as a mode of human remains was his most consistent contribution to contemporary debates about social progress, a belated development of Dugald Stewart's contention in the 1790s that print technology constituted an essential change in the human condition. This literary project is not only essential to a sound understanding of Godwin's career; more broadly, it shows us that the book's material properties played crucial and conflicting roles in writings about national identity, literary canon and cultural futurity in nineteenth-century Britain. Godwin's work thus offers us one way to explore the interface of figure and fact in media history, according to which representation is a condition of historical action. It also indicates that, as Leah Price observes, 'the history of books is centrally about ourselves' – it enables us to contextualise and make sense of our own media environments and norms of media engagement.[50] Godwin reminds us that media technology has a track record of representing and furthering our most cherished beliefs about the ends and possibilities of human life.

Notes

1. Godwin, 'Of an Early Taste for Reading', *The Enquirer: Reflections on Education, Manners, and Literature*, *PPW*, vol. 5, p. 95.

2. Marilyn Butler, *Romantics, Rebels and Reactionaries* (Oxford University Press, 1981), p. 182.
3. Ina Ferris, 'Introduction', *Romantic Circles Praxis Series*, Romantic Libraries issue, ed. Ina Ferris (University of Maryland, 2004) <https://www.rc.umd.edu/praxis/libraries/index.html> (last accessed 19 February 2019 (para. 2)); Ferris, 'Book Fancy: Bibliomania and the Literary Word', *Keats-Shelley Journal* 58 (2009): 33–52 (p. 52). See also Ina Ferris and Paul Keen, 'Introduction: Towards a Bookish Literary History', in *Bookish Histories* (Basingstoke: Palgrave Macmillan, 2009), pp. 1–15; Andrew Piper, *Dreaming in Books: The Making of the Bibliographic Imagination in the Romantic Age* (Chicago: University of Chicago Press, 2009).
4. Christina Lupton, *Knowing Books: The Consciousness of Mediation in Eighteenth-Century Britain* (Philadelphia: University of Pennsylvania Press, 2012); Paula McDowell, *The Invention of the Oral: Print Commerce and Fugitive Voices in Eighteenth-Century Britain* (Chicago: Chicago University Press, 2017). See also Clifford Siskin, *The Work of Writing: Literature and Social Change in Britain, 1700–1830* (Baltimore: Johns Hopkins University Press, 1998).
5. Ferris and Keen, 'Introduction: Towards a Bookish Literary History', p. 5.
6. Work on the history of books and the book trade in the British Romantic period is too extensive to cite here comprehensively. For detail on the above generalisations see William St Clair, *The Reading Nation in the Romantic Period* (Cambridge: Cambridge University Press, 2004), especially Chapters 6 and 11; James Raven, *The Business of Books: Booksellers and the English Book Trade, 1450–1850* (New Haven: Yale University Press, 2007); Lee Erikson, 'The Romantic-Era Book Trade', *A Concise Companion to the Romantic Age*, ed. Jon Klancher (Oxford: Blackwell, 2009), pp. 212–31; Michael F. Suarez, 'Introduction', *The Cambridge History of the Book in Britain: Vol. V, 1695–1830*, ed. Michael F. Suarez and Michael F. Turner (Cambridge: Cambridge University Press, 2009), pp. 1–35; David McKitterick, 'Introduction', *The Cambridge History of the Book in Britain: Vol. VI, 1830–1914*, ed. David McKitterick (Cambridge: Cambridge University Press, 2010), pp. 1–74.
7. Clifford Siskin and William Warner, 'This Is Enlightenment: An Invitation in the Form of an Argument', in *This Is Enlightenment* (Chicago: Chicago University Press, 2010), pp. 1–33 (pp. 19–20).
8. Maria Jane Jewsbury, *Phantasmagoria: Or, Sketches of Life and Literature*, vol. 1 (London: Hurst, Robinson and Co., 1825), p. 3.
9. See Ina Ferris, *Book-Men, Book Clubs, and the Romantic Literary Sphere* (Basingstoke: Palgrave Macmillan, 2015).
10. For a good summary of these issues surrounding the activity of reading see Felicity James, 'Romantic Readers', in *The Oxford Handbook*

to *British Romanticism*, ed. David Duff (Oxford: Oxford University Press, 2018), pp. 478–94.
11. Among the many studies in this area are McDowell, *Invention of the Oral*; Julia Carlson, *Romantic Marks and Measures: Wordsworth's Poetry in Fields of Print* (Philadelphia: University of Pennsylvania Press, 2016); Jon Mee, *Conversable Worlds: Literature, Contention, and Community 1762 to 1830* (Oxford: Oxford University Press, 2011); Maureen McLane, *Balladeering, Minstrelsy, and the Making of British Romantic Poetry* (Cambridge: Cambridge University Press, 2008); Katie Trumpener, *Bardic Nationalism: the Romantic Novel and the British Empire* (Princeton: Princeton University Press, 1997); Penny Fielding, *Writing and Orality: Nationality, Culture, and Nineteenth-Century Scottish Fiction* (Oxford: Clarendon, 1996).
12. Kevis Goodman, *Georgic Modernity and British Romanticism: Poetry and the Mediation of History* (Cambridge: Cambridge University Press, 2004), especially the introduction and Chapter 1; John Guillroy, 'Enlightening Mediation', in *This Is Enlightenment*, pp. 37–63. See also Siskin and Warner, 'This Is Enlightenment: An Invitation in the Form of an Argument'; Mary Favret, *War at a Distance: Romanticism and the Making of Modern Wartime* (Princeton: Princeton University Press, 2010); McDowell, *The Invention of the Oral*, Introduction and Chapter 1.
13. See Paul Heyer, *Communications and History: Theories of Media, Knowledge, and Civilization* (Westport, CT: Greenwood Press, 1988); McDowell, *The Invention of the Oral*, pp. 252–3, 281–3; Jon Klancher, 'Wild Bibliography: The Rise and Fall of Book History in Nineteenth-Century Britain', in *Bookish Histories*, pp. 19–40.
14. Tim Fulford, 'Millenarianism and the Study of Romanticism', in *Romanticism and Millenarianism*, ed. Tim Fulford (Basingstoke: Palgrave, 2002), pp. 1–22.
15. Thomas Carlyle, 'Signs of the Times' (1829), in *A Carlyle Reader*, ed. G.B. Tennyson (Cambridge: Cambridge University Press, 1984), pp. 31–54 (p. 36); Godwin, *Thoughts on Man, His Nature, Productions, and Discoveries. Interspersed with Some Particulars Respecting the Author*, PPW, vol. 6, p. 248.
16. Adrian Johns, *The Nature of the Book: Print and Knowledge in the Making* (Chicago: Chicago University Press, 1998). On imagining the future in this period see especially Emily Rohrbach, *Modernity's Mist: British Romanticism and the Poetics of Anticipation* (New York: Forham University Press, 2016); Jonathan Sachs, *The Poetics of Decline in British Romanticism* (Cambridge: Cambridge University Press, 2018); Christina Lupton, *Reading and the Making of Time in the*

Eighteenth Century (Baltimore: Johns Hopkins University Press, 2018); James Chandler, *England in 1819: The Politics of Literary Culture and the Case of Romantic Historicism* (Chicago: University of Chicago Press, 1998).

17. See, for example, Alberto Manguel, *The Traveler, the Tower, and the Worm: The Reader as Metaphor* (Philadelphia: University of Pennsylvania Press, 2013); essays in *Bookish Histories*, ed. Ferris and Keen; Brian Allen Cummings, 'The Book as Symbol', in *The Oxford Companion to the Book*, ed. Michael F. Suarez and H. R. Woudhuysen (Oxford: Oxford University Press, 2010), pp. 63–5; Piper, *Dreaming in Books*; Johns, *The Nature of the Book*, especially Chapter 5 on the 'cultural construction' of printing history; Régis Debray, 'The Book as Symbolic Object', in *The Future of the Book*, ed. Geoffrey Nunberg (Berkeley and Los Angeles: University of California Press, 1996), pp. 139–52.

18. Piper, *Dreaming in Books*, p. 11. Cf. Christopher Flint, *The Appearance of Print in Eighteenth-Century Fiction* (Cambridge: Cambridge University Press, 2011), according to which eighteenth-century novels 'recorded the self-conscious manipulation of [their] typographical nature' in order to interrogate the period's developing print culture (pp. 1–2).

19. Jonathan I. Israel, *Enlightenment Contested: Philosophy, Modernity, and the Emancipation of Man 1670–1752* (Oxford: Oxford University Press, 2006), p. 23.

20. [Anon.], 'Review of "Life of Geoffrey Chaucer"', *Critical Review, or, Annals of Literature* 1.1 (January 1804): 60.

21. My understanding of Godwin's career has been guided primarily by Mark Philp, through *Godwin's Political Justice* (London: Duckworth, 1986), introductions to *PPW* and *CNM* (the latter co-written with Marilyn Butler), and his entry for Godwin in the *Oxford Dictionary of National Biography* (2004). Biographies of Godwin by Don Locke, *A Fantasy of Reason: The Life and Thought of William Godwin* (London: Routledge and Kegan Paul, 1980), Peter H. Marshall, *William Godwin* (New Haven: Yale University Press, 1984) and William St Clair, *The Godwins and the Shelleys: the Biography of a Family* (London: Faber, 1989) remain very useful; Pamela Clemit's ongoing work on Godwin's letters enables deeper knowledge of his life, career and self-understanding; and Julie Carlson's 'literary biography' of the Godwin-Shelley family is valuable as the only monograph that explicitly addresses Godwin's interest in books and reading (although without systematic treatment): *England's First Family of Writers: Mary Wollstonecraft, William Godwin, Mary Shelley* (Baltimore: Johns Hopkins University Press, 2007).

22. See especially Philp, *Godwin's Political Justice* and 'Introduction' to *PPW*, vol. 1, pp. 7–45. A broad overview of the concept of perfectibility

in Western culture is provided by John Passmore in *The Perfectibility of Man*, 3rd ed. (Indianapolis: Liberty Fund, 2000) and Godwin's commitment to intellectual perfectibility is situated briefly within 'British anarchism' on pp. 277–80, 321–3.
23. Transcribed in Philp, 'Introduction' to *PPW*, pp. 17–18.
24. William Hazlitt, 'The Spirit of the Age', in *The Collected Works of William Hazlitt*, ed. A. R. Waller and Arnold Glover, vol. 4 (London: J. M. Dent & Co., 1902), pp. 185–368 (p. 212). See Godwin's preface to the 1796 edition of *Political Justice* (*An Enquiry Concerning Political Justice: Variants*, *PPW*, vol. 4, pp. 6–7) and his 'Thoughts occasioned by the perusal of Dr Parr's Spital Sermon [. . .] being a reply to the attacks of Dr. Parr, Mr. Mackintosh, The Author of an Essay on Population, and others' [hereafter 'Reply to Parr'], *PPW*, vol. 2, pp. 163–208.
25. See Philp, *Godwin's Political Justice*, and D. H. Monro, *Godwin's Moral Philosophy: an Interpretation of William Godwin* (London: Oxford University Press, 1953), pp. 36–56.
26. Godwin, 'Essay of Scepticism', *PPW*, vol. 5, pp. 302, 309. A similar passage can be found in his 1801 'Reply to Parr', pp. 171–2.
27. *Political Justice: Variants*, pp. 7–8. See also his defence of principles 'fundamental to the system' of *Political Justice* in the preface to *St Leon; A Tale of the Sixteenth Century*, *CNM*, vol. 4, pp. 10–11.
28. *Thoughts on Man*, p. 292. Cf. 'Reply to Parr', pp. 207–8.
29. *Thoughts on Man*, p. 42.
30. *Political Justice*, p. 106; *Political Justice: Variants*, p. 143. See Philp's discussion of Godwin's view of private judgement in his *Godwin's Political Justice*. For three typologies of private judgement in eighteenth-century religious discourse, see Chapter 1 of Daniel Patrick L. Huang, '"Private judgment" in the Anglican writings of John Henry Newman (1824–1945)', (doctoral dissertation, The Catholic University of America, 1996), *ProQuest Dissertations Publishing*. For the generation of 'perfectibility' as a more general social assumption in eighteenth-century culture, see James Sambrook, *The Eighteenth Century: The Intellectual and Cultural Context of English Literature, 1700–1789* (London: Longman, 1986), pp. 229–33; David Spadafora, *The Idea of Progress in Eighteenth-Century Britain* (New Haven: Yale University Press, 1990); and Basil Willey, *The Eighteenth Century Background: Studies on the Idea of Nature in the Thought of the Period* (London: Chatto & Windus, 1940).
31. *Political Justice*, p. 397. This particular phrase is removed in subsequent editions, but the argument remains the same: see *Political Justice: Variants*, pp. 295–6.
32. *Political Justice*, p. 76 (retained in all editions).

33. Ibid. p. 106 (emphasis mine).
34. For examples of this 'transition' focus, see Marshall, *William Godwin*, p. 404, and Passmore, *The Perfectibility of Man*, pp. 278–89.
35. For details on Godwin's fluctuating public reputation, see Pamela Clemit and Avner Offer, 'Godwin's Citations, 1783–2005: Highest Renown at the Pinnacle of Disfavor', *Nineteenth-Century Prose* 41 (2014): 27–52.
36. 'Considerations on Lord Grenville's and Mr Pitt's Bills, concerning treasonable and seditious practices and unlawful assemblies, by a lover of order', *PPW*, vol. 2, pp. 123–62.
37. Thomas Robert Malthus, *An Essay on the Principle of Population, as it affects the future improvement of society, with remarks on the speculations of Mr. Godwin, M. Condorcet, and other writers* (London: J. Johnson, 1798); a substantially revised second edition appeared in 1803. See Philip Connell, *Romanticism, Economics and the Question of 'Culture'* (Oxford: Oxford University Press, 2001); Catherine Gallagher, 'The Romantics and the Political Economists', in *The Cambridge History of English Romantic Literature*, ed. James Chandler (Cambridge: Cambridge University Press, 2009), pp. 71–100 (pp. 75–6).
38. Godwin, *Of Population. An Enquiry concerning the Power of Increase in the Numbers of Mankind, being an Answer to Mr. Malthus's Essay on that Subject*, *PPW*, vol. 2, p. 295. Wollstonecraft, *Letters Written in Sweden, Norway, and Denmark*, in *The Works of Mary Wollstonecraft*, ed. Janet Todd and Marilyn Butler, vol. 6 (London: Pickering and Chatto, 1989), p. 279. On Wollstonecraft's position see John Whale, *Imagination Under Pressure, 1789–1832: Aesthetics, Politics and Utility* (Cambridge: Cambridge University Press, 2000), Chapter 3.
39. *Political Justice*, pp. 27–31, 141.
40. 'Considerations on Lord Grenville's and Mr Pitt's Bills', p. 155.
41. Antoine-Nicolas de Condorcet, *Sketch for a Historical Picture of the Progress of the Human Mind* (1795), trans. June Barraclough (London: Weidenfeld & Nicolson, 1955), pp. 99, 101.
42. Dugald Stewart, *Elements of the Philosophy of the Human Mind* (1792), in *The Collected Works of Dugald Stewart*, ed. Sir William Hamilton (London: Thoemmes Press, 1994), vol. 2, p. 242; Stewart, *Account of the Life and Writings of Adam Smith, LL.D* (1793), in *Collected Works*, vol. 10, p. 54.
43. 'Reply to Parr', pp. 207–8.
44. *Thoughts on Man*, p. 248.
45. *The Genius of Christianity Unveiled: In A Series of Essays*, *PPW*, vol. 7, pp. 75–240 (p. 235). This is a repetition from an earlier section: see p. 132.

46. Manuscript note as cited in Philp, 'Introduction' to *PPW*, p. 23.
47. *LWG*, vol. 2, p. 253. See also Chapter 5 on Godwin's heated correspondence with Richard Phillips concerning the production of his *Life of Chaucer*.
48. On the Godwins' business venture see Mark Philp, 'Godwin, William (1756–1836)', *Oxford Dictionary of National Biography* (Oxford University Press Online, 2004); William St Clair, 'William Godwin as Children's Bookseller', in *Children and Their Books: A Celebration of the Work of Iona and Peter Opie*, ed. Gillian Avery and Julia Briggs (Oxford: Clarendon, 1989), pp. 165–79.
49. 'Of the Length of the Life of Man: A Confession', *CNM*, vol. 1, pp. 61–5.
50. Leah Price, 'Reading: the State of the Discipline', *Book History* 7.1 (2004): 303–20 (p. 318).

Chapter 1

The Matter of the Reader: Materialism and Private Judgement

For many eighteenth-century philosophers and educators, the activity of reading had a clear and yet elusive goal: the genesis of independent thought. John Locke's posthumously published treatise *Of the Conduct of the Understanding* (1706) claims that 'Reading furnishes the mind only with materials of knowledge; it is thinking makes what we read ours.'[1] Reading matter is here distinguished from an agential cognitive act, by which the reader acquires an emphatically personal kind of intellectual substance. If the reader stops short of this act, however – and Locke implies that they frequently do – they are to be considered a mere bookshelf or storage facility, furnished with the materials of knowledge while remaining lifeless and impersonal. These concerns were developed in a range of educational writings across the ensuing decades. Isaac Watts, for instance, cautioned the aspiring student in 1741 that 'if all your learning be nothing else but a mere amassment of what others have written [. . .] I do not see what title your head has to learning above your shelves'.[2] Like Locke, Watts was concerned to distinguish the autonomous thought of his reader ('your head') from the material bulk of the library ('your shelves'). This genesis of independent judgement, he argued, was the *raison d'être* of reading, and it was what made the reader truly human.

William Godwin's depictions of readers at the turn of the century intensified these concerns about autonomous thought and negotiated their complex literary and political legacies. His writing about reading and thinking unearths a network of inherited questions about the relationship between matter and mind – where does one end and the other begin? – which were themselves bound up with live debates about epistemology, causation and the principle of biological life itself. Much was at stake here for Godwin, for at the heart of his account of human nature and society was the goal of enabling and exercising private judgement, each person's perfectible capacity for independent thought and evaluation. He understood this faculty to be the medium of all desirable change in individual and social life, and the activity of reading to be integral to its development. Amid this vision of intellectual possibility, however, he frequently described the human mind in terms that suggested it was necessarily subject to an impersonal realm of matter. In both philosophy and fiction, Godwin dwells upon readers whose minds and bodies cannot be distinguished in any meaningful way from the substances of their immediate environments, and whose judgements are consequently in no sense autonomous or 'private'. This is especially the case in his novels, in which readers are possessed by books rather than possessing them and 'thought' as an agential medium seems to be lost. As Marilyn Butler observes, Godwin's novels consistently threaten the 'conscious, sentient, unique individual' that he relied upon in his philosophy.[3]

Godwin was not unaware of this threat. In fact, he was employing a recognised tension between mind and matter to both imagine and empower the elusive autonomous thinker of his philosophical theory. An ambivalent or 'double' reading of mind was integral to the epistemological and physiological writing of the eighteenth century – including that of John Locke, David Hume and Joseph Priestley – and within this the concept of figuration was central. Godwin exploited the uncertain line between literal and metaphoric meaning in these accounts of relations between bodies, minds and material environments, and, like other writers in his social circle, turned it to literary purpose. His fiction and philosophy use the equivocality of 'thought' to emphasise both the formative power of educational circumstances and the ability of the individual mind to escape its confines. His writing thus illuminates a literary subculture that used the ambiguous nature of thought in the contemporary imagination to signal the emancipatory potential of individual judgement, while simultaneously painting a vivid picture of the sinister formative power of corrupt social environments. In other words, Godwin represents a movement that was attuned to ways in which 'reading matter' could be transformed through fiction from an intellectual problem into a space for imagining social possibility.

Political Justice and the Problem of Thought

An Enquiry Concerning Political Justice (1793) was founded upon an assumption about the importance of independent thought, an ideal to which Godwin most frequently referred using the loaded term private judgement.[4] For Godwin, as for many educated in dissenting Protestant communities, private judgement was not simply the result of an enlightened and emancipated society; it was the means of achieving it. 'The proper method for hastening the decay of error, is not, by brute force, or by regulation', he contends, 'but on the contrary by teaching every man to think for himself.'[5] In both substantially revised editions of the treatise (1796, 1798) he continues to describe private judgement as 'a doctrine [. . .] unspeakably beautiful' and his analyses of social institutions and customs consistently take the principle as their reference point. National assemblies, for example, are considered pernicious because they encourage a false sense of unanimity and so foster intellectual passivity in the individual.[6] Significantly, Godwin writes about the activity of reading in ways that make it essential to private judgement's development. Thorough engagement with literature (in the generous eighteenth-century sense of that term) produces 'salutary' effects upon the mind, he contends, helping to disentangle it from prejudice and mistake.[7]

Despite this foundational commitment to independent thinking, however, the mind is threatened from every side in Godwin's *Enquiry*. Political institutions infect and corrupt human faculties to such an alarming extent that escape from prejudice is made to seem almost impossible. The influence of government 'fastens itself upon us like an incubus, oppressing all our efforts' towards independent judgement.[8] There are social threats to its operation, too; everyday conventions of politeness, custom and 'domestic tactics' alienate people from 'the pursuit of truth'.[9] This apparent paradox has been widely noted in the work of Godwin, Wollstonecraft and their literary-intellectual milieu, and is aptly described by Barbara Taylor as an example of the 'corruption/progression antinomy haunting eighteenth-century thought' at large.[10] Widespread belief in inevitable national and even universal improvement – signalled by stadial historiographies, technological utopianism and revivals of millenialist eschatologies – clashed with a plethora of ultra-negative analyses of current society, embodied in an array of forms including radical sermons, political polemic and novels depicting the moral bancruptcy of contemporary communities.[11]

In *Political Justice*, however, independent thought is troubled on a level more basic even than this. An epistemological threat develops over successive editions of the treatise, as Godwin increasingly uses the vocabulary of the materialist to describe the production of knowledge in the human mind. Knowledge is a process of 'impression' from external forces, in which minds can be 'ductile', 'stiff' or 'elastic'. While he constructs the spread of truth in abstract, ethereal terms – 'diffusion', 'dissemination' – practical encounters with ideas are corporeal and tactile. This language is peppered throughout the treatise from the earliest printed version, but it becomes more concentrated as the editions progress and more problematic for Godwin's ideal of independent thought.[12]

A good example of these troubling implications is found in the section on 'The Cultivation of Truth', in which Godwin equates virtue with one's ability to understand circumstances clearly in the mind. Where the first edition describes the need for 'clear and distinct perception' of these circumstances, in subsequent editions this is changed to 'strong and vivid perception'.[13] Godwin replaces an intellect that is imagined in visual terms, implying a degree of distance and independence from the circumstances under consideration, with one defined by the material force of impressions upon sensory faculties. This appears to jeopardise his ideal of the impartial thinking agent; rather than describing the mind as separate from the material processes of the body, it employs the discourse of corporeal cause and effect, implying that the human mind is at the mercy of impersonal external forces that manipulate its most basic operations.

The consequences of Godwin's altered language in this example indicate that accounts of matter and mind were closely affiliated with debates about determinism in this period, as they still are today. A great variety of British thinkers – from Ralph Cudworth and Humphrey Ditton to Thomas Reid – had argued that if the phenomenon of mind was defined or explained primarily in terms of matter, it would legitimise the equation of human life with machinery, a position that became associated mid-century with the notorious *L'Homme machine* of the French materialist philosopher La Mettrie (1748). Many feared that if the accepted definition of mind failed to include a dimension beyond matter, then human action would be understood as determined solely by the cause-and-effect conditions of the natural world. Free choice would be reduced to a psychological illusion and the domain of ethics left largely redundant. Strict materialism where the mind was concerned was inextricable from charges of atheism – a term covering a range of non-orthodox positions – and specifically the irreverance associated with the French *philosophes*. It was for these reasons, as John Yolton has detailed, that eighteenth-century fascination with lifelike automata went hand in hand with a profound fear that modern natural philosophy was 'mechanising' humankind.[14]

Godwin's writing about the mind often appears to make just such a mechanising move. In the first edition of *Political Justice* he states:

> Though mind be a real and efficient cause, it is in no case a first cause. It is the medium through which operations are produced. Ideas succeed each other in our sensorium according to certain necessary laws. The most powerful impression, either from without or from within, constantly gets the better of all its competitors, and forcibly drives out the preceding thought, till it is in the same irresistible manner driven out by its successor.[15]

This description of mind as a 'medium', in which ideas compete for prominence in a process akin to natural selection, positions the thinker as fundamentally passive. Ideas are received according to 'necessary laws' and the subject's power to filter or select them is limited. By the third edition, however, Godwin has altered the first sentence to read, 'Though mind be a real and proper antecedent, it is in no case a first cause, a thing indeed of which we have in no case any experimental knowledge.'[16] The mind can now only be described as an antecedent rather than an efficient cause – it precedes action, but it does not by any original force of its own determine the nature of that action. This signals increased scepticism about the degree to which thinkers can be said to have agency, even in a secondary sense. The most powerful impressions always imprint themselves upon the mind, and the mind itself appears to be merely their receptacle.

When it comes to reading, this approach to mental life has sinister implications. If the mind is necessarily subject to the most powerful ideas that it encounters, are its judgements at the mercy of its reading matter? As Godwin describes his ideal of an intellectually virtuous community in the *Enquiry*, he does indeed appear to position the reader in a materialist's universe:

> Having ventured to state these hints and conjectures, let us endeavour to mark the limits of individuality. Every man that receives an impression from any external object, has the current of his own thoughts modified by force; and yet without external impressions we should be nothing. We ought not, except under certain limitations, to endeavour to free ourselves from their approach. Every man that reads the composition of another, suffers the succession of his ideas to be in a considerable degree under the direction of his author. But it does not seem as if this would ever form a sufficient objection against reading. One man will always have stored up reflections and facts that another wants; and mature and digested discourse will perhaps always, in equal circumstances, be superior to that which is extempore [. . .] conversation and the intercourse of mind with mind seem to be the most fertile sources of improvement.[17]

The tension within Godwin's approach to intellectual activity is clearly shown here. The reader is depicted at the mercy of external impressions that battle for impact upon the mind. Their ideas are 'modified by force', suggesting reading to be a kind of coercion by which the mind is manipulated by its reading materials. This language allows Godwin to explain the power and importance of reading from the standpoint of empiricist philosophy, yet it seems to eliminate from the picture any sense of the reader's independence. At the same time, however, he suggests that such coercion can be a necessary, even positive, process. Because each person 'will always have stored up reflections and facts that another wants', reading is an activity of sharing that enlarges its participants. It is 'fertile', an activity which generates something new in the mind and causes 'improvement'. In other words, while Godwin's descriptions of mind as matter threaten his central claims about the development of intellectual autonomy, he also strives to keep the reader-as-agent on centre stage.

Later editions of the *Enquiry* – in which the materialist language is most explicit – contain an insightful comment upon this very tension. In a discussion of education designed to refute those who explain intellectual ability by reference to predetermination by innate qualities, Godwin remarks that:

> Multitudes will never exert the energy necessary to extraordinary [educational] success, till they shall dismiss the prejudices that fetter them, get rid of the chilling system of occult and inexplicable causes, and consider the human mind as an intelligent agent, guided by motives and prospects presented to the understanding, and not by causes of which we have no proper cognisance and can form no calculation.[18]

The emancipatory energy necessary for intellectual independence is to be achieved, Godwin implies here, through an act of the imagination.[19] We must renounce determinism and instead '*consider* the human mind as an intelligent agent' – believe that this is the case – and by doing so, we will find ourselves transformed for the better. This act of belief is far from a naive or unreasonable gesture: in fact, it is crucial for understanding Godwin's depictions and discussions of reading in later works.

Godwin's explicitly stated model of the human mind in *Political Justice* allows for this imaginative operation. His account cannot be classified straightforwardly as materialist or immaterialist in the strict senses of those terms, but rather exhibits what Yasmin Solomonescu describes as a 'dialogical relationship between idealism and materialism', which, she argues, structured the scope of Romantic-period writing like 'double-helix DNA'.[20] In a chapter 'Of the Mechanism of the Human Mind' Godwin describes mind as a mechanism like the body, and allows that we can use the vocabulary of physical process to describe its operation, but he argues that we must understand it to be 'a mechanism of a totally different kind'.[21] There is an overt element of mystery at play here, which has an important function. Godwin observes that we cannot know exactly how thought produces physical consequences, but he claims that this realm of unknowing does not mean that it cannot produce them or that thought therefore does not exist. This aspect of his account resonates indirectly with Kant's observation about biological life in the *Critique of the Power of Judgment* (1790) that 'the organization of nature is [. . .] not analogous with any causality that we know'. Godwin's most intentional source is Hume, however, betrayed by his ensuing claim that we cannot empirically know how anything causes anything; habit simply leads us to assume that it does.[22] Godwin deploys Hume's sceptical approach to knowledge of causation in order to urge that we embrace the assumption supplied by common sense that thought is a meaningful and largely independent cause of action.

Godwin uses this framework in *Political Justice* to argue that we must believe that the substance of the mind transcends matter, even though we cannot prove it by empirical method. This is important because it is only by ascribing mind a dimension beyond matter that we are able to explain some of the most fundamental elements of human life, experience of intellectual agency being an example. A later undated manuscript note reinforces this idea, suggesting that although thought is non-material, it is not *im*material – it is just as tangible as 'the vegetation & life of a plant', which cannot be materially located but nevertheless exists in and affects the physical world.[23] As this comment implies, the nature of thought for Godwin was interlaced with contemporary ideas about the principle of biological life or 'animal vitality', a hot topic of debate in 1790s London. While many associated the so-called vital principle with empirically observed phenomena such as blood or electricity, the language used to account for vitality in itself remained inescapably analogous and slippery. In what way did it exist – as a substance, an emergent property, or something else entirely?[24] Godwin's foray into physiology employs a recognised field of linguistic and conceptual ambiguity in order to sustain his imperative to 'consider the human mind as an intelligent agent'.

Godwin was not unusual for this account of human thought. Thought had long been considered an ambiguous mediator between realms of mind and matter, and his writing indexes and responds to many other thinkers in a long-standing and complex debate about its nature and mediatory operations.[25] Locke's dualism, in which thought was essentially 'superadded' to matter by God, came under pressure early in the eighteenth century. Natural scientists and philosophers began to grapple with the physiological applications of what Newton termed 'subtle elastic fluid', a concept which appeared to problematise the nature of matter as traditionally conceived. If matter had aspects of what had formerly been considered the immaterial, was the latter realm still necessary to explain human experience of the mind? A wide range of thinkers increasingly described moral and intellectual activity in physiological terms.[26] David Hartley, for example, investigated the relationship between ideas and the operation of the nerves, and his explanatory discourse of vibration influenced British culture for decades. Although Hartley made a distinction between ideas and the material vibrations that supposedly corresponded with them, his claim about their correlation was often understood to blur the boundaries between thought and its materials. Joseph Priestley adapted Hartley's account, breaking down the traditional distinction between 'material' and 'immaterial' – all matter, in his account, is porous and defined solely by forces of attraction and repulsion – and claiming that 'thought' is a property of a system of such matter, the nervous system.[27]

Godwin wrote at a time in which the nature of thought was much debated, due in part to many medically significant neurological discoveries that occurred in Britain and on the Continent.[28] As he began his career as a writer in the 1780s and 90s he socialised regularly with prominent figures of London's scientific community, including the chemist William Nicolson and the surgeon Anthony Carlisle; he also began a close friendship with John Thelwall, whose paper on the physical nature of the mind, delivered to the Guy's Hospital Physical Society in 1793, caused controversy and charges of atheism.[29] Godwin's work suggests that he largely espoused Joseph Priestley's views, as did many from dissenting communities. Like Priestley, he described himself as modifying Hartley's system in order to avoid the 'material automatism with which it was unnecessarily clogged'.[30] Fascinated as he was by the possibilities entailed by new research into the brain and the nervous system, he was keenly aware of the undesirability of exclusively material explanations of thought and its relation to behaviour.

Godwin's open or ambiguous view of the mind was also intended as a means to sidestep the problems he perceived in the accounts of reading, thinking and enlightenment produced by French *philosophes* with materialist leanings, many of whom he read and admired. Helvétius's *Essays on the Mind* (1758), for example, describes the predicament of the poor labourer who 'prefers the blue library, to the writings of St. Real, Rochefoucault, and cardinal de Retz' and needs to be awakened to his 'true interest' in advancing the welfare of society through political and social reform.[31] The means by which the labourer might transcend the affinity of his ideas to his uninspiring reading matter is conspicuously lacking in Helvétius's materialist framework, however. The mechanics of the intellect render reading choice a matter of necessary 'attachment', implying that the reader is ultimately passive. Godwin confronted this problem as a student at Hoxton Academy and during his early years as a writer, becoming convinced that, if the activity of reading was to be given emancipatory potential, then thought must be considered in some way independent of matter.

Another key influence upon the way Godwin used materialist language, and perhaps the most significant for understanding his enduring confidence in independent thought, is the way in which physiological vocabulary was operating in works of empiricist philosophy. Brad Pasanek describes the eighteenth century as being 'in the grips of an indirect or figurative empiricism', according to which the mind was understood through '*metaphors* drawn from the sensuous impressions'.[32] Locke's *Essay Concerning Human Understanding* (1690), for example, had described knowledge production in terms of sensation and reflection, using verbs such as 'impress' and 'strike' to conjure up an explanatory picture of the genesis of ideas – yet Locke did not intend his work to be an anatomy of ideas. Indeed, he almost apologises for his discussion of physical sensation, admitting, 'I have [. . .] been engaged in physical inquiries a little further than perhaps I intended.'[33] He later attests that

> We have the *Ideas* of *Matter* and *Thinking*, but possibly shall never be able to know, whether any mere material Being thinks, or no; it being impossible for us, by the contemplation of our own *Ideas*, without revelation, to discover, whether Omnipotency has not given to some Systems of Matter fitly disposed, a power to perceive and think, or else joined and fixed to Matter so disposed, a thinking immaterial substance.[34]

As Ann Jessie Vant Sant observes, Locke's work features 'a fusion of traditional metaphor with the natural scientist's and the physiologist's understanding of sensation [. . .] despite Locke's deliberate avoidance of the physicality of sensation, he cannot do without its vocabulary'.[35] In this way his corporeal language of thought hovers between the metaphorical and the literal, inhabiting a realm of deliberate unknowing.

While this equivocality of signification may have allowed Locke to avoid a problem, it became a feature of more sceptical empiricist works. David Hume's *Treatise on Human Nature* (1739–40) capitalises on the limits of human knowledge, maintaining that 'Nothing is ever present to us but our perceptions.'[36] All we experience of reality, according to Hume, is a succession of vivid impressions in the theatre of the mind. Undermining the common anti-materialist argument which claimed matter could never give rise to thought – and therefore that the substances must be distinct – Hume asserted that as far as our knowledge goes, 'any thing may be the cause or effect of any thing'. Our idea of causation derives only from an experience of constant conjunction.[37] The nature and cause of the impressions in our mind, whether material or immaterial, can never ultimately be known; and the question of whether the language of 'impression' is literal or metaphoric must therefore be eternally ambiguous. This ambiguity proves essential, in Hume's *Treatise*, for the pragmatics of living. Although there is very little ground, according to its system, for proving notions such as individual agency, personal identity and moral value to be things-in-themselves rather than social fantasies, he concludes that the philosopher must act *as if* they were things-in-themselves in order to live practically in the world. In everyday life the sceptic is obligated to 'yield to the current of nature' and 'live, and talk, and act like other people in the common affairs of life'.[38] The language of 'impression' for Hume thus takes on an element of extra significance than it does for Locke – the relationship of its imagery to reality cannot be known, but Hume insists that we assume it to have explanatory power, or else cease to function as social beings.

Godwin was by no means a strict Humean: he remained committed to a view of 'truth' as an objective entity that was external to the knower and had great epistemological authority.[39] Yet his elusive language of matter in *Political Justice* exhibits a clear legacy of the figurative empiricism of Hume's *Treatise*. Moreover, as Amanda Goldstein shows, a vocal strand of Romantic-period materialism, inspired by Lucretius' *De rerum natura*, was promoting the view that figuration was in fact 'central to the reality of things', a belief that placed poetic knowledge at the heart of scientific endeavour.[40] In other words, Godwin wrote at a time when, for some thinkers, both mind and body were essentially modes of figuration. All these contexts help us to see that Godwin's description of the mind in materialist terms recruited an acknowledged tension in a range of philosophical and physiological writings. He emphasised foremost the formative power of material circumstances in his account of human intellect, yet the overtly ambivalent status of his sensory vocabulary – is it literal, metaphorical, or somehow both? – allows Godwin to imagine and assert what he cannot prove, his sacred ideal of independent thought. Thought is couched in physiological language, and is more than analogous to matter, and yet it escapes the confines of the material system through its mysterious status as a mechanism 'of a totally different kind'.

Godwin continued to negotiate the tension entailed by this view of the mind in Humean style, as his treatment of the mind-matter theme almost forty years later, in his collection of essays *Thoughts on Man* (1831), strongly suggests. 'The mind may aptly be described under the denomination of the "stranger at home"', he argues in his opening essay 'Of Body and Mind':

> Where [the mind] resides we cannot tell, nor can authoritatively pronounce, as the apostle says, relatively to a particular phenomenon 'whether it is in the body, or out of the body.' Be it however where or what it may, it is this which constitutes the great essence of, and gives value to, our existence [. . .][41]

Godwin appeals once again to mystery here; his quotation from 2 Corinthians 12 associates the mind with religious experience, a real aspect of human life that lies both within and beyond the scope of human knowledge. The great value and meaning that the mind has for human life, he argues, has a sort of obvious authority; it trumps physiological or philosophical conclusions about the nature of matter. Godwin spells this out in a subsequent essay 'Of the Material Universe', directly echoing Hume:

> The speculator in his closet is one man: the same person, when he comes out of his retirement, and mixes in intercourse with his fellow creatures, is another man. The necessarian [. . .] proves to his own apprehension irrefragably, that he is a passive instrument [. . .] But no sooner does this acute and ingenious reasoner come into active life and the intercourse of his fellowmen, than all these fine-drawn speculations vanish from his recollection. He regards himself and other men as beings endowed with a liberty of action [. . .] Nature is too strong, to be prevailed on to retire, and give way to the authority of definitions and syllogistical deduction.[42]

The double standard of the materialist is adjacent to that of the necessarian: both are different men in the studious 'closet' to those that they are in everyday life. Godwin uses this discussion to contend that all persons must imagine themselves to be intellectual agents – they must act as though this is the case – no matter what theoretical conclusions about materialism or determinism they reach in private. This imaginative pragmatism, and its implications for the language used to describe acts of reading, took on an explicit role in works of fiction by Godwin and the writers of his literary circle in the 1790s.

Reading Matter in *Caleb Williams* and *Mandeville*

Descriptions of childhood reading feature in each of Godwin's full-length novels. The young, impressionable reader was a common literary trope by the late eighteenth century, often used to code character type or signal quixotic dispositions with an eye to social commentary, as in Charlotte Lennox's *The Female Quixote* or Jane Austen's *Northanger Abbey*. For Godwin this trope was a means of placing the matter of the mind upon centre stage; and perhaps the most striking example is found in the changes he made to the opening of *Caleb Williams* in its second and third editions (1796, 1797). In the first edition (1794) Caleb is described as being 'engrossed' by reading as a child, 'neglect[ing] no means of information from conversation or books'.[43] The second edition inserts a new paragraph, which describes how he 'delighted to read of feats of activity' and connects this propensity to his supple and vigorous physical frame.[44] The 1797 text further expands this account, and its changes are retained in subsequent editions. It details at length how Caleb's mental disposition and reading matter mutually reinforce each other, culminating in irresistible cravings:

> The spring of action which, perhaps more than any other, characterised the whole train of my life, was curiosity. [. . .] In fine, this produced in me an invincible attachment to books of narrative and romance. I panted for the unravelling of an adventure with an anxiety, perhaps almost equal to that of the man whose future happiness or misery depended on its issue. I read, I devoured compositions of this sort. They took possession of my soul; and the effects they produced were frequently discernible in my external appearance and my health.[45]

Caleb's physical and mental faculties merge as he is shaped by reading material. His preference for 'narrative and romance' is a process of positive feedback and has uncertain origins: it is determined partly by a prior internal disposition of curiosity, partly by his athletic physique and partly by the books themselves, which 'took possession of my soul'. As Caleb compares his absorption in each tale to that of the person whose fate is determined by its issue – the fictional protagonist – he registers the quixotic extent to which his existence is governed by what he reads. The term 'attachment' encapsulates the ambiguity of Caleb's situation, as it implies both material connection (the mind's fusion with its educative environment) and subjective bias (a preference for one thing over another). What kind of attachment is Caleb's attachment to his books? Can mental and physical attachment be distinguished? The origins and nature of mental and physical states collide in this account of reading experience.

This growing preoccupation with the effects of reading upon his protagonist's appearance and personality corresponds to the changes of language in *Political Justice* explored above: in both texts, matter seems to encroach upon mind. Godwin revised both for new editions during the same period in the mid-1790s (the second and third editions of *Political Justice* were published in 1796 and 1798). These years also saw the publication of *The Enquirer* (1797), a collection of essays on 'Education, Manners, and Literature', which describes the process of reading using similar corporeal language and addresses the issue of literary determinism head-on. As the 1790s progressed, the boundary between the sensory and the intellectual became increasingly hard to distinguish across Godwin's work, problematising his attention to the individual's capacity for independent thought. A close look at scenes of reading in *Caleb Williams* and *Mandeville* suggests to us one reason why Godwin made intellectual determinism such an explicit theme in his fiction.

Caleb's early interaction with reading matter shapes the quality and disposition of his mind as a medium of experience and judgement, and in this respect it has hermeneutical significance for the novel as a whole. In other words, Caleb's childhood reading determines the way that he perceives, evaluates and communicates lived experience in narrative. Most significantly, his undisciplined interaction with tales of action, excitement and novelty render his mental character 'irresolute and pliable'.[46] This resonates with and intensifies his physical characteristics, according to which his limbs are flexible and active, and his body lends itself to manipulation and disguise. His mind is portrayed throughout the novel in similar terms of material pliability, impressionability and ductility; its characteristics are also associated with heat, the 'burning', 'boiling' and 'glowing' of an inflamed imagination.[47] Godwin's prose style formalises this intellectual state, its vehement, hyperbolic rhetoric and long, often disjointed sentences embodying the sensitive fluidity of Caleb's mental life.

This disposition determines the passionate and impetuous nature of Caleb's subsequent judgements, feelings and decisions. Despite his frequent resolve to display 'firmness' and 'unalterable constancy', he describes his mental experience as akin to being blown about and driven by powerful winds, each one driving out the other with superior force.[48] An early example of this behaviour is found when Thomas is sent to fetch Caleb after his first departure from the Falkland estate. Initially Caleb describes in the strongest terms his conviction that to return would be impossible: 'I have taken my resolution [. . .] all the world shall never persuade me to alter'. Upon reading Forrester's letter, however, he experiences a dramatic reversal of ideas, and resolves to return with Thomas immediately. 'The letter overwhelmed every quality of my mind', Caleb records; 'The ideas it suggested had a tendency to fill the mind, and shut out the possibility of competition.'[49] Mental processes are signified here in spatial terms – ideas fill, shut out and overwhelm like wind or waves. The description directly references Godwin's account of the genesis of ideas in *Political Justice*: 'The most powerful impression [. . .] constantly gets the better of all its competitors, and forcibly drives out the preceding thought, till it is in the same irresistible manner driven out by its successor.'[50] Caleb appears to be at the mercy of external impressions, which battle for impact upon his mind. Any independent conviction or resolve that he reaches – any hope of truly private judgement – is instantly overridden.

This characterisation of intellectual life was intrinsically political for Godwin. As Chapter 4 of this book explores in detail, he used the language of rapidity and heat across his writings in the 1790s to censure political reform movements for promoting weak, dependent judgements – notably radical working-class organisations such as the London Corresponding Society, which he critiqued for using demagogy and group solidarity in order to ensure uniformity of opinion among its members. For Godwin, the passions incited by these reformist meetings and their charismatic leaders encouraged the slumber of rational thought; they were simply another way in which the members' potentially independent minds capitulated to an external authority. As the example of Forrester's letter indicates, Caleb's judgement is similarly overwritten by those outside of him, supremely Falkland. The plot is driven by the interplay between Caleb's resistive energy in the face of Falkland's demands and his ongoing subjection to Falkland's power, a dynamic that is often considered the novel's most compelling feature.

For our purposes here, the materialist vocabulary used to establish Caleb's essential passivity indicates the strong connection between accounts of the mind in Godwin's time and politically motivated critiques of social and educational subordination. This was a literary culture dominated by physiological imagery, in which the language of the body was often used to signal ideas about the body politic. Many associated materialist accounts of biological life with republicanism; terms such as 'quickening', 'circulation' and 'vitality' certainly resonated with the ideals of democratic knowledge exchange that animated many reformist writers and speakers, including Godwin's friend John Thelwall.[51] In *Caleb Williams*, however, these ideals are subverted by materialist vocabulary and its necessarian implications for the mind. The imagery provided him with a framework for depicting the slavish dependence of individuals to systems of unjust government.

Falkland, of course, participates in this climate of intellectual passivity as much as he perpetuates it. Just like Caleb, he is given a childhood reading experience that is couched in the language of physical incorporation: he 'imbibed the love of chivalry and romance'.[52] These tales of chivalric code, combined with a classical education and a fascination with the histories of 'great men', shape him into a staunch upholder of tradition, a patron of the *ancien régime*. He is described as 'inflexible', 'rigid' and 'cold', terms that apply both to his mental disposition and his physical features.[53] Indeed, by the time Caleb becomes his secretary, his battle to preserve chivalric ideals has become 'inscribed in legible characters upon his countenance'.[54] Capitalising on the various meanings annexed to the eighteenth-century term *character*, Godwin depicts Falkland according to the literal sense of a typographical mark, suggesting that the stamp of his material environment has determined his personal characteristics. Like Caleb, he is ultimately depicted as critically passive, physically inscribed by his reading material.

When Caleb and Falkland meet in the novel's final scene, they are extreme physical confirmations of the mental dispositions that their reading experiences have set in train. Caleb shakes with emotion, while Falkland appears shrivelled, hardened and corpse-like.[55] Although their reconciliation may be interpreted as signalling the possibility of revolution in opinion through honest discourse, their characters remain fundamentally unchanged. Falkland is still 'the fool of honour and fame', for he cannot survive without being 'the guardian of [his] reputation', and promptly dies.[56] Caleb's reasoning remains subservient to impulse and enthusiasm, epitomised by the fact that he finally becomes possessed by Falkland's reputation worship. He concludes by stating his allegiance to Falkland's tale, subverting his original statement of narrative intent with his claim that he finishes the memoirs 'that *thy* story may be fully understood'.[57] Once again his pliable mind has been usurped by the most powerful impression; he is arguably just as defeated here as he was in the original manuscript ending, in which he was left drugged and incarcerated. Both the language and plot of *Caleb Williams* signal that its two main characters have been at the mercy of their reading materials. With 'things as they are', any hope of autonomous enquiry is precluded.

Twenty years later, Godwin intensified this picture of intellectual subordination in his thrillingly dark *Mandeville* (1817). The trajectory of childhood reading had become a trope in Godwin's novels: the hero of *St Leon* (1799) is enslaved to 'the first lesson imprinted upon my infant mind' (the love of fame), and in *Fleetwood* (1805) early bookish isolation instils in the protagonist a stubborn and misanthropic cast of mind, with tragic consequences.[58] Yet Godwin depicted Mandeville as determined by his material environment and trapped within his mental dispositions more overtly than any of his other characters. He particularly exploited the Gothic potential of this determinist theme, using it to consider the interplay between religious experience, mental illness and community fracture.

From *Mandeville*'s opening pages, Godwin's narrator-protagonist constructs an account of his character formation in explicitly material terms. Describing the details of his childhood residence, he observes that

> they insensibly incorporated themselves as it were with the substance of my mind; and my character, such as it was afterwards displayed, owed much of its peculiarity to the impressions I here received.[59]

This comment merges together different kinds of 'substance'. The material features of the house, the reclusive and strange personalities that populate it, the sombre violence of the waves against the rocks – all converge in the mind of the young man, producing formative 'impressions'. These forces confound any distinction between body and mind, for Mandeville's physical appearance takes on the tenor of his environment in tandem with his intellectual disposition. In suggesting that his character may be read in its subsequent display, Mandeville portrays his life as irrevocably stamped by the particulars of its educational context. Once again, a key aspect of this environment is reading material:

> A book that my preceptor particularly recommended to my attention, was Fox's Acts and Monuments of the Church; nor did I need much persuasion to a study, to which my temper inclined me, and which occasions that sort of tingling and horror, that is particularly inviting to young persons of a serious disposition. In this tremendous volume the engravings eminently help to inforce the dead letter of the text. The representation of all imaginable cruelties, racks, pincers and red-hot irons [. . .] combined with my deep conviction that the beings thus treated, were God's peculiar favourites [. . .] produced a strange confusion and horror in my modes of thinking, that kept me awake whole nights, that drove the colour from my cheeks, and made me wander like a meagre, unlaid ghost, to the wonder and alarm of the peaceable and well-disposed inhabitants of my uncle's house.[60]

The *Book of Martyrs* has a coercive effect, 'inforc[ing]' its text and images upon the reader, manipulating not just his thoughts but his very 'modes of thinking'. In a similar fashion to Caleb, the incorporation of reading matter into mental substance is visibly manifested, expressed through his skin colour, constitution and bodily stature, reinforcing the idea that reading is a process of physical possession. Godwin's own attitude towards this particular text corresponds well to his novel's image of readerly subjection: in an unpublished essay on the composition of history he attacked the *Acts and Monuments* for its propagandistic bias and dubious sources, contending that it manifested the common tendency for 'a book of reasonable dimensions, of a grave & measured style' to smuggle prejudice to its audience undetected.[61] Mandeville's experience of the weighty tome instils precisely this latent prejudice, leading him to embody its horror and gloom. The *Book of Martyrs* is integral to his mental and physical identity, welding both together.

This sharing of substance that Mandeville experiences during childhood is presented thereafter in the novel as something that has irrevocably determined his character, trapping him in a trajectory of jealousy and isolation against which he is powerless. The narration is littered with retrospective reflections that call this process to mind, and the plot is frequently interrupted with seemingly impotent laments: 'What a being I was, and for what a fate I was reserved!' Terms such as 'fate' and 'destiny' are ubiquitous, and Mandeville's retrospective speculations include the claim that his 'character was fixed'.[62] Indeed, he reflects upon the early formation of his mind in terms of physical deformity:

> There were certain muscles of my intellectual frame that had never been brought into play; there were arteries of my heart through which the blood never rushed. My character was withered: not chilled; but dried, and stiffened, and changed to a yellow, death-like hue, like the confected carcasses of ancient Egypt. [. . .] My education I had derived from a formal, rigid, pedantic, pharisaical priest. Other inmates of the roof under which I dwelt I had had none, except my unfortunate uncle, and his servants, who were more like *automata*, than human beings.[63]

Mandeville describes the development of his mind through the language of the body. Certain 'muscles' and 'arteries' of his immaterial person have been deprived of use and sustenance, left to wither. Images of lifeless bodies – mummified corpses and automata – reflect both the mechanistic framework in which Mandeville's life is imagined (he has no intellectual independence or vitality), and the uncanny effects to which it is put. Similar themes shape *Fleetwood*, in which the protagonist's creation of wax dummies representing his wife and supposed lover symbolises his own intractability of mind and dehumanisation of others. In both novels, imagery associated with materialistic ontology is used to pinpoint the spooky effects that their unpropitious social climates have had upon the mind. In Mandeville's case, distorted intellectual and bodily identities fully align through his literal disfigurement in the final scene. He ends his tale with a climactic assertion of possession, similar to that of *Caleb Williams*: 'Clifford had set his mark upon me, as a token that I was his forever.'[64] This final surrender into past tense, combined with the imagery of branding, reinforces the novel's characteristic sense of no return.

Reviewers of *Mandeville* were quick to identify this dark picture of material trajectory as the work's central concern, and many considered it to be in conflict with the reformist views of Godwin's political philosophy. Percy Shelley aptly captured the impression that the novel gave to its first readers:

> The events of the tale flow on like the stream of fate, regular and irresistible, and growing at once darker and swifter in their progress; – there is no surprise, there is no shock; we are prepared for the worst from the very opening of the scene, though we wonder whence the author drew the shadows which render the moral darkness every instant more profound and, at last, so appaling [*sic*] and complete.[65]

Shelley's sense of wonder and profundity at *Mandeville*'s exploration of material determinism was not shared by the majority of reviewers, most of whom were repulsed rather than thrilled. Their comments identify a contrast between Godwin's ideal of reform through independent thought in *Political Justice* and his bleak depiction of historical and social determinism in *Mandeville*. One writer suggested that Godwin's repeated analyses of 'whatever is deplorable in the constitution of society' had led him to despair of his system, and accused him of 'complaining of, and railing at, what he cannot hope to reform'.[66]

Notably, however, this review equates Godwin's own conception of reality with the constructions of his fictional narrator. It pinpoints the paradox of corruption and perfectibility that all Godwin's novels explore, yet it is driven by contestable assumptions about the nature and method of the reform that he hoped his literary work would achieve. Close attention to the formal features of his novels and their place within Romantic-period literary culture suggests that Godwin was presenting the materially determined lives of Caleb and Mandeville within his framework of perfectibility, trading upon the double reading of thought that *Political Justice* established. As Jon Klancher puts it, they bring 'Godwin on Possibility' to the fore, by using 'the sign of fiction and its possible or virtual worlds' as a mode or symbol of social redress.[67] In other words, at the same time that Godwin used his novels as troubling windows into interior lives, he also used them to imagine and assert the social possibility of independent thought by exploiting the figurative empiricism introduced in his philosophical work.

Godwin's mode of first-person narration provides the foundation upon which this figurative empiricism is built. Caleb and Mandeville are made the narrators of explicitly subjective accounts that derive their energy from the tale-tellers' internal responses to circumstances. The novels adapt a tradition of confessional perspective pioneered by Defoe a century earlier, which had placed psychological experience and questions of veracity at the helm of the action. Epistolary novels, novels of sensibility and, in particular, the Gothic novel as developed by Ann Radcliffe further honed an array of literary techniques by which psychological states were dramatised. This context encourages us to read the sensory language of mind dominating Godwin's novels as an experiential language: his narrators communicate the *felt* nature of social formation. And this self-conscious subjectivity is not simply an attempt at emotional realism, for he uses it to develop his readers' sense that the narrators are flawed, unstable and potentially unreliable. Mandeville's increasingly disturbing psychological condition casts his explanation of childhood events into doubt, for example, and the open-ended conclusion of his tale invites speculation as to its true import. Caleb's constant fluctuation in convictions and opinions, culminating in the dramatic reversal in his interpretation of his own story, performs a similar function. We are even encouraged to read his history of Falkland in the first volume with caution, given that he openly admits he cannot vouch for its veracity.[68] Godwin used his narrators to introduce tales of psychological experiences and their attendant conditions, as opposed to authoritative chronicles of events.

This experiential mode of narration, then, implicitly upholds the possibility of private judgement by interpolating the reader themselves as a judge. Godwin's novels deliberately provoke multiple and conflicting readings and in doing so, as Pamela Clemit writes, they place the 'burden of interpretation and decision' upon the reader.[69] This feature is epitomised by the central mystery devices of *Caleb Williams* and *St Leon*, by which the elusive contents of Falkland's chest and St Leon's alchemical secret become sites of endless conjecture for readers inside and outside the narratives, appropriated in ways that drastically alter interpretations of their confessions. As St Leon moves through history he is at times a philanthropic hero and at others a manipulative villain, and Falkland's chest symbolises the unrealised promise of what Caleb calls a 'faithful narrative', a definitive version of events.[70] These speculative trajectories of Godwin's novels – which critics note are bound up with self-conscious reflection on the mediatory properties of written and spoken words – invite readers to invent the faithful narrative for themselves, to judge and interpret the accounts they have received.[71]

This narrative context manoeuvres the deterministic language of mental development in *Caleb Williams* and *Mandeville* into a realm of possibility and speculation. In other words, Godwin used the novel form to provoke double readings of matter even more explicitly than he had done in *Political Justice*. Ambiguity surrounding the metaphorical status of words such as 'impulse' and 'impression' allows for open-ended readings of character development: the terms express the influential nature of material circumstances yet also reflect subjective experience, inviting readers to judge for themselves the authority and scope of the formative conditions that Caleb and Mandeville recall. This dual perspective is evident in Mandeville's account of his childhood influences:

> they insensibly incorporated themselves as it were with the substance of my mind; and my character, such as it was afterwards displayed, owed much of its peculiarity to the impressions I here received.

The substances of mind and matter here are analogous – 'as it were' – and their relations 'insensibl[e]'. Although felt to be literally incorporated into one another, they can be described as distinct. Mandeville also uses overtly performative terms: he considers his character 'such as it was afterwards displayed', evoking the most literal meaning of *display* in Godwin's time, to unfold to view like a banner or naval signal. This kind of language tacitly registers the figurative aspect to

Mandeville's tale, the way in which his confession renders or bodies forth subjective experience in narrative form. Godwin exploits the recognised ambiguity of materialist discourse in order to encapsulate the psychological pressure of Mandeville's early environment while simultaneously implying that it may be transcended. He allows us to read matter in two ways: as a literal confinement in the material realm on the one hand, and as an experience of formative coercion in a prejudiced society on the other hand, which may be reinterpreted and surpassed.

It was this second kind of reading that provided the reformist energy for Godwin's critique of societal conditions. In *Political Justice* he repeatedly argued that any institution, convention or habit that encouraged the mind to be passive was in fact 'reducing men to the state of machines'.[72] Coding the mental lives of his fictional characters with mechanical language was a political statement, implying that their environments were in effect dehumanising. The particular ways in which books trouble his protagonists suggest that he was pinpointing specific realms of social prejudice: Falkland's elitist environment warps his mind towards the quixotic and destructive ideals of his chivalric tales; Caleb's under-resourced and untutored upbringing suffers his mind to overindulge in the thrills of adventure, generating dispositional hastiness and malleability which might have been balanced by a more disciplined and wide-ranging textual diet; Mandeville's cultish religious climate encourages hatred and suspicion to the extent of insanity. Godwin thus depicts a world in which class structure and religious bigotry disfigure the development of private judgement, as symbolised by Mandeville's disfigured face. Only a new social order that respects foremost the operation of individual judgement, he implies, will redeem the humanness of humanity. It is a reversal of the closet situation described in *Thoughts on Man*: in lived experience Caleb and Mandeville are positioned in the realm of necessity, described as subject to the pressures of their political, educational and social environments, but when incorporated into a realm of readerly speculation they offer the possibility of future reform and independence.

In this respect Godwin was furthering a literary movement. Similar motivations underlay many of the novels produced in the 1790s by writers associated with the publisher Joseph Johnson – often referred to as 'Jacobin' writers, a contemporary slur now adopted for critical convenience – including Elizabeth Inchbald, Mary Wollstonecraft and Thomas Holcroft. Their novels, as Jonathan Sachs highlights, draw attention to discursive practices such as reading and writing in order to indicate correctives for the negative habits they believed were perpetuated by educational norms.[73] Inchbald's *Nature and Art* (1796), for example, uses the reading habits and speech of Henry, who has been raised in seclusion and independence, to expose the artifice of his urbane cousin William. Holcroft's *Hugh Trevor* (1794–7) uses Hugh's tortuous course of writing, feedback and revision in contact with Turl in order to model an ideal process by which the unintelligent spin-doctoring promoted by the classical education of the privileged is replaced by plain, forceful, accessible speech. Such tales of self-improvement through reading or the failure thereof resonated with the increasingly popular autobiographies of working-class reformers such as Francis Place, Thomas Hardy, James Lackington and John Thelwall, which often idealised the struggles of the poor to improve their minds through reading and participate in political debate. Godwin's fictional characters do not inhabit such clear moral ground or follow a straightforward trajectory; instead the reader of the novel is interpolated as the ultimate agent in the process of advancement.

The writing of Mary Hays attests most clearly to the creative influence of Godwin's attention to the reading mind per se. Hays was one of several women to whom Godwin became literary advisor in the mid-1790s, and she drew directly from Godwin's fictional accounts of reading in her semi-autobiographical novel *Memoirs of Emma Courtney* (1796), employing a troubled reader-protagonist to comment upon the pernicious nature of social convention.[74] She borrowed heavily from her discussions of philosophy with Godwin, which had centred around questions of personal agency. Like Godwin, Hays exploited materialist language in her novel in order to raise questions about the ability of individuals to transcend the state of 'things as they are'. Yet the social evil to which she drew attention, gender convention, was one that she believed Godwin had neglected.

In a written 'confession', Emma describes her own character as determined by the material impressions upon her mind, aiming to demonstrate the irresistible power of circumstances, modifying and controuling [*sic*] our characters, and introducing, mechanically, those associations and habits which make us what we are; for without outward impressions we should be nothing.[75]

This account of determination frames the novel from start to finish, casting Emma as trapped within predetermined dispositions and tendencies. The novel relates her struggle to negotiate the tensions between an overly sentimental disposition and a rigidly stratified community, in which patriarchal values govern sanctioned behaviour. Emma's disposition is fashioned, in a large part, by reading material. At her most formative age she develops an ungoverned penchant for novels from the circulating library: 'Every day I became more attached to my books', she records, to the extent that she 'devoured' them.[76] Her reading is a corporeal experience of attachment and impression that prefigures the 1797 *Caleb Williams*, and Hays similarly incorporates the vocabulary of ingestion, indicating that the assimilation of pages involved in Emma's intellectual formation is a physical and vulnerable process. This initial, unchecked consumption of sentimental tales grates against Emma's subsequent engagement with classical history and metaphysical enquiry through the works of Plutarch and Descartes, for her fundamental tendency towards sentiment has been irrevocably set. Agony results: the uneven reading diet produces an irrevocable fault line between 'rational' and 'sentimental' matter, which compose her mind like layers of sediment. 'I went through, by my father's direction, a course of historical reading, but I could never acquire a taste for this species of composition', she relates; though it sometimes inspired 'pleasure and enthusiasm' it mostly left her 'fatigued and disgusted', craving the solace of poetry and fiction.[77]

The internal conflict that this reading produces in Emma's mind determines an external social conflict. While she ardently desires to participate in the rational detachment and critical autonomy to which Mr Francis (the Godwinian philosopher figure) urges her, the sentimental bedrock of her disposition renders these exhortations impotent and obsolete. Emma is trapped within herself, unable to process or progress beyond her all-consuming feelings for Harley. The materialistic language used to describe her mind suggests that she is unable to escape the 'modes of thinking' initially instilled through her reading material.

Emma's disqualification from the 'masculine' arena of critical autonomy has been understood by some to signal a fundamental disagreement with or departure from Godwin's work. Marilyn Brooks, for example, argues that *Emma Courtney* turns the Godwinian exhortation to rational enquiry into 'a public debate about an inadequate discourse'; it points out the felt incompetence of Godwin's entire theory of social change through rationality.[78] This view assumes that Emma's sentimental temperament is fully endorsed by Hays (which is far from clear), and also takes for granted that Godwin's social theory excludes sentiment (which is untrue). It accurately pinpoints a perceived problem concerning the process of individual reform, but this problem is one with which both Hays and Godwin were centrally concerned. Just like Godwin, Hays describes Emma's intellectual formation in vividly corporeal language in order to raise questions about the extent to which certain kinds of people can develop critical autonomy: she holds the discourse of gradualist intellectual reform up to scrutiny. In doing so, the novel performs a similar function to *Caleb Williams* and *Mandeville*, portraying the formation of private judgement in current society to be a brutal struggle. The experience of individuals such as Emma, Hays suggests, testifies to the sinister power of 'things as they are'.

Just as Godwin's novels incorporate an aspect of faith in human potential for independent thought, *Emma Courtney* also expresses confidence in the positive power of reading through its narrative frame. Emma's story is an epistolary 'confession' to her adopted son, who remains a textually absent figure, the symbol of a new generation. Through this addressee the novel appeals to a judgement external to its confines: this future reader is urged to 'exercise your understanding, think freely, [. . .] Rouse the nobler energies of your mind'.[79] Such overt summons to critical reinterpretation continue until the final pages, in which the novel's readers are imagined as harbingers of intellectual emancipation:

> Posterity will plant the olive and the laurel, and consecrate their mingled branches to the memory of such, who, daring to trace, to their springs, errors the most hoary, and prejudices the most venerated, emancipate the human mind from the trammels of superstition, and teach it, *that its true dignity and virtue, consist in being free.*[80]

Rather than espousing the determinism with which the novel began, Hays's narrator prophesies autonomy. New generations of readers will attain freedom of judgement as they trace the sources of error in Emma's restrictive educational circumstances. Alongside Godwin's novels, then, *Emma Courtney* transcends the confining language of mechanism and asserts the triumph of autonomous thought – although it is worth noting that Emma addresses a son, rather than a daughter, a fact that arguably casts a shadow over this imagined trajectory.

Hays's interest in reading was thus conceptually prior to her critique of gender conventions and not derivative from it, as some critics have assumed.[81] Her negative assessment of the intellectual arena available to women relied upon a more basic conviction about the nature of all human flourishing, which she shared with Godwin, and according to which universal development of healthy judgement was the ultimate social good. Such development was disabled by the restrictions placed on female education, and therefore these restrictions were a social evil. In Godwin's novels, similarly, the activity of reading was not an afterthought thrown in to back up an argument about the operation of social class; his depictions of class conventions are reliant upon fundamental assumptions about the power of reading and its potential to enhance every mind.

Reading held a similarly basic position for other writers in Godwin's literary-intellectual circle. In Inchbald's *A Simple Story* (1791), Miss Milner's concern for the material appearance of books rather than their content both signals and fuels her intellectual superficiality, which has disastrous relational consequences. Her faulty relationship to reading matter is used as incriminating evidence against educational norms: as the final pages ominously attest, Miss Milner's father should have 'bestowed upon his daughter a PROPER EDUCATION'.[82] In *A Vindication of the Rights of Woman* (1792), Mary Wollstonecraft's assertion of men and women's equal capacity to develop their mental faculties through suitable education led her to castigate the common social practice of limiting women's reading to romances and behavioural instruction books. This textual diet, she argued, promoted intellectual feebleness and triviality. While advocating reading as a key means of female emancipation, her work simultaneously analysed in scathing detail the role of certain books and reading habits in perpetuating the eighteenth-century woman's 'infantine' position. Like Inchbald,

Holcroft, Hays and Godwin, she indicated the need for a transformation of reading practice that would actualise books' potential to precipitate intellectual and social reform.[83] Godwin developed many of his *Enquirer* essays on education in conversation with Wollstonecraft during their brief marriage; both were passionate advocates of reading equality. They shared a conviction that reading had existential consequences, and was thus of primary importance to any account of social and political life.

Godwin's work from the 1790s and beyond thus illuminates a group of writers and intellectuals for whom the activity of reading brought into clear focus the hopes, anxieties and opportunities that sprung from contemporary understandings of the human mind. His fiction and philosophy unearth complex debates about the nature of thought and its mediation between realms of matter and mind, especially questions concerning its location along conceptual axes of activity and passivity, autonomy and dependency, agency and determinacy. Godwin drew from the ambivalent language of mental formation emerging from these debates in order to express and enact his enduring faith in literature's capacity to stimulate and strengthen independent judgement in readers. This faith fuelled his engagement with the novel form and inspired others to do the same. As Sachs notes, a unifying feature of the Jacobin writers is their shared attempt to 'carve the process of novel reading as a new locus of virtue for their readers'.[84] That pursuit was inseparable from a turbulent context of philosophy of mind and physiology of thought, which offered new, complex vocabularies and frameworks for radical social critique.

Notes

1. Locke, *Of the Conduct of the Understanding* in *Posthumous Works of Mr. John Locke* [. . .] (London: printed by W. B. for A. and J. Churchill at the Black Swan in Pater-Noster-Row, 1706), p. 60.
2. Watts, *The Improvement of the Mind* in *The Works of the Late Reverend and Learned Isaac Watts, D.D* [. . .], 6 vols (London: printed for T. and T. Longman, J. Buckland et al., 1753), vol. 5, pp. 185–358 (p. 189).
3. Marilyn Butler, *Jane Austen and the War of Ideas* (Oxford: Clarendon, 1988), pp. 55, 58. Butler argues that Godwin partially succeeds in vindicating this 'individual', unlike the other writers of his literary circle.

4. For detailed discussion of private judgement in Godwin's work, see Philp, *Godwin's Political Justice*. For the resonance of private judgement in eighteenth-century religious discourse, see Huang, '"Private judgment" in the Anglican writings of John Henry Newman', Chapter 1.
5. *Political Justice*, p. 450.
6. Ibid. pp. 76, 306–7.
7. Ibid. pp. 14–15.
8. *Political Justice: Variants*, p. 125.
9. *Political Justice*, p. 120 (retained in all editions).
10. Barbara Taylor, *Mary Wollstonecraft and the Feminist Imagination* (Cambridge: Cambridge University Press, 2003), p. 162; Peter Marshall, *William Godwin*, p. 404.
11. Barbara Taylor, *Mary Wollstonecraft and the Feminist Imagination*, p. 162; Peter Marshall, *William Godwin*, p. 404.
12. See Philp, *Godwin's Political Justice*, for full analysis of Godwin's changing language across successive editions of the *Enquiry*.
13. *Political Justice*, p. 143; *Political Justice: Variants*, p. 169.
14. John W. Yolton, *Thinking Matter: Materialism in Eighteenth-Century Britain* (Oxford: Blackwell, 1983), especially pp. 30, 45, 119, 124–5; Robert E. Schofield, *Mechanism and Materialism: British Natural Philosophy in an Age of Reason* (Princeton: Princeton University Press, 1970).
15. *Political Justice*, p. 185.
16. *Political Justice: Variants*, p. 195.
17. *Political Justice*, p. 452 (virtually unchanged in subsequent editions).
18. *Political Justice: Variants*, p. 24.
19. See James Engell, *The Creative Imagination: Enlightenment to Romanticism* (Cambridge, MA: Harvard University Press, 1981), pp. 7–8, for wider discussion about the extent to which the imagination was held to offer reconciliation between different conceptual realms in this period.
20. Yasmin Solomonescu, *John Thelwall and the Materialist Imagination* (Basingstoke: Palgrave Macmillan, 2014), pp. 141–2.
21. *Political Justice*, p. 176.
22. *Political Justice*, p. 177. Immanuel Kant, *Critique of the Power of Judgment*, ed. and trans. Paul Guyer (Cambridge: Cambridge University Press, 2000), p. 246.
23. Godwin, 'Untitled [on Matter, Thought, Motion and Identity]', n.d., Oxford, Bodleian Library, Abinger Collection, MS. Abinger c. 36 Fol. 3. See also Godwin's *Essay on Sepulchres*, in which he confesses himself 'more inclined to the opinion of the immaterialists; than of the materialists' concerning the nature of thought', *PPW*, vol. 6, pp. 1–30 (p. 8).

24. On vitalism in the 'long' eighteenth century see Amanda Jo Goldstein, *Sweet Science: Romantic Materialism and the News Logics of Life* (Chicago: Chicago University Press, 2017); Solomonescu, *John Thelwall and the Materialist Imagination*, Chapter 1; Catherine Packham, *Eighteenth-Century Vitalism: Bodies, Culture, Politics* (Basingstoke: Palgrave Macmillan, 2012); Denise Gigante, *Life: Organic Form and Romanticism* (New Haven: Yale University Press, 2009).
25. For an overview of this debate in the eighteenth century see Yolton, *Thinking Matter*; on Romantic-period theories of mind see Alan Richardson, *British Romanticism and the Science of the Mind* (Cambridge: Cambridge University Press, 2001); on the specifically mediatory work of the nervous system in Romantic-period writing, see Kevis Goodman, 'Reading Motion: Coleridge's "Free Spirit" and its Medical Background', *European Romantic Review* 26.3 (2015): 349–56.
26. For an insightful case study of this broad movement, see Isabel Rivers, *Reason, Grace, and Sentiment: A Study of the Language of Religion and Ethics in England, 1660–1780*, 2 vols (Cambridge: Cambridge University Press, 1991; 2000).
27. See David Hartley, *Observations on Man: His Frame, His Duty, and His Expectations* (Cambridge: Cambridge University Press, 2013); Joseph Priestley, *Disquisitions Relating to Matter and Spirit. [. . .]* (London: printed for J. Johnson, No. 72, St. Paul's Church-Yard, 1777), pp. 16–18.
28. See Richardson, *British Romanticism and the Science of the Mind*, pp. 5–7.
29. Sharon Ruston, *Creating Romanticism: Case Studies in the Literature, Science and Medicine of the 1790s* (Basingstoke: Palgrave Macmillan, 2013), pp. 81–8; Somolonescu, *John Thelwall and the Materialist Imagination*, pp. 3–4, 26.
30. *Political Justice*, p. 176.
31. Claude Adrien Helvétius, *De L'Esprit: Or, Essays on the Mind, and Its Several Faculties* (London: Vernor, Hood, and Sharpe, 1810), pp. 51–3. Godwin's Preface to the first edition of *Political Justice* records his reading of Helvétius (p. iv); on his engagement with eighteenth-century *philosophes* more generally see Philp, *Godwin's Political Justice*, Chapter 2.
32. Brad Pasanek, *Metaphors of Mind: an Eighteenth-Century Dictionary* (Baltimore: Johns Hopkins University Press, 2015), p. 21 (emphasis mine).
33. Locke, *An Essay Concerning Human Understanding*, 7th edn, vol. 1 (London: J. Churchill and Samuel Manship, 1715), p. 102.
34. Locke, *An Essay Concerning Human Understanding*, 7th edn, vol. 2 (London: J. Churchill and Samuel Manship, 1715), pp. 140, 167 [quotation interrupted by long footnote] (emphasis original). On the philosophical and theological context of Locke's account of relations between

thought, matter and personal identity see Jon W. Thompson, 'Personal and Bodily Identity: The Metaphysics of Resurrection in 17th Century Philosophy', PhD thesis (Kings College London, 2019), esp. pp. 156–7.
35. Ann Jessie Van Sant, *Eighteenth-Century Sensibility and the Novel: The Senses in Social Context* (Cambridge: Cambridge University Press, 1993), p. 90.
36. David Hume, *A Treatise of Human Nature: A Critical Edition*, ed. David Fate Norton and Mary J. Norton (Oxford: Clarendon Press, 2007), p. 137.
37. Ibid. pp. 161–3 (p. 163).
38. Ibid. p. 175. My reading here is indebted to discussions of Hume and the sceptical imagination in Fred Parker, *Scepticism and Literature: An Essay on Pope, Hume, Sterne, and Johnson* (Oxford: Oxford University Press, 2003), and Ian Duncan, *Scott's Shadow: The Novel in Romantic Edinburgh* (Princeton: Princeton University Press, 2007).
39. See Chapter 4. For a detailed account of Godwin's selective appropriation of Humean language, see Philp, *Godwin's Political Justice*, pp. 142–4, 154–6, 159–67.
40. Goldstein, *Sweet Science*, p. 4.
41. *Thoughts on Man*, pp. 44, 42–3. The phrase 'stranger at home' is unattributed but may be drawn from Edward Young's *The Complaint: or, Night-Thoughts on Life, Death, and Immortality* (London: R. Dodsley, 1742), p. 6: 'At home a stranger / Thought [. . .]'.
42. *Thoughts on Man*, pp. 274–5.
43. *Caleb Williams*, p. 7.
44. Ibid. p. 280.
45. Ibid.
46. *Caleb Williams*, p. 248.
47. See, for example, *Caleb Williams*, pp. 109, 141, 248; I note that Caleb's assertion that he is 'no longer irresolute and pliable' (p. 248) is ironically followed by an experience of mental turmoil and manipulation (p. 258).
48. Ibid. p. 258.
49. Ibid. pp. 142–3.
50. *Political Justice*, p. 185.
51. See Solomonescu, *John Thelwall and the Materialist Imagination*, pp. 21–4 and *passim*.
52. Ibid. p. 11.
53. Ibid. pp. 6–7.
54. Ibid. p. 247.
55. *Caleb Williams*, pp. 271–2.
56. Ibid. p. 90.

57. Ibid. p. 277 (emphasis mine).
58. *St Leon*, p. 155.
59. *Mandeville; A Tale of the Seventeenth Century in England*, CNM, vol. 6, p. 23.
60. Ibid. p. 52.
61. 'On the Composition of History; An Occasional Reflection', n.d., Oxford, Bodleian Library, Abinger Collection, MS. Abinger c. 29 fols. 5–16 (7–8).
62. *Mandeville*, p. 307.
63. Ibid. p. 131.
64. Ibid. p. 174.
65. E. K. [Percy Bysshe Shelley], 'Godwin's Mandeville', *The Examiner*, Iss. 522 (Dec 28, 1817): 826–7 (p. 827).
66. [Anon.], 'Review of Mandeville; A Tale of the Seventeenth Century by William Godwin', *The North-American Review and Miscellaneous Journal* 7.19 (1818): 92–105 (p. 92).
67. Jon Klancher, 'Godwin and the Republican Romance: Genre, Politics, and Contingency in Cultural History', *Modern Language Quarterly* 56.2 (1995): 145–66 (p. 164).
68. See *Caleb Williams*, p. 95.
69. Pamela Clemit, *The Godwinian Novel: The Rational Fictions of Godwin, Brockden Brown, Mary Shelley* (Oxford: Clarendon Press, 1993), p. 6.
70. *Caleb Williams*, p. 267.
71. See, for example, Angela Esterhammer, 'Godwin's Suspicion of Speech Acts', *Studies in Romanticism* 39.4 (2000): 553–78; Tilottama Rajan, *Romantic Narrative: Shelley, Hays, Godwin, Wollstonecraft* (Baltimore: Johns Hopkins University Press, 2010); Noelle Gallagher, 'Don Quixote and the Sentimental Reader of History in the Works of William Godwin', in *Historical Writing in Britain, 1688–1830: Visions of History* (Basingstoke: Palgrave Macmillan, 2014), pp. 162–81.
72. *Political Justice*, p. 449.
73. See Jonathan Sachs, *Romantic Antiquity: Rome in the British Imagination, 1789–1832* (Oxford: Oxford University Press, 2010), pp. 80–3, 107.
74. See Pamela Clemit, 'Godwin, Women, and "the collision of mind with mind"', *Wordsworth Circle* 35.2 (2004): 72–6. For further detail on the Hays-Godwin intersection, see 'Hays/Godwin Correspondence 1794–1800', in *The Correspondence (1779–1843) of Mary Hays, British Novelist*, ed. Marilyn L. Brooks (Lewiston, NY: Edwin Mellen Press, 2004).
75. Mary Hays, *Memoirs of Emma Courtney*, ed. Marilyn L. Brooks (Peterborough, ON: Broadview, 2000), p. 44.
76. Ibid. p. 49.

77. Ibid. p. 59.
78. Marilyn L. Brooks, 'Hays/Godwin Correspondence 1794–1800', in *The Correspondence (1779–1843) of Mary Hays, British Novelist* (Lewiston, NY: Edwin Mellen Press, 2004), pp. 363–81 (p. 376).
79. Hays, *Memoirs of Emma Courtney*, ed. Marilyn L. Brooks (Peterborough, ON: Broadview, 2000), p. 42.
80. Ibid. p. 221 (emphasis original).
81. See for example: Richard De Ritter, *Imagining Women Readers, 1789–1820: Well-Regulated Minds* (Manchester: Manchester University Press, 2015); Katherine Binhammer, 'The Persistence of Reading: Governing Female Novel-Reading in "Memoirs of Emma Courtney" and "Memoirs of Modern Philosophers"', *Eighteenth-Century Life* 27.2 (2003): 1–22; Jacqueline Pearson, *Women's Reading in Britain, 1750–1835: A Dangerous Recreation* (Cambridge: Cambridge University Press, 1999), e.g. p. 4.
82. Elizabeth Inchbald, *A Simple Story*, ed. J. M. S. Tompkins (London: Oxford University Press, 1967), pp. 146, 338.
83. Mary Wollstonecraft, *A Vindication of the Rights of Woman*, ed. Janet Todd (Oxford: Oxford University Press, 1994), pp. 71–5. On this see Katie Halsey, 'The Home Education of Girls in the Eighteenth-Century Novel: "the pernicious effects of an improper education"', *Oxford Review of Education* 41.4 (2015): 430–46; Taylor, *Mary Wollstonecraft and the Feminist Imagination*, pp. 71–2, and Carlson, *England's First Family*.
84. Sachs, *Romantic Antiquity*, p. 110.

Chapter 2

The Ethics of Novel-Reading: Fiction and Moral Law

William Godwin ended his preface to the 1832 edition of *Fleetwood* on a disturbing note. After giving a lengthy retrospective account of the composition of his most famous novel, *Caleb Williams* (1794), he recollected the experience of one of its first readers:

> And, when I had done all, what had I done? Written a book to amuse boys and girls in their vacant hours, a story to be hastily gobbled up by them, swallowed in a pusillanimous and unanimated mood, without chewing and digestion. I was in this respect greatly impressed with the confession of one of the most accomplished readers and excellent critics that any author could have fallen in with (the unfortunate Joseph Gerald [*sic*]). He told me that he had received my book late one evening, and had read through the three volumes before he closed his eyes. Thus, what had cost me twelve months' labour [. . .] he went over in a few hours, shut the book, laid himself on his pillow, slept and was refreshed, and cried,
> 'To-morrow to fresh woods and pastures new.'[1]

Godwin was drawing from a familiar bank of gustatory imagery in his description of this reading experience ('gobbled' 'swallowed'), and in doing so was rooting it within a rich field of moral and pedagogical discourse. Writers of the late eighteenth century were fascinated by the image of the binge-reader, a figure who consumed novels for temporary pleasure at the expense of lasting inner nourishment. Such a person (usually young and female) was ascribed 'a weakened and depraved stomach', as Clara Reeve expressed it in 1785, and censured accordingly.[2] In applying these descriptors to Joseph Gerrald, a political reformer and member of the London Corresponding Society with whom he had associated frequently in the 1790s, Godwin was expressing his alarm that even otherwise 'accomplished readers' allowed fictional fare to bypass the mind and cater only to bodily sensation.[3] His image of eating 'without chewing or digestion' turns it into a deliberately absurd picture: such a mindless way of reading, he implies, is like dining without a digestive system.

Earlier in the *Fleetwood* preface, Godwin had described his original ambition for *Caleb Williams* in strikingly different terms. In the glow of success that he had experienced following the publication of *Political Justice*, he was 'unwilling to stoop to what was insignificant' and had thus said to himself, 'I will write a tale, that shall constitute an epoch in the mind of the reader'. He envisaged his novel as a reformatory influence upon human lives, a work that would ensure 'no one, after he has read it, shall ever be exactly the same man as he was before'.[4] These lofty hopes jar with Godwin's subsequent description of the work's reception: the text he had hoped would induce a new stage of mental development in its readers instead became a shallow stimulant. This has led some critics to conclude that by the 1830s he had lost his faith in the power of fiction to benefit society, or even that he had developed a general 'pessimism regarding print culture'.[5]

Thwarted literary ambition and careless readers were not new themes in Godwin's work, however; neither was their prominence a sign of diminished faith in the potential of novels to enhance minds. His writings of the 1830s were in fact the climax of a career-long attempt to express the value of fiction in specifically ethical terms. His prefaces to reprinted novels during this decade and his final novel *Deloraine* (1833) gave renewed public expression to critical concepts that had germinated in the 1790s, and they reveal a bold, tenacious vision for the novel's role in moral life. Godwin built upon philosophies of sentiment that had dominated eighteenth-century moral theory and which found ambivalent aesthetic expression in so-called novels of sensibility, yoking them to the focus upon intellectual judgement that he had inherited from his rational dissenting background. True virtue, he claimed, depends upon the cooperation of social feeling and independent reasoning, both of which are regulated by the mind and are innately perfectible. Novels instigate virtue insofar as they facilitate social sympathy while also empowering readers to make autonomous judgements about the objects of their sympathy. For Godwin, this process required readers and writers with dispositions hard to come by in the contemporary world. His reflections upon it were consequently haunted – as *Fleetwood*'s preface shows – by prospects of failure.

Godwin's anxious insistence upon the novel's capacity to become a medium of moral reform is significant, in part, because it elucidates something of the novel's mercurial public status in the later Romantic period. Critics including Ina Ferris, Katie Trumpener and William Warner have described the early decades of the nineteenth century as a time of unique contention over novels' potential civic value, during which, in Ferris's words, 'fictions assumed public resonance through techniques of generic hybridisation and contestation learned from the aggressive interventions of the 1790s'.[6] *Deloraine* dramatises the creative dimensions of this controversial process. Both the formal dimensions and subject matter of his novel launch an apologetics of literary form, offering 'confessional' fiction as an antidote to moral shortcomings associated with institutional law and popular journalism. Godwin's literary reflections and experiments of the 1830s thus illuminate a public discourse that allied novel-reading to ethics – a discourse that was echoed in the writings of fellow dissenters such as Anna Barbauld and William Hazlitt, and which became one of the many factors behind the novel form's cultural 'elevation' in Britain. His contribution to this movement suggests ways in which the concept of private judgement shaped evaluations of the novel's social role in the early nineteenth century.

Novels and the Mind

Godwin attempted to make an ethical case for novel-reading at various points during his literary career. One of the best-known articulations of his position appeared as a letter to the *British Critic* in 1795, in which he replied to an accusation by one of the paper's correspondents that his goal in writing *Caleb Williams* had been to 'throw an odium on the laws of my country'. Godwin's response was to claim a loftier intention: 'to disengage the minds of men from prepossession, and launch them upon the sea of moral and political enquiry'.[7] In this statement he connects the mind, specifically, to the development of moral and political good. Novels can stimulate independent judgement in their readers, which, as he had made clear in *Political Justice*, he considered the first and fundamental step towards reforming the ethical priorities and social structure of modern life. It was a vision of the literary world that Godwin reiterated in more general terms in his preface to *The Enquirer* (1796), describing himself as 'persuaded that the cause of political reform, and the cause of intellectual and literary refinement, are inseparably connected'.[8]

Anticipating a second *Enquirer* volume, Godwin drafted an essay in 1797 which made a more detailed case for 'that species of literature, which [. . .] calls itself romance or novel'. His 'Essay of History and Romance' is concerned with ascertaining which sorts of prose narrative are best suited to improving the minds of readers: 'My first enquiry is, Can I derive instruction from it?'[9] Godwin contrasts different styles of narrative history in order to commend the unique benefits of narrative fiction. He begins by arguing that historiography is at its best when it facilitates personal encounters between readers and characters:

> The men I would study upon the canvas of history, are men worth the becoming intimately acquainted with. [. . .] Superficial acquaintance is nothing. A scene incessantly floating, cannot instruct us; [. . .] I would stop the flying figures, that I may mark them more clearly. There must be an exchange of real sentiments, or an investigation of subtle peculiarities, before improvement can be the result. There is a magnetical virtue in man, but there must be friction and heat, before the virtue will operate.[10]

Godwin uses the language of visual portraiture to make a connection between detailed textual characterisation and the moral improvement of readers. Only if the author facilitates an intimate encounter between reader and character will the opportunity arise for an 'exchange of real sentiments', which engenders virtue. His vocabulary is rooted in the mid-century ethical theories of Scottish Enlightenment thinkers such as Adam Smith, according to which the human capacity for imaginative sympathy upon the perception of suffering or injustice provided the basis of a shared moral sense.[11] The vocabulary of the body was often used to describe this sentimental experience, reflecting the ambiguous line it trod between philosophy and physiology. This moral framework had been influential in Godwin's training at Hoxton Academy, especially regarding the engendering of piety in parishoners through preaching. It had also deeply impacted British novels in the latter half of the eighteenth century, many of which were geared towards training the reader in sentimental responses to word and image – implementing, in Janet Todd's words, 'a kind of pedagogy of seeing and of the physical reaction that this seeing should produce'.[12] Throughout the 1760s–80s, fiction was both conceived as an aesthetic means of cultivating virtue in this way and used to probe its own limits as such a means.[13]

Godwin was not new to writing about moral sentiment; it was central to the devotional logic of his published sermons (1784), as Daniel White has pointed out.[14] Yet he made a renewed effort to emphasise the positive role of interpersonal attachment towards the end of the 1790s, notably in his preface to *St Leon* (1799) and 'Reply to the attacks of Dr. Parr' (1801), after he was accused of ignoring it completely in the first edition of *Political Justice*.[15] Private affections were 'the most admirable instruments in the execution of the purposes of virtue', he wrote, yet he cautioned against the isolation of feeling from judgement: 'A truly virtuous character is the combined result of regulated affections.'[16] Rowland Weston describes Godwin's concern as an increasing emphasis upon moral knowledge, or the personal-ethical dimension that must infuse propositional knowledge in order to induce historical change.[17] In 'History and Romance' Godwin directed this alliance of feeling and reason to the experience of reading historical narrative, contrasting abstract accounts of national events to the 'friction and heat' engendered by character studies. The latter sort of prose encourages the reader to imaginatively identify with the text's subject, triggering the same moral sentiment that would be facilitated by a real interpersonal encounter. Yet Godwin is careful to offset its 'friction and heat' with the language of visual perception – and to simultaneously underscore his goals of instruction and 'improvement' – thus fusing sentimental experience to the imperative of cognitive judgement.

Godwin notes in 'History and Romance' that such character-oriented historiography is inevitably speculative, rendering it a sort of fiction. But the line between fact and fiction is in fact far from clear: 'True history consists in a delineation of consistent human character, in a display of the manner in which such a character acts under successive circumstances.'[18] In other words, Godwin argues that *real* histories are those that offer a reliable account of the relationship between character, context and action, using a specific individual to illustrate something general and timeless. It follows from this, he claims, that novelists are the best historians, for they have more scope to render their accounts convincing and give them representative power. 'The writer of romance [. . .] is to be considered as the writer of real history', Godwin announces:

> The writer of romances collects his materials from all sources, experience, report, and the records of human affairs; then generalises them; and finally selects, from their elements and the various combinations they afford, those instances [. . .] which he judges most calculated to impress the heart and improve the faculties of his reader. In this point of view we should be apt to pronounce that romance was a nobler species of composition than history.[19]

Godwin situates the activity of this idealised writer in a framework of moral perfectibility that encompasses both feeling and reason: the aim of a good novel is to 'impress the heart and improve the faculties'. It is not simply that the novelist is able to give a better psychological portrait and thus portray the human condition more vividly than the historian. His real advantage lies in the relationship he opens up between reader and textual subject, the 'exchange of real sentiments', which recruits and develops the reader's moral capacity.

Godwin is far from sanguine here about the social reality of novel-reading, however. As he introduces his conception of the novel's contribution towards moral improvement, he pauses to make a preliminary distinction between the 'true' novel and the novel 'as an object of trade among booksellers'. Novels are disreputable because of a 'class of readers, consisting of women and boys, [. . .] considerably numerous', whose undiscriminating demand encourages booksellers to pursue quantity rather than quality. To make a moral case for the form in general, then, Godwin contends that we must ignore the 'scum and surcharge of the press' and 'consider only those persons who had really written romance, not those who had vainly attempted it'.[20] We must divide the literary field into two categories: real novels, which benefit the mind, and pseudo-novels, which don't.

Godwin was rehearsing a familiar jeremiad about the oversupply and quality decline of printed matter. As he sought to disassociate works of cultural value from the promiscuous world of literary commerce, his 'true' novel emerges as a somewhat immaterial or abstract entity – a critical strategy that would resonate, albeit with different inflection, in the writings of contemporaries such as Wordsworth and Coleridge. However, as his 'Essay of History and Romance' draws to a close, Godwin complicates the distinction by arguing that all novels inevitably fall short of their moral potential. Hard on the heels of his proclamation that romance is true history, he suddenly announces 'a deduction to be made from this eulogism' because the production of true romance is a task for which the faculties of the best novelist are incompetent. The writer of abstract history at least implicitly acknowledges that 'events are taken out of his hands and determined by the system of the universe'; the novelist, however, 'is continually straining at a foresight to which his faculties are incompetent, and continually fails'. To accurately portray the relationship between character, context and action is impossible, and Godwin concludes that 'To write a romance is a task too great for the powers of man.'[21]

The essay's final paragraph makes an ambivalent move towards situating this state of affairs in a trajectory of perfectibility. Godwin suggests that the inevitable failure of novelists reflects the fact that all 'the sciences and the arts of man are alike imperfect', constantly in progression towards something better.[22] This is the situation we have to work with, he implies; we need to recognise a mismatch between aspiration and reality in the current state of society. The tensions inherent to the novel in fact encapsulate the defining tension of human life for Godwin, as expressed in *Political Justice*, according to which minds are caught between forces of corruption and improvement.

'Essay of History and Romance' was not published in Godwin's lifetime, but its ideas surfaced publicly in his preface to *Cloudesley* (1830). *Cloudesley* was the first novel that Godwin had produced since *Mandeville* in 1817, and his diary suggests renewed interest in the novel form more generally around the time of its composition: his reading entries for 1829 include novels by Daniel Defoe, Henry Mackenzie, Ann Radcliffe, Elizabeth Inchbald, Walter Scott, Edward Bulwer-Lytton and James Fennimore Cooper. It was also a period in which he was revisiting his previous fictional work pending its republication in Henry Colburn and Richard Bentley's *Standard Novels* series, which was conceived according to a 'conscious editorial policy to secure revised texts and new Prefaces in which the author's mature judgement was passed on his earlier work'.[23] It was thus a time of critical and autobiographical reflection for Godwin, which had been manifest in germinal form throughout his writings of the 1820s.

Cloudesley's preface makes a case for the novel in a manner similar to the 'Essay of History and Romance', opening with the shortcomings of the historian's work. Godwin subtly develops his previous account by placing greater emphasis upon the internal dimensions of character:

> [N]o man thoroughly understands himself: how then is it to be expected, that the historian, who looks at him through a narrow aperture, and sees but a small part of his thoughts, his words and his actions, should arrive at a sounder result?

The historian's work only allows for 'a narrow aperture' into human character, Godwin argues, and this is a deficiency because it 'render[s] the attempt to pass a *sound judgment* upon the characters of men to a great degree impossible'.[24] In other words, neither the writer nor the reader of history have the inside information that they need in order to acquire moral knowledge. He then introduces and specifies his previous claim about 'real history':

> When the creator of the world of imagination, the poet, or writer of fiction, introduces his ideal personage to the public, he enters upon the task with a preconception of the qualities that belong to his being, the principle of his actions, and its necessary concomitants. [. . .] In this sense then it is infallibly true, that fictitious history, when it is the work of a competent hand, is more to be depended upon, and comprises more of the science of man, than whatever can be exhibited by the historian [. . .][25]

Fiction discloses greater knowledge of human nature than so-called historical writing, Godwin argues, because the author has greater freedom to unveil and explore the very things that make their agents human: qualities of being, principles of action, webs of contingency. He evokes and adapts Aristotle's famous claim that 'poetry is more philosophical and more serious than history' because it addresses, not 'what *has* happened', but 'the kind of thing that *would* happen, i.e., what is possible in accordance with probability or necessity'.[26] By maximising these 'universal' elements of human existence and eliciting the judgement of the audience upon their particular manifestations in plot and character, prose fiction can provide a better means of moral literacy than other social codes. In this sense it 'comprises more of the science of man' than anything pretending to be factual.

In his preface to the 1832 edition of *Fleetwood*, Godwin further developed these claims about the moral significance of having access to the principles and inside details of a character, connecting them to the specifics of narrative technique. During his retrospective account of *Caleb Williams*'s composition, he explains his choice of first-person perspective by allying it to the 'science of man' that *Cloudesley*'s preface described:

> I [. . .] assumed the first person, making the hero of my tale his own historian; and in this mode I have persisted in all my subsequent attempts at works of fiction. It was infinitely the best adapted, at least, to my vein of delineation, where the thing in which my imagination revelled the most freely, was the analysis of the private and internal operations of the mind, employing my metaphysical dissecting knife in tracing and laying bare the involutions of motive, and recording the gradually accumulating impulses, which led the personages I had to describe primarily to adopt the particular way of proceeding in which they afterwards embarked.[27]

Godwin was justifying his choice of confessional narrative by casting it as a facilitator of the moral knowledge he had previously described as the 'true' novel's prerogative. First-person perspective gives readers access to complex relationships between character, context and action: it exposes 'the private and internal operations of the mind', 'the involutions of motive' and 'the gradually accumulating impulses' that underlie human events. This intimate portrait thus engages the reader's moral faculties by encouraging them to imaginatively identify with the character, and by giving them the inside information they need in order to interpret and judge the character's actions. Godwin incorporates the language of natural science ('dissecting') in order to lend authority to this enterprise.

Godwin's focus here upon 'the private and internal operations of the mind' indicates that he continued to place the life of the individual mind at the helm of his ethics in the 1830s. This position stemmed from his basic conviction that humans were distinguished from animals and automata by their perfectible intellectual lives, which was partly inherited from the dissenting educational culture in which he was schooled. It is the logic of his critique of historical narrative; his call to 'stop the flying figures' was about rescuing past lives from the sort of 'superficial acquaintance' that effaced their personhood. *Cloudesley*'s preface makes this explicit through a comparison of page and stage, according to which the novelist contributes more to the moral development of society than the dramatist because he has more scope to render the unique details of intellectual life: he 'explains the inmost thoughts that pass in the bosom of the upright man and the perverse'.[28] Reviewers of *Cloudesley* noticed this connection that Godwin was making between individual minds and collective moral improvement – one noted that he 'makes the analysis of our inmost thoughts the *materiel* for melioration of the human species'.[29]

As all these comments indicate, Godwin was participating in a longstanding debate about the moral significance of novel-reading, which had been a feature of public discourse since at least the 1740s.[30] His work represents one aspect of a critical movement in the early nineteenth century that strove to link the sensitive reader of fiction to the sensitive reader of the moral landscape, while also avoiding the self-indulgence or social impotence associated with the aesthetics of sensibility exploited in novels of the 1760s–80s. This movement included the rhetorical and formal emphasis upon rational judgement that marked out many works of the 1790s, especially those self-conscious about their perceived role in political controversy. Charlotte Smith noted in her preface to *Desmond* (1792) that novels had the potential to both regulate readers' affections and to display the 'predominant power of truth and reason' over error and vice. In his preface to *Hugh Trevor* (1794), Holcroft argued that good novels were 'very essentially connected with moral instruction' because they represented 'so many histories of the progress of mind'.[31] These comments were not only attempts to deflect anticipated accusations of seditious content, but also emergent claims about what a good novel can do – by representing moral enquiry it could instigate it in readers.

Dissenting-educated thinkers such as Godwin tended to understand the disclosure or 'confession' of private thoughts as a particular force for social good, something with the potential to activate the independent moral judgement of readers. This sprang from the principle of candour, fundamental to the pedagogy of the English dissenting academies, which invested 'the honest mind' with immense reformatory potential.³² This concept shaped many understandings of the ethics of fiction as the nineteenth century dawned. It underlay, for example, Anna Barbauld's claim that novels could have 'a very strong effect in infusing principles and moral feelings' in her essay 'On The Origin And Progress Of Novel-Writing' (1810). It was more explicit in William Hazlitt's *Lectures on the English Comic Writers* (1819), which argued that through novels we 'imbibe our notions of virtue and vice from practical examples, and are taught a knowledge of the world'. We gain this knowledge not from the 'professed moralist', Hazlitt argues, but from 'the painter of manners' who 'gives the facts of human nature, and leaves us to draw the inference'.³³ There is a clear similarity to Godwin's ideas here, in the supposition that a clear apprehension of human experience will necessarily inculcate sound moral judgement.

These kinds of arguments were integral to the novel's social elevation in the early nineteenth century – its journey from an unrespectable form to one with recognised public value. Ina Ferris has shown that the novel in the 1810s and 20s attempted 'deliberate self-alignment with non-fictional genres' and argues that this was an attempt 'to harness for itself the cultural power of modern fact and to transform itself into a properly public genre'.³⁴ Godwin's language of ethics (as 'the science of man'), alongside his claims about the novel as 'true history', were similar endeavours to ally his fiction to discourses of social authority. Indeed, the very contexts of this growing body of critical comments about the novel (prefaces, essays, lectures, reviews) are significant, showing that it was becoming a form with a history, deemed worthy of theorisation and canonisation.³⁵

This social and material context helps to illuminate Godwin's ending to the 1832 *Fleetwood* preface. This was his own critical introduction in a collection of reprints, the successful *Standard Novels* series – begun in 1831 by Henry Colburn and Richard Bentley but soon continued by Bentley alone after the partnership disintegrated – which, by reissuing popular three-volume novels in a more affordable one-volume format, was a major contributor to the cultural 'assimilation' of the novel in the early nineteenth century.³⁶ Godwin was required once again to reflect upon his fictional craft, and this time was speaking into a context in which the novel was rapidly rising in public grace. His emphasis was thus less upon defending the moral status of the form (as it had been in 1797), and more upon criticising those readers who missed its moral potential. To recount the ways in which *Caleb Williams* was 'hastily gobbled up' was to echo the anxieties of his 'Essay of History and Romance' about the class of readers which lowered the novel's standard of production and reception – those who consumed the story but failed to extract moral nutrition from the lives it mediated.

Yet the boundaries of this class are more troubled in 1832 than they were in 1797, for they include Joseph Gerrald, a fellow reformist with whom Godwin had associated before his trial for sedition in 1794 and eventual transportation in 1795. He was apparently the ideal reader for *Caleb Williams*, someone well attuned to the social and political issues Godwin was raising. His superficial encounter unsettles distinctions between 'true' and 'false' novel-readers, in much the same way that the ending of 'History and Romance' unsettled distinctions between 'true' and 'false' novel-writers. Godwin was placing the weight of moral responsibility for the novel form upon readers, but if 'one of the most accomplished readers' could fail, what hope was there for others?

The Case of *Deloraine*

Godwin's final novel *Deloraine* was conceived in direct dialogue with these critical writings. It was composed while he revised the 1832 *Fleetwood*, begun almost immediately after *Cloudesley*'s publication, and it shares the orienting question of their prefaces: what renders a life morally legible?[37] Like *Caleb Williams*, *Deloraine* is centred around a murder – literally, in this case, for the act occurs in the middle of the second volume – and is rendered in Godwin's trademark confessional mode. Shortly after the eponymous narrator's second marriage to the delicate Margaret, he encounters her in the presence of her former lover William, who had been presumed dead: Deloraine impulsively shoots William, causing Margaret to die from shock, and flees abroad with his daughter Catherine to escape the ramifications of his deed. The tale thus pursues not factual knowledge of the perpetrator's identity or proceedings, but moral knowledge. Godwin dramatises two reductive systems of moral representation in his narrative – institutional criminal law and popular journalism – and implicitly upholds confessional narrative as their radical counterpoint.

Representatives of the British criminal justice system appear in *Deloraine* as defunct storytellers, whose narratives obscure, rather than disclose, moral knowledge. This criticism is not only implicit – the legal narrative jars against the personal experience presented to the reader by the narrator – but also explicit in Deloraine's direct reflections upon his circumstances. These reflections commence immediately after he kills William: 'I knew enough of the laws of my country to know that that which in my mind was a vindication, would not be so received in an English court of justice.' This conflict of interpretations is shortly explained by a description of the law's fundamental approach to moral knowledge:

> Nothing [is] more precise than the expounding and application of the English law in the case of murder. It is like the application of a cloth-yard in a mercer's shop. [. . .] The only question is, Does the deed under consideration come up to the rule? Just as in the shop of the mercer we decide, Does the cloth measure three feet of twelve inches each? [. . .] No consideration is had of the character of the parties, or the nature of the provocation. The heart of the judge is dead within him, and so of the rest. The whole is determined, in a way that more resembles the turning of a machine, than the decision of that complicated being called man, endowed with eyes to see, and an understanding to discriminate, and a heart to feel, and a moral sense to judge according to the eternal law written in the skies.[38]

Institutional law obscures moral knowledge, Deloraine claims, because it is based upon the wrong sort of measurement. It works according to rules, categories and terms, which are appropriate for representing inanimate materials such as cloth, but of little use when it comes to understanding 'that complicated being called man'. It upholds a story about human behaviour that is untrue to life. Deloraine assumes that this mechanistic approach to public judgement not only harms the person accused, who is 'disposed of' according to the rules, but also damages the judicial authorities themselves, whose abilities to reason and feel are overridden and blunted by the legal machinery. Criminal law dehumanises all participants because it replaces the living capacity for moral judgement with rigid, insensible measures.

Deloraine's view of criminal law is confirmed by the actions of the legal authorities once he has fled the scene of violence. The local magistrate organises an inquest, assisted by a doctor, coroner and hastily assembled jury. They process the available information solely according to 'the principal constituents of what the law denominates the crime of murder', valuing only those categories of legal measurement that Deloraine had bitterly critiqued. After interviewing witnesses they conclude with a judgement of wilful unprovoked homicide, finding no evidence for 'a charge of previous malice' but sufficient time lapse before the act itself for 'malice aforethought'. Godwin's matter-of-fact, list-like prose affirms the mechanistic impression of the meeting: 'This verdict was accordingly found and recorded; and the coroner in conclusion issued his warrant for my apprehension.'[39] It jars with the preceding relation of the actual killing, which after nearly two volumes of context is embedded in a matrix of relational and psychological pressure. The inquest narrative accounts insufficiently for the event, extracting it unnaturally from its proper home.

The law is critiqued again in similar terms by Deloraine's daughter and ally Catherine, in an eloquent appeal that brings the plot to its climax and finally ends the flight/pursuit motif of the third volume. Boldly confronting Travers, who has tracked them across Europe in the name of English justice, she states:

> I know how the law construes all this. It scorns to take account of previous circumstances, of any of the strings that twine themselves round the human heart. It comes with its scales, and weighs every thing to the partition of a hair. It comes with its measures, and takes account of roods, and yards, and inches of space, and reckons hours, and quarters of an hour, and minutes, and seconds of time. And it finds in the present case the required sum of space and time, and pronounces a crime of malice prepense, and a verdict of wilful murder. It hurries the actor therefore to an ignominious death. [. . .] Deloraine, however unfortunate in the offence he has committed, has not deserved the retribution you seek. He has no felonious qualities. He is neither profligate nor malicious. Though he shed the blood of William, he did not imbrue his hands in guilt. He has contracted no moral defilement.[40]

Catherine appropriates the language of the law here in order to attack the way that it 'construes' events. Blackstone's *Commentaries* had distinguished between 'excusable' and 'felonious' homicide, for example, and her claim that Deloraine 'has no felonious qualities' is a deliberate subversion of accepted criminal categories.[41] While the action itself, extracted from its context, falls under the definition of felonious homicide (an unlawful deliberate killing), the personal qualities of the perpetrator himself resist the category and trouble its authority. Catherine thus presents the 'scales' and 'measures' of the law as Deloraine had done previously, as insufficient for attaining moral knowledge. Her speech in its entirety contains a radically alternative narrative about Deloraine's action, presented in a manner deliberately antithetical to the stories circulated by social authorities, in which Deloraine is a tragic figure and Travers the one morally 'degraded' by his role as 'a hunter of human blood'. This climactic appeal reinforces the novel's central theme of defunct legal judgement, and positions it in a framework of narrative conflict.

These were critiques with political resonance, given that criminal law – and especially the issue of capital punishment – was a hot topic of parliamentary debate in the 1820s and 30s. Many of the so-called 'Newgate novels' of the 1830s were conceived in implicit reference to contemporary attempts to consolidate and clarify the justice system, for which Sir Robert Peel as Home Secretary became the figurehead and which brought a dramatic reduction to the list of offences carrying the death penalty.[42] Godwin was clearly interested in these developments, but he was also revisiting an intervention that he had made four decades ago in *Political Justice*. All editions of that treatise had argued that criminal law per se was flawed because it took insufficient account of the contingency, complexity and individuality of human action. In fact, Godwin had begun by redefining the term 'law' itself: 'Reason is the only legislator [. . .] The functions of society extend, not to the making, but to the interpreting of law.'[43] In other words, the law of reason – apprehended by human beings through the faculty of private judgement in an interminable, yet perfectible process – should be the only fixed principle that determines society's response to wrongdoing. Legal codes and structures sustained over time by societies tend to ossify the faculty of private judgement and thus obscure the true law of reason:

> Law tends no less than creeds, catechisms and tests, to fix the human mind in a stagnant condition, and to substitute a principle of permanence, in the room of that unceasing perfectibility which is the only salubrious element of mind.[44]

Institutional law, Godwin argues, makes judgements about future behaviour by constraining it to the precedents and frameworks of the past, thus hampering the basic human capacity for intellectual improvement. This tension between law and justice became a central theme of many so-called Jacobin novels in the 1790s, perhaps most explicitly in Holcroft's *Hugh Trevor*, which contains an extended discussion of institutional law owing much to *Political Justice*.[45] It surfaced again in Godwin's plans, around the time of *Deloraine*'s composition, for a novel based upon the life of the infamous eighteenth-century convict Eugene Aram (plans he may have given to Edward Bulwer-Lytton, whose own novel *Eugene Aram* appeared in 1832).[46] The tension is fully explicit in Deloraine's contention that the English legal system neglects 'the eternal law written in the skies': its fixed regulations are unable to account for the unusual, ambivalent nature of his situation, which the reasoning mind would apprehend and prioritise.

Much more could be said about Godwin's discussion of criminal law in *Political Justice*, but most germane is his interest in describing the flaws of the legal system in narrative terms. Its fixed categories confound all the subtleties of thought, motive and psychology that every case involves, and thus tell defunct stories about the mind. Or rather, they tell defunct stories about human life that fail to take the centrality and complexity of the mind into account:

> This part of the subject will be put in a striking light, if we recollect the narratives that have been written by condemned criminals. In how different a light do they place the transactions that proved fatal to them, from the construction that was put upon them by their judges? [. . .] Who will say that the judge with his slender pittance of information was more competent to decide upon the motives, than the prisoner after the severest scrutiny of his own mind? How few are the trials which an humane and a just man can read, terminating in a verdict of guilty, without feeling an uncontrolable [*sic*] repugnance against the verdict? If there be any sight more humiliating than all others, it is that of a miserable victim acknowledging the justice of a sentence, against which every enlightened reasoner exclaims with horror.[47]

Past events may be represented more or less faithfully by the parties involved, yet the judge – with his scanty information and predetermined behavioural categories – will always tell an obfuscatory tale.

The prisoner himself will tell a better one, Godwin claims, since he knows instinctively to prioritise and scrutinise 'his own mind'. The legal rendering of the story is invasive and manipulating, however, often leading the accused to 'acknowledg[e] the justice' of its conclusion. The audience member, if he be 'enlightened', will intuit that the label 'guilty' is nearly always reductive and therefore a distorted interpretation of the circumstances under investigation. *Political Justice* thus contains a germinal form of Godwin's argument about narrative fiction in the 'Essay of History and Romance' and the preface to *Cloudesley*.

In *Deloraine*, Godwin emphasises this narrative dimension to institutional judgement by giving it an overtly textual embodiment. The protagonist becomes aware of the legal rendering of his case solely through newspapers, and these printed forms pursue him across Europe with aggressive, distorted tales about his life and character. Godwin was not only tapping into the familiar trope of popular journalism as an agent of corruption – he was specifically associating official legal judgements with the lurid stories of downmarket Newgate literature, in a similar manner to Falkland's handbills in *Caleb Williams*.[48] Deloraine is expecting to confront his case in print, yet the initial encounter still affects him powerfully:

> Though all this was matter of course, was drawn up in the ordinary forms, and might have been anticipated by me almost word for word as I found it, yet such is the nature of the human mind, that a stronger and almost a new effect is produced upon us, when it comes to be subjected to our sense. It lost its vagueness, the misty and obscure form it previously bore, and thrilled through the marrow in my bones.[49]

This newspaper makes no allowance for ambivalence, nuance or uncertainty; the events are (literally) presented in black and white. Its materiality reinforces this, for as an object 'subjected to our sense' it makes clear and stark what Deloraine knows to be obscure. It is an unnatural embodiment, and as such elicits horror. It also precipitates violence:

> The paragraph I beheld struck at my liberty and my life. Till the hour of the rash act I had committed, I had been a recognised and authentic member of the aristocracy of my country, protected by its laws and with all my

> immunities and privileges, and honoured by my fellow-citizens. [. . .] Now I was proclaimed as a loathsome and rejected member of the community, and a price was fixed upon my head. [. . .] My head was devoted, a victim to the demands of criminal law; and the code of civilization could not be satisfied without my extirpation.[50]

The narrative is inherently hostile: it strikes, demands, victimises. And a key mechanism of its violence is typology, its recognition and sorting of subjects via institutional code, which Deloraine describes elsewhere as 'the vocabulary of undistinguishing law'.[51] His status as 'authentic' and 'honoured' is suddenly reversed to 'loathsome' and 'rejected' in accordance with the law's unreasoning measures. The newspaper's ultimate contribution is to exacerbate and reinforce this categorisation through public embodiment.

As the novel progresses, newspapers take licence with the content of Deloraine's story and distort it more obviously. They are simultaneously associated with Gothic literary tropes: the newspaper assumes the role of the omnipresent persecutor, energising a long flight-and-pursuit narrative across Europe that evokes Victor's flight in Shelley's *Frankenstein* (1818). Deloraine is never safe from the reductive version of his life story. Even when he shelters in a remote half-ruined castle, a 'French periodical *brochure*' finds its way to his patron and its edition of the tale initiates betrayal.[52] As Deidre Lynch notes, Gothic fiction of this period is marked out by its interest in narrative possession. Characters are routinely 'hemmed in by others' stories' and dogged by literary legacies, and these circumstances provide a means for authors to explore systemic aspects of cultural interpretation.[53] This comes to the fore in *Deloraine* as the protagonist is haunted by the monstrous double of his own narrative and is never able to put it to rest. Godwin implies that institutional justice spawns reductive stories about human behaviour for the purposes of irrational coercion.

This inadequate narrative system is overtly challenged, however, by Godwin's mode and style of narration. *Deloraine* shares the first-person perspective with his preceding novels yet, in accordance with *Fleetwood*'s 1832 preface, is particularly self-conscious about the ways in which that perspective might redress the obfuscations of institutional law. The moral landscape of the protagonist's confession emerges in radical contrast from that sketched by legal representatives.

Whereas legal narrative begins with the criminal act, for example, Deloraine's confession embeds that act within his entire unwieldy personal history, revealing something about the violence which the law never could – that its deepest roots lay in his idealisation and objectification of women. This shifting of the moral coordinates through narrative perspective was a belated development of Defoe's confessional novels, as several critics have noted. Defoe used the conventions of spiritual autobiography and criminal tale to present events exclusively from the position of the social deviant – Moll Flanders, or Roxana – thereby drawing readers into 'imaginative complicity' with their actions.[54] Confessional models resonated variously as the novel developed in the eighteenth century, including in the interpersonal disclosures of epistolary fiction. A conscious inheritor of this tradition, Godwin drew from formal aspects of the memoir, epistle and criminal tale in order to undermine representations of Deloraine that arrive from sources other than his own introspection. *Deloraine* thus makes a statement about public ethics, attempting to redress both the perceived displacement of private judgement in moral discrimination and institutional neglect of the complexity, necessity and irreducibility of individual lives.

Godwin also alienates legal narrative from lived experience through what he leaves absent from the novel. Deloraine is never tried. He immediately flees after he kills William, assuming that the system of criminal law will be inadequate in its moral judgement upon the case. Official legal spaces, procedures and apparatus are thus conspicuously absent from the novel, unlike in *Caleb Williams*: it is as though the system has been denied a home. Criminal law is represented in ghost form, through Travers, through the mob, through the newspapers. It is always on foreign territory, an alien force that invades human life. The legal story, moreover, is denied an ending: Catherine's climactic appeal is successful and Travers ceases his European pursuit, but Deloraine remains in exile from England, knowing that a price remains upon his head. The justice that has been recognised and felt between two personal parties cannot be mirrored by institutional justice, Godwin implies. Criminal law remains suspended in its task, and the psychological effects of this give the novel its bittersweet ending. Lack of closure was a recognised feature of Godwin's novels and annoyed most reviewers – particularly those of *Mandeville*.[55] In *Deloraine*, however, this kind of ending was bound up with a specific attempt to show the inadequacy of legal narrative. By leaving its 'official' story pending, Godwin disrupts the law's drive towards simplified case-closure.

This simplifying tendency of legal narrative is counteracted further by the temporal ambiguity of Deloraine's narration. Although the story begins rather conventionally with his birth, Deloraine builds temporal disruption into it as he proceeds: he started composing the tale at a certain point in his flight from the law, he records, and signals that the narrative is being continued in the present around its crisis point, rather like in *Caleb Williams*. Throughout his account Deloraine draws attention to the fact that he is including information inaccessible to him at the time of action and thus only gained at a later date, sometimes presumably after the climax itself.[56] The tale ends by placing the process of composition into the preceding narrative, and imagining its moral tendency upon future generations. Yet it also deliberately evades historical location, conjecturing that it will be most of use centuries down the line, when the particulars of names and dates have been forgotten.[57] The narrator is thus anxious to position himself and his narrative in time, and yet simultaneously highlights his non-linear (even atemporal) rendering of events. By contrast, the demands of the law are portrayed in terms of precise time measurement: it 'reckons hours, and quarters of an hour, and minutes, and seconds of time'. Indeed, the verdict of malice prepense hangs upon these measures. Godwin's conscious temporal disruption of Deloraine's tale undermines the authority of these minutes and seconds, placing their strictures in a disorienting web of past, present and future.

The style in which Deloraine's perspective is rendered also implicitly recruits readers to the judgement task. Godwin's syntax mirrors his subject's thought processes, which respond to a new event or intelligence with a sequence of reflections, questions and imagined possibilities. Deloraine's receipt of William's ship letter, for example, initiates such a string of reactions. He begins with a question of knowledge – 'What was I to believe?' – and after contemplating historical possibilities, considers a question of action, the appropriate response to the unopened letter: 'On what was I to resolve?' After reading it, he wonders what the letter means for his own being, and poses a question of identity: 'What was I now?'[58] Such pockets of intellection cluster around key plot developments, framing them as matter for thought and offering them up to scrutiny: Godwin prompts his readers to pause and consider the significance of events for themselves. Moreover, by highlighting the contingent and protean nature of Deloraine's judgements, he positions the narrator's mind itself as a key object of investigation, discouraging readers from complacently assuming its perspective. Contemporary reviewers recognised the importance of this: *Deloraine* is 'full of thought, and the matériel of thought', wrote one, articulating the link he established between the mental lives of his protagonist and his readers.[59]

Deloraine's confession finishes on a deeply ambivalent note, however, which underscores the vulnerability of judgement to institutional power rather than the possibility of its independence. This is precipitated by the second newspaper, which paints a picture so grotesque that it initially prompts him to defend himself: 'I felt in my heart that I was justified.' Yet Deloraine soon slips into a train of anxious reflections, questioning his motives for taking action. 'This paper [. . .] first suggested to me a doubt of the all-sufficiency of the evidence upon which I had acted', he records. This possibility precipitates an increasingly negative stream of thoughts, which revise or contradict his earlier convictions. He soon asserts: 'never did I regard [my action] but as the most aggravated and atrocious crime that imagination itself could devise'.[60] His language echoes that of the newspaper article, suggesting that he has absorbed its two-dimensional construction of his character.

As the tale draws to a close, Deloraine appears to be completely overpowered by these reductive stories. While he was on the run, he claims, his 'thoughts were beguiled', but now 'I have nothing to do, but to ruminate on what I have committed. [. . .] And the more I revolve in my secret soul the deed I have perpetrated, the blacker does it shew itself.' Like Caleb in the printed ending of *Caleb Williams*, Deloraine enters a realm of self-abasement and narrative revision, concluding that his character is 'odious, horrible even to the imagining, and past all redemption', once again echoing the second newspaper account (which described him as 'an unparalleled monster, heartless, selfish and sanguinary').[61] Although Catherine is able to heal, Deloraine's moral sense has been irrevocably warped by public interpretations of his life. In his short, awkward 'Conclusion', he questions the import of his narrative and frames it as a moral fable, committing it to the use of future readers.[62]

Why finish with this nightmarish portrayal of institutional power over the mind's moral judgement? Godwin's preface to *Fleetwood* in 1832 ended with a disordered reading experience, and the final scene of his final novel provides a similar close-up of a weak mind, a reader whose capacity for ethical knowledge has been overwhelmed by social climate. This conclusion represents a tension that remains as unresolved in *Deloraine* as it does anywhere in Godwin's writing: the capacity of the mind to launch into independent territory is set starkly against its tendency to capitulate to the status quo. We might consider this as a version of the preoccupation with the limits of individual agency that marked out novels of this period more generally, from novels of manners to travel narratives and national tales. The identity and role of the individual within a wider social complex is a puzzle that energises plot structures across this varied landscape of fiction, including those by writers as stylistically divergent from Godwin as Jane Austen and Walter Scott. For Godwin, the reading mind was the key battleground upon which individual potential conflicted with social habit and behaviour; his fiction and his criticism therefore do all they can to encourage reading experiences that flex the moral muscles of the mind.

Godwin's theorisation of narrative fiction in terms of moral knowledge was an attempt to direct public conversations about the social significance of the novel. He made a renewed effort to link the novel form to intellectual perfectibility in the early 1830s, exploiting a moment in which novelists were increasingly associating their work with the cultural authority of non-fictional genres in order to imbue his particular sort of novel with ethical credentials. Simultaneously, however, he was preoccupied with exposing the intellectual atrophy and subjection of the existing reading nation. His later writings in and about the novel form juxtapose idealistic belief in human perfectibility with anxious assessments about the means by which it may be realised in the messy material world of the present. What emerges is a problem of mediation. How might fiction mediate truth, justice and virtue to its readers? And what conditions are necessary for the mind to successfully receive and be formed by them? One of Godwin's ongoing responses to this tension was to write about good reading practice; in fact, one of the consistent features of his writing is an appeal to the notion of 'true reading'. The next chapter examines Godwin's practical reading advice in detail, and explores some of the assumptions about the mediating properties of the mind upon which it was based.

Notes

1. *Fleetwood: or, The New Man of Feeling*, CNM, vol. 5, p.12.
2. Clara Reeve, *The Progress of Romance, through Times, Countries, and Manners* [. . .], vol. 2 (Colchester: Keymer, 1785), p. 78. For the wider contexts of gustatory imagery see Denise Gigante, *Taste: A Literary History* (New Haven: Yale University Press, 2005), especially pp. 13–21.
3. See *LWG*, vol. 1, p. 93 n.1.
   Gerrald died in 1796 after being transported to Australia, hence Godwin's reference to him as 'unfortunate'.
4. *Fleetwood*, pp. 8, 10.
5. Garrett Sullivan, '"A Story to Be Hastily Gobbled Up": *Caleb Williams* and Print Culture', *Studies in Romanticism* 32 (1993): 337.
6. Ina Ferris, 'Transformations of the Novel – II', *The Cambridge History of English Romantic Literature*, ed. James Chandler (Cambridge: Cambridge University Press, 2009), p. 478. See Ferris *The Achievement of Literary Authority: Gender, History, and the Waverley Novels* (Ithaca, NY: Cornell University Press, 1991); Katie Trumpener, *Bardic Nationalism: the Romantic Novel and the British Empire* (Princeton: Princeton University Press, 1997); William Warner, *Licensing Entertainment: the Elevation of Novel Reading in Britain, 1684–1750* (Berkeley: University of California Press, 1998), pp. 8–9.
7. *LWG*, vol.1, pp. 116–17.
8. *The Enquirer*, p. 79.
9. 'Essay of History and Romance', *PPW*, vol. 5, pp. 297, 298.
10. Ibid. p. 294.
11. See Smith, *The Theory of Moral Sentiments*, ed. D. D. Raphael and A. L. Macfie (Oxford: Clarendon Press, 1976).
12. Janet Todd, *Sensibility: An Introduction* (London: Methuen, 1986), p. 4.
13. See, for example, Maureen Harkin, 'Mackenzie's Man of Feeling: Embalming Sensibility', *ELH* 61.2 (1994): 317–40. On the discourse of sentiment more generally and its theological nuances see Isabel Rivers, *Reason, Grace, and Sentiment: a Study of the Language of Religion and Ethics in England, 1660–1780*, vol. 2 (Cambridge: Cambridge University Press, 2000).

14. Daniel E. White, *Early Romanticism and Religious Dissent* (Cambridge: Cambridge University Press, 2006), p. 113.
15. In his unpublished writings Godwin attributed this neglect to the influence of 'Calvinist system' and linked his subsequent attempts to remedy it to his reading of Hume: 'Autobiographical Fragments and Reflections', *CNM*, vol. 1, pp. 53–4.
16. 'Reply to Parr', *PPW*, vol. 2, pp. 182–3.
17. Rowland Weston, 'History, Memory, and Moral Knowledge: William Godwin's "Essay on Sepulchres"', *The European Legacy* 14.6 (2009): 651–65.
18. 'Essay of History and Romance', p. 301.
19. Ibid. pp. 301, 299.
20. Ibid. pp. 298–9.
21. Ibid. p. 301.
22. Ibid. p. 301.
23. 'Introductory note', *Fleetwood*, p. v.
24. Preface to *Cloudesley*, *CNM*, vol. 7, p. 7 (emphasis mine).
25. Ibid. pp. 7–8.
26. Aristotle, *Poetics*, trans. Malcom Heath (London: Penguin, 1996), p. 16.
27. *Fleetwood*, p. 10.
28. Preface to *Cloudesley*, p. 8; Godwin makes Shakespeare an exception to this rule. For his attitude and contribution to drama, see David O'Shaughnessy, *William Godwin and the Theatre* (London: Pickering & Chatto, 2010).
29. [Edward Bulwer-Lytton], 'Cloudesley, by the Author of Caleb Williams', *The New Monthly Magazine and Literary Journal* 28.109 (January 1830): 368.
30. For a concise summary see Warner, *Licensing Entertainment*, pp. 1–19.
31. Charlotte Smith, *Desmond. A Novel*, in *The Works of Charlotte Smith*, vol. 5, ed. Stuart Curran (London: Pickering & Chatto, 2005), p. 3; Thomas Holcroft, *The Adventures of Hugh Trevor*, ed. Seamus Deane (London: Oxford University Press, 1973), pp. 3–4.
32. See Tessa Whitehouse, *The Textual Culture of English Protestant Dissent 1720–1800* (Oxford: Oxford University Press, 2015), p. 30; D. O. Thomas, *The Honest Mind: The Thought and Work of Richard Price* (Oxford: Clarendon Press, 1977); Pamela Clemit, 'Self-Analysis as Social Critique: The Autobiographical Writings of Godwin and Rousseau', *Romanticism* 11 (2005): 161–80 (p. 164).
33. Anna Barbauld, *The British Novelists*, vol. 1 (London, York and Edinburgh: Rivington et al. 1820), pp. 46–7; Hazlitt, *Lectures on the English Comic Writers* (London: Taylor and Hessey, 1819), pp. 209, 211.
34. Ferris, 'Transformations of the Novel', pp. 473, 489.

35. See Michael Gamer, 'A Select Collection: Barbauld, Scott, and the Rise of the (Reprinted) Novel', Heydt-Stevenson and Sussman, *Recognizing the Romantic Novel: New Histories of British Fiction, 1780–1830*, ed. Jillian Heydt-Stevenson and Charlotte Sussman (Liverpool: Liverpool University Press, 2008).
36. See Alan Downie, 'The English Novel at the End of the 1820s', *The Oxford Handbook of the Eighteenth-Century Novel* (Oxford: Oxford University Press, 2016), p. 582.
37. See *Deloraine*'s preface (*CNM*, vol. 8, p. 5). *Deloraine* appears almost daily in *DWG* from April 1831 until November 1832.
38. *Deloraine*, pp. 148, 152.
39. Ibid. p. 183.
40. Ibid. p. 279.
41. Sir William Blackstone, *Commentaries On the Laws of England* [. . .], vol. 4 (London: Strahan et al., 1787), p. 177.
42. See David Bentley, *English Criminal Justice in the Nineteenth Century* (London: The Hambledon Press, 1998); Randall McGowen, 'The Image of Justice and Reform of the Criminal Law in Early Nineteenth-Century England', *Buffalo Law Review*, 32.1 (1983): 89–125; Philip Handler, 'James Mackintosh and Early Nineteenth-Century Criminal Law', *The Historical Journal* 58.3 (2015): 757–79.
43. *Political Justice*, p. 95.
44. Ibid. p. 413.
45. *Hugh Trevor*, pp. 255–6.
46. For these notes and Godwin's relations with Bulwer-Lytton, see C. Kegan Paul, *William Godwin: His Friends and Contemporaries*, vol. 2 (Boston: Roberts Brothers, 1876), pp. 304–5. On Aram's renewed significance in the early nineteenth century, see Nancy Jane Tyson, *Eugene Aram: Literary History and Typology of the Scholar-Criminal* (Hamden, CT: Archon Books, 1983).
47. *Political Justice*, pp. 386–7.
48. See Aled Jones, *Powers of the Press: Newspapers, Power and the Public in Nineteenth-Century England* (Aldershot: Scolar Press, 1996). For the significance of this dynamic to the history of the novel, see Jessica Valdez, *Plotting the News in the Victorian Novel* (Edinburgh: Edinburgh University Press, 2020).
49. *Deloraine*, p. 209.
50. Ibid.
51. Ibid. p. 233.
52. Ibid. p. 243.
53. Deidre Lynch, 'Transformations of the Novel – I', *The Cambridge History of English Romantic Literature*, ed. James Chandler (Cambridge:

Cambridge University Press, 2009), p. 468; see also the preface to Hal Gladfelder, *Criminality and Narrative in Eighteenth-Century England: Beyond the Law* (Baltimore: Johns Hopkins University Press, 2001).
54. Gladfelder, *Criminality and Narrative*, p. 9; see also Clemit, *The Godwinian Novel* (Oxford: Clarendon, 1993), pp. 55–6.
55. See, for example, [Anon.], 'Remarks on Mandeville', *Blackwood's Magazine*, 2 (January 1818): 402–8. For this writer the ending of the novel was 'a conclusion "so lame and impotent," that but for the words THE END, at the bottom of the page, we would naturally turn over the leaf for another chapter. [. . .] to leave everything unsettled, as in the conclusion of Mandeville, is to part with the reader on bad terms' (p. 408).
56. *Deloraine*, e.g. pp. 125, 129, 137, 186–7, 219, 277.
57. Ibid. p. 286.
58. Ibid. pp. 110–13.
59. [Anon.], 'Deloraine. By the Author of "Caleb Williams",' *Literary Gazette* 838 (1833): 81.
60. *Deloraine*, pp. 245–6, 263.
61. Ibid. pp. 284, 285, 245.
62. On this see Esterhammer, 'Godwin's Suspicion of Speech Acts', esp. pp. 577–8.

Chapter 3

The Discipline of Reading: 'Enquiry' and Religious Dissent

'[F]ew men have sufficiently reflected on the true mode of reading', Godwin declared in his essay 'Of Learning' in *The Enquirer* (1797).[1] The comment reflects his long-standing interest in reading as a practical task and simultaneously advertises an exclusive attitude towards it: the fact that reading had a 'true mode' also meant that it had a false one. Writing to Percy Shelley a few years later, Godwin argued that 'True reading is investigation, [. . .] an active enquiry.'[2] Ways of reading were important because they facilitated particular postures of mind towards the world. Healthy reading, he believed, was integral to healthy judgement. Such a crucial activity was not to be taken lightly, and accordingly practical advice about how to read appears throughout Godwin's correspondence and writings on education.

It is the noetic significance of Godwin's reading advice that concerns this chapter – the beliefs his instructions betray about the nature and operation of the mind as a medium of knowledge. Adrian Johns observes of the early modern period that 'accounts of the practical experience of reading came to play a central role in arguments about the status of claims to knowledge',[3] and Godwin's instructions for 'true reading' performed a similar function in his own day. His advice was rooted in an educational subculture of Protestant dissent, spearheaded by John Jennings, Philip Doddridge and Isaac Watts, according to which reading was conceived as a discipline – in the sense of a field of study and also in the sense of a programme of training, such as those associated with military, medical and moral regimes. Through the correct discipline of reading, it was understood, the mind developed a disposition of cautious receptivity or 'enquiry' towards the world it encountered, which enabled it to make sound judgements. Godwin's adaption of this educational tradition – and especially the habitual aspect of its reading advice – is noteworthy in part for its conflicting assumptions about sources and modes of epistemic authority. His growing insistence that writing practice was a necessary element of successful reading, moreover, testifies to the way that this uneasy pedagogical emphasis upon discipline fertilised understandings of literary production, an intersection that studies of Romantic-period literature increasingly underscore.[4]

To maximise the role of discipline and habit in this reading advice is to depart in some measure from critical trends. In recent years Godwin's writings on education have been reassessed from a political perspective – along with the period's pedagogy and literature for children more widely – in justified response to the oversight of preceding histories that represented them as a retreat from political intervention towards 'neutral subjects'.[5] Godwin is often cast as an unusually liberal voice amid the increasing conservatism of 1790s Britain, and *The Enquirer* cited to the near exclusion of other writings. The conclusion is that his reading advice was designed to inculcate freedom above all other principles, in defiance of prevailing restrictions – freedom of choice, freedom of judgement, freedom of imagination.[6] It is easy to interpret Godwin's understanding of 'freedom' anachronistically, however, especially when its roots in dissenting culture are neglected. Rather than an attitude of self-sufficiency or a blanket rejection of all social authorities, educational freedom for Godwin meant a form of structured exposure to heterogeneous beliefs and choices, which in turn fostered a mental disposition favourable to the apprehension of truth. Such exposure was only beneficial insofar as it was directed by particular reading skills and undertaken in a context of routine. When we recognise this overriding disciplinary imperative, we uncover the equivocal view of the mind's tendencies that Godwin, like other writers of his time, inherited from dissenting educational culture. Great confidence in the mind's discriminating powers converged with great fear of its adverse principles, such as passivity, distraction and rebellion.

Godwin's advice is not limited to childhood reading and often does not make a clear distinction between the reading practices of different age groups. The child became a new object of social and commercial interest during his lifetime, and children's literature emerged as a recognisable category – indeed, Godwin and his second wife Mary Jane were involved in the business of children's books through their Juvenile Library venture at the beginning of the nineteenth century. Childhood functions in Godwin's reading advice not as a separate category, however, but as a temporal window for instilling habits that set the tenor for later life. Godwin adhered to a version of the environmentalist view of the child, which was manifest variously in Romantic-period culture and often traced back to Locke; the mind was in some measure 'neutral' or 'blank' at birth and acquired its lasting character through the impressions it received during early education and experience. Young minds, Godwin observed, are 'peculiarly ductile'.[7] Childhood reading practices were thus of enormous import for future development, but Godwin did not stop there and undoubtedly conceived of education as a lifelong process. He also gave specific advice for mature readers, which included revisiting books read in former days, exploiting old reading notes, and making the composition of new works an integral part of the reading life.

Unlike Watts, Godwin did not devote a book or series of essays purely to the topic of 'how to read well', but instead dispersed his ideas throughout a range of writings over forty years. His instructions are often parenthetical or exemplary within broader, abstract discussions of communication and pedagogical method. Even an essay with the title 'Of Choice in Reading' is primarily concerned with power relations and epistemic authority – choice – rather than reading in and of itself. Despite these disparate contexts, however, a clear pattern of reading advice emerges from Godwin's work, especially from his essay collections *The Enquirer* (1797) and *Thoughts on Man* (1830); his correspondence with Marmaduke Martin (1798) and Percy Shelley (1812); and his 'Letter of Advice to a Young American' (1818), a pamphlet that responded to the enquiries of an aspiring student and incorporated aspects of his previous correspondence with Martin.[8] In fact, the dispersed nature of Godwin's reading advice is itself significant, reflecting something crucial about his approach to reading. For Godwin 'true reading' was not a study skill that could be segregated from others but rather an outworking of a way of life, an action that sprung naturally from the enquiring disposition. By writing the bulk of his educational advice as essays and weaving reading instructions throughout them, Godwin was attempting to instil this enquiring disposition as he described it. According to *The Enquirer*'s preface, his essays were 'the materials of thinking [. . .] the hints of enquiry rather than actual enquiries: but hereafter perhaps they may be taken under other men's protection, and cherished to maturity'.[9] In other words, Godwin chose the essay form in order to embody his educational advice, to initiate his audience into the discipline of true reading.

Reading and Dissenting Education

The dissenting academies are now viewed – and were often viewed at the time – as the highest-quality option available to young men in eighteenth-century England's very eclectic educational landscape. Most academies encompassed aspects of what we would now term secondary education, higher education and ministerial training; they were known for their expansive curricula at a time when Oxford and Cambridge were increasingly accused of retaining narrow, irrelevant educational programmes and outdated systems of examination.[10] Godwin was educated at Hoxton Academy, within a subculture of dissent that was especially shaped by the pedagogical and intellectual legacies of John Jennings, Philip Doddridge and Isaac Watts.

One of the most important contexts for understanding his subsequent literary work is the emphasis that this educational environment placed upon 'free enquiry' – a somewhat fluid term, which operated here both as an ideal of intellectual animation and honesty and as an exhortation to a specific set of habits that was understood to form a disposition favourable to that ideal's achievement.[11] Of particular significance for Godwin was the way that attention to reading practice in this subculture crystallised an inherent complication in its concept and practice of free enquiry. Theoretical confidence in the salutary results of a flexible and open mental disposition converged with practical caution concerning the means by which that disposition could be realised. This complication would become an explicit tension in Godwin's work, whereby he navigated uncertain territory concerning the degree of trust warranted by the mind as a medium of knowledge.

The nature of intellectual enquiry and its appropriate role within the pious life were contentious issues among eighteenth-century dissenters. Among the many things at stake was the mode of relation between the human faculty of reason, on the one hand, and special forms of divine revelation, on the other. Three unifying beliefs held by the majority of dissenting denominations were commonly summarised as '1. The right of private judgement, 2. Liberty of conscience, and 3. The perfection of scripture as a Christian's *only* rule of faith and practice'.[12] The potential for tension between the first and third tenets was manifest in clashes over their relative practical authority between dissenters of more 'rationalist' persuasion and those of more 'evangelical' persuasion.[13] Terms of debate were complex and the denominational terrain shifted as the century progressed; Godwin became familiar with the landscape during his childhood, which was shaped by the exclusive rationalistic sect of Sandemanianism.

Jennings, Doddridge and Watts were among those dissenters in the first half of the century who negotiated the potential conflict via a belief that rational enquiry, if undertaken properly, would necessarily support revealed truth (defined as their version of Protestant orthodoxy).[14] This core assumption fuelled their understanding of education as a means of 'free enquiry' and became integral to the ethos of several prominent dissenting academies. Uninhibited questions were encouraged, and in many cases a pattern of teaching emerged that tended to emphasise methods of critical activity over and above specific doctrinal tenets. These educational programmes were far from sceptical or secular; as Tessa Whitehouse underscores, 'theological education [was] the core aim of academies, even those with a markedly liberal approach to education'.[15] Yet within this theological agenda, many tutors became known for the belief – as Richard Price put it later in the century – that the task of education 'should be to teach *how* to think, rather than *what* to think; or to lead into the best way of searching for truth, rather than to instruct in truth itself'.[16] One consequence was that the practice of reading took on particular significance within this academy movement.

John Jennings (1687–1723) was convinced that the mind's critical powers were strengthened through exposure to a broad range of views, and accordingly pioneered a programme of wide-ranging reading at his Kibworth academy. Doddridge, who was one of his pupils, recorded that he 'encourages the utmost freedom of inquiry. He furnishes us with all kinds of authors of every subject, without advising us to skip over the heretical passages for fear of infection.' In his lectures 'Mr Jennings does not follow the doctrines or phrases of any particular party; but is sometimes a Calvinist, sometimes an

Arminian, and sometimes a Baxterian, as truth and evidence determine him.'[17] Jennings's approach followed Milton's *Areopagitica* (1644), which in its campaign against press licensing had claimed robust reasoning skills as a product of uncensored reading.[18] Such exposure was not unprincipled or freeform, however; it was subordinate to a strict critical regime. Jennings would regularly interrogate his students to ensure that they were actively evaluating their books' contents, for example.[19] Extensive reading was a means of provoking the mind to reason independently, to prevent it from passively accepting a position while remaining unable to defend it. This standpoint was controversial even among dissenters, many of whom did not share its exalted view of human intellectual capacity and feared that young readers, if introduced to unorthodox or immoral texts, would be corrupted. As early as 1703, Samuel Palmer wrote a pamphlet that defended dissenting schools against charges of licentious and lewd reading, indicating that their affiliation with unrestricted reading practice was already a contentious issue.[20]

Philip Doddridge (1702–51), who became leader of the academy at Northampton, admired and developed Jennings's pedagogical emphasis upon extensive, rigorous reading.[21] He was the first tutor to establish an academy library – others relied on private collections – and he gave lectures to his students on its contents and proper use. In lectures Doddridge would assemble opposing arguments from several authors representing the main approaches to his topic and discuss his views of their merits; students would then receive a broad reading list to follow up for several hours in the library. At the next lecture he would question his pupils concerning their opinions before proceeding to the next subject, and – while making his personal beliefs clear – his concern to foster proper investigative method in his students came over and above his own doctrinal convictions. Certainly, as Isabel Rivers points out, the rhetoric of free enquiry had limitations in practice; dissenting academies were governed by denominational and ministerial agendas, and their library resources were limited.[22] Nevertheless, Doddridge was convinced that unrestricted reading, if undertaken correctly, would foster sound critical judgement; reason would be strengthened through the habitual practice of discernment, leading to more reliable knowledge of God's truth. In a letter to John Wesley, he argued that 'in order to *defend the truth*, it is very proper that a young minister should know the chief strength of error'.[23]

Wesley, like others, strongly objected. Their divergence highlights theological disagreements about the nature of the mind, which were endemic to both the established church and nonconformists in this period, and which often revolved around the extent to which human reason was affected by sin. A liberal approach to rational enquiry was an essential part of the religious life for Doddridge, and this was reflected in his confidence in wide reading.

Doddridge qualified this recommendation of reading scope, however, by underscoring in his teaching that it was only valuable insofar as it was undertaken in a disciplined manner. This included strategic deployment of time: an early memorandum entitled 'Rules for the Direction of my Conduct While a Student' contains the commitment to 'Never [. . .] trifle with a book with which I may have no present concern.'[24] Such caution over irrelevant or superficial reading was expressed in his own strict schedule of study, according to which he often read for several hours before breakfast. The most important discipline, however, was a method of careful, critical reading. Books, Doddridge advised a friend, are 'a food we ordinary sort of animals cannot live without; and yet we may possibly be overcharged, if we cram ourselves with more than we can digest'.[25] Job Orton – Doddridge's pupil and subsequent colleague – testified to these habits of 'Care and close Study' in a biography, remembering him as a keen note-taker who sought out books with large margins.[26] Orton recalled his teaching and example with admiration:

> As he cautioned his *Pupils* against that indolent and superficial Way of Reading, which many Students fall into, so he took Care that his own Example should enforce his Precepts. His usual Method was, to read with a Pen in his Hand, and to mark in the *Margin* particular Passages, which struck him. Besides which, he often took down Hints of what was most important, or made References to them, in a *blank Leaf* of the Book, adding his own reflections on the Author's Sentiments.[27]

This close, analytical sort of reading was important to Doddridge not simply because it clarified meaning, but because it was integral to the formation of individual reasoning powers. It was about adopting and honing the critical skills that would ensure one's faculty of judgement was effective. As Orton noted, Doddridge believed that 'the true End of Reading [was] only to furnish the

Mind with *Materials* to exercise its own Powers'.²⁸ To unite the practice of reading with one's own writing, in particular, was to take a crucial step in the formation of private judgement – a conviction that Godwin would endorse and expand upon during his literary career.

This nascent pattern of reading instruction was articulated most fully in the writings of scholar, minister and hymnodist Isaac Watts (1674–1748). Although he never held a tutorial post himself, Watts's educational advice was very influential among the dissenting network and he maintained a close literary relationship with Doddridge.²⁹ *The Improvement of the Mind* (1741, 1751), a sequel to his enormously popular *Logick; Or, the Right Use of Reason in the Inquiry After Truth* (1725), translated convictions about the centrality of independent reason in education into a set of practical instructions for conversation, meditation and reading. Its reading advice built upon the principles of exposure, routine and skill that were expressed in Doddridge's teaching. Watts depicted reading as a discipline for the mind, akin to physical exercise or labour, and expanded in detail upon particular strategies for promoting critical health.

Like Jennings and Doddridge, Watts presented exposure to a variety of viewpoints through reading as essential to the healthy development of the mind. While he eulogised the proliferation of printed material throughout history as a divinely ordained process,³⁰ his emphasis was less upon extensive reading per se and more upon extensive thinking – an open mental disposition that expressed itself in critical investment or sympathy when reading. Quoting the Book of Proverbs, Watts instructed readers to 'Cry after knowledge, and lift up thy voice; seek her as silver, and search for her as for hidden treasures.'³¹ This involved placing oneself in the author's shoes and viewing things from his or her perspective: 'Enter into the sense and argument of the authors you read.'³² Only readers that are imaginatively open to the viewpoints they come across will be able to accurately judge the merit of the text.

Watts was careful to clothe this process of mental flexibility or freedom in the language of discipline, however. Readers, he contended, must seek 'by degrees *an Habit* of judging justly, and of reasoning well'.³³ This meant that they had to work regularly at their task: do not 'abandon reading and labour', he urged, listing the verbs side by side to imply their affinity.³⁴ He repeatedly used agricultural imagery to emphasise his point that good reading was formed over time through habit and hard work: 'infinite errors will overspread the mind, which [. . .] lies without any cultivation', he argued, warning against idle or half-hearted reading.³⁵ Watts was reacting strongly against the idea that intellectual ability could be exclusively intuitive or unschooled. He was not denying the existence of talent, but attacking the idea that talent could bring itself to fruition unaided by educational discipline. 'Presume not too much upon a bright genius', he cautions from the beginning of *Improvement of the Mind*, 'for this without labour and study will never make a man of knowledge and wisdom.'³⁶ This sort of presumption was particularly pernicious because it threatened the dissenting conviction that truth must always be examined for oneself through private judgement, and not chosen by instinct or blind trust. Watts is thus at pains to present reading as an 'industry' and frequently warns against the mental and spiritual dangers of apathy.³⁷

Watts expressed this conflation of reading and labour practically through the endorsement of strict reading routine, giving instructions, like Doddridge, for the efficient use of time. 'Let every particular study have due and proper time assigned it', he advised; 'Order and method in a course of study will have a happy influence to secure you from trifling and wasting your minutes in impertinence.' When organising this schedule, it was also important to be aware of the mind's limits: 'Do not apply yourself to any one study at one time longer than the mind is capable of giving a close attention to it without weariness or wandering'; 'Don't over-fatigue the spirits at any time.'³⁸ Habits of private judgement would be formed most effectively through reading schedules that maximised attentive capacities.

Routine wasn't enough on its own, however: 'There are many who read with constancy and diligence, and yet make no advance in true knowledge by it.'³⁹ Watts recommended specific techniques of critical engagement with one's reading matter, describing practical strategies that would render the labour of the reader effective and fruitful. While he separated reading and meditation into separate sections in *The Improvement of the Mind*, he made it clear that 'meditation, or study' was an integral part of truly profitable reading, and encapsulated this contention in gustatory metaphor. If reading was like eating, then critical engagement with one's reading was the digestive process:

> It is meditation and study that transfers and conveys the notions and sentiments of others to ourselves, so as to make them properly our own. It is our own judgment upon them as well as our memory of them that makes them become our own property. It does as it were, concoct our intellectual food, and turns it into a part of ourselves: Just as a man may call his limbs and his flesh his own, whether he borrowed the materials from the ox or the sheep, from the lark or the lobster [. . .] it is all now become one substance with himself.[40]

In expressing the need to 'digest' reading by means of this extra dimension, Watts was drawing from a long tradition of reading-eating metaphor. As Denise Gigante notes, the imagery of digestion in eighteenth-century writing had two major strands of meaning: it could suggest the drive of corporeal, Hobbesian appetite, as well as an older idea of holistic engagement with authoritative revelation, 'a presecular ontology of eating based on the edible Word of Christianity'.[41] Watts was exploiting both connotations: readers could be shallow gobblers, concerned merely with their transient appetites, or devoted recipients who responsibly assimilated reading matter into their contitution. He was implying that intellectual health and growth could only be acquired from reading matter if it was skilfully processed, integrated into a larger critical economy. As he wrote elsewhere in the treatise, 'Readers may cram themselves in vain with intellectual food, and without real improvement of their minds, for want of digesting it by proper reflections.'[42] Most significantly, Watts allied this practice to the formation of an independent intellect. Shallow readers merely regurgitate the arguments of the books they read, but digesting readers transform them into their 'own property'.

Watts gave various practical instructions for reading in this meditative manner. He advised readers to work through books slowly, after a quick initial survey of the contents and structure. He recommended that books were read more than once, with the occasional exception of history, travels or 'poesy'.[43] He also directed readers in habits of notation; commonplace books were a popular educational resource at the time, but Watts's treatise transcended commonplacing conventions and expanded their usual role.[44] He recommended that students mark up their books with questions and comments, create their own index systems, and even rewrite original texts into more convincing arguments. He argued that particularly worthy books should be written out in an abridged form for personal use, a suggestion that was popular in dissenting academy teaching and may well have inspired the practice that Godwin prescribed, discussed below. '[O]ne book read over in this manner, with all this laborious meditation, will tend more to enrich your understanding, than the skimming over the surface of twenty authors', Watts claimed.[45] It forced the reader to verbalise their interaction with the text, bringing their response into clear formation and enabling them to reflect upon it; it was a safeguard against thoughtless reading, prejudice and the passive absorption of error.

Watts's treatise, then, encapsulates the importance of reading to dissenting educationists mid-century and shows how their models of successful reading aimed to train students towards particular habits and practices in order to achieve the ideal of free enquiry. This intersection of discipline and independence remained a prominent principle of dissenting writings on education throughout the century. As Richard Price expressed it in the 1780s:

> [H]itherto education [. . .] has been a *contraction*, not an *enlargement* of the intellectual faculties; an *injection* of false principles hardening them in error, not a *discipline* enlightening and improving them. Instead of opening and strengthening them, and teaching to think *freely*; it hath cramped and enslaved them, and qualified for thinking only in *one* track.[46]

Contrasts abound here: contraction and enlargement, rigidity and flexibility, slavery and freedom. But the opposition of injection and discipline is perhaps the most telling of Price's inherited view of education, which is understood as participation in a method, regime or approach rather than the passive reception of input. The language of enslavement further pictures this process in a hostile environment: the would-be enquirer must resist an inherited climate of complacency and prejudice in order to attain independence of thought. As with Doddridge and Watts, then, the view of the mind entailed by these instructions is less radically optimistic than the rhetoric of freedom encourages us to assume. The tenor of discipline in these writings reveals a profound fear of mental tendencies to passivity, indolence and usurpation, especially as exacerbated by contemporary norms of education. Through reading advice, dissenting culture was grappling with key philosophical and theological questions about the innate qualities of the mind: Where should its various faculties be located on scales of activity and passivity, or honesty and deception? What degree of confidence should we place in its judgements?

Despite this foundational caution, the approach to learning instigated by dissenters such as Doddridge and Watts was best publicised for its confidence in the mind's ability to develop sound judgement through critical exposure. Its emphasis upon extensive reading in this vein brought much ridicule and censure, which was not helped by the careers of Doddridge's students, many of whom subsequently assumed heterodox theological positions.[47] A particularly infamous attack was levelled by Edmund Burke in 1790, as part of his intervention in British debates about the significance of revolutionary events in France. 'His zeal [. . .] is not for the propagation of his own opinions, but of any opinions', he observed sardonically about Richard Price. 'It is not for the diffusion of truth, but for the spreading of contradiction.'[48] For Burke, the emphasis that dissenting teachers of more rationalist persuasion placed upon method meant that they failed in substance, opening a gateway to public disarray. The educational paradigm of Doddridge and Watts had considerable influence, however, external hostility and internal tension notwithstanding. Doddridge's lectures were revised, annotated and circulated for about seventy years after his death, and were consequential among dissenting teachers and a wider public; they were even used by some Oxbridge tutors.[49] Watts's books were especially well received, and Samuel Johnson asserted of *The Improvement of the Mind* that 'Whoever has the care of instructing others, may be charged with deficience in his duty if this book is not recommended.'[50] The treatise remained popular in Romantic-period Britain, going through several new editions in the late eighteenth and early nineteenth century.

Godwin's Discipline of Reading

Godwin's early life was profoundly shaped by the Doddridge-Watts educational tradition. His grandfather, a dissenting minister, had been a friend of Doddridge, and his father and uncle were educated at Doddridge's Northampton academy; two of his tutors at Hoxton, Andrew Kippis and Samuel Morton Savage, had also been friends and disciples of Doddridge. He was familiar with Watts's educational writings, and recorded reading *Logick* as late as 1792.[51] Godwin clearly had an eye for pedagogical theory: one of his first published works is a prospectus for an academy of his own, which was never actualised. Notably, this 'Account of the Seminary That Will Be Opened [. . .] at Epsom' (1783) gives reading a special importance, assuming that a child's education should be tailored to instil within them a love of reading and to encourage critical engagement with books.[52] This reflects the prominence he gave to memories of reading at Hoxton in his unfinished autobiography, and suggests his personal experience of its centrality in academy life.[53]

Godwin's debt to dissenting education surfaces explicitly in his articulation of true education as initiation into a set of practices, rather than reception of content. This is the unifying principle of his essays in *The Enquirer* and expressed in similar terms to Price: 'It is of less importance that a child should acquire this or that species of knowledge, than that, through the medium of instruction, he should acquire *habits* of intellectual activity.'[54] Godwin placed the activity of reading at the heart of such habit formation, both in *The Enquirer* and in later writings, and attached momentous consequences to particular strategies. He believed that the development of good reading practice would ultimately lead to mass social improvement because it was integral to the development of private judgement – a mental faculty that assumed somewhat eschatological significance for Godwin. This underlies his claim in *The Enquirer* that 'He that loves reading, has every thing within his reach.'[55] Such a high view of reading informs Godwin's sustained appeal to the abstraction of his title, the enquirer, an idealised figure whose fundamental priority is to cultivate intellectual life. Godwin echoed Watts's caution, however, in his practical instructions for achieving this ideal, specifying 'true reading' as a rigorous training regime or battle drill.

Like Jennings and Doddridge, Godwin claimed that wide-ranging reading was essential to the development of discernment. This was a particular focus of his *Enquirer* essays, several of which recommended that readers be exposed to a variety of languages, genres and viewpoints from childhood. 'It must probably be partial, not extensive, information, that is calculated to lead us astray', he contended in his essay 'Of the Utility of Talents'.[56] His essay 'Of Choice in Reading' is devoted to the argument that textual restriction is always detrimental to the young. Like many writers of dissenting tradition Godwin echoed Milton's *Areopagitica*, which had allied the licensing of the English press with the perceived intellectual oppression of European Catholicism. He asks,

> Is it our duty to digest for our offspring, as the church of Rome has been accustomed to digest for her weaker members, an *Index Expurgatorius*, a catalogue of those books in the reading of which they may be permitted to indulge themselves?[57]

Censoring a child's reading, Godwin argues, is a harmful and authoritarian practice; it undermines relational trust and results in critical naivety. Only the reader with unrestricted access to reading matter from the earliest age will be properly trained to reason, distinguish and judge. That this training will necessarily be successful, given the right circumstances, is inferred from the assumption that 'Truth is powerful, and [. . .] will make good her possession.' Parents and teachers are therefore urged to 'Suffer [the child] to wander in the wilds of literature.'[58]

This argument had obvious political inflections given the timing of its publication. Godwin had claimed in *Political Justice* that the major evil of political institutions was their inherent narrowness or fixity of ideas, which hindered accurate judgement of alternative viewpoints because it excluded them a priori. Recent government legislation against sedition reinforced this view, and Godwin's 'Considerations on Lord Grenville's and Mr Pitt's Bills' (1795) makes similar use of Milton and the Catholic Index in order to protest against political censorship.[59] From this perspective, 'Of Choice in Reading' is an intervention in public debates about freedom of communication and its relation to social structure and authority. In Godwin's understanding, giving a new generation complete freedom of reading choice was one way to protect them from institutional indoctrination and thus a mode of effecting political change.

More fundamentally, however, Godwin was drawing from a Doddridgian view of the mind's development through critical exposure, according to which students can only understand and defend truth if they 'know the chief strength of error'. It was like a soldier's experience of conflict: it was essential to know your opponents, to learn how to fight from repeated engagement with the enemy. Priestley had encapsulated this view in his *Observations Relating to Education* (1778), arguing that shielding a student from certain writers amounted to 'committing him with an enemy, of whom he had no previous knowledge'.[60] Through constant exercise of judgement, the reader attained a posture of mind that enabled a successful encounter with everything they read. This is the tradition from which Godwin drew when he insisted in his essay 'Of Choice in Reading' that the mind's 'temper' or 'spirit' determined the way in which it received textual content. '[T]he impression we derive from a book, depends much less upon its real contents, than upon the temper of mind and preparation with which we read it', he wrote. 'Every thing depends upon the spirit in which [books] are read. He that would extract poison from them, must for the most part come to them with a mind already debauched.'[61] This interest in the reader's prior disposition of mind and the habits that create it marks out every essay in the *Enquirer*, all of which can be fruitfully read as extensions of the first essay 'Of Awakening the Mind'. '[H]e who reads in a proper spirit, can scarcely read too much', Godwin reiterates in 'Of Learning'.[62]

Godwin's specific focus upon very young readers, however, coupled with its loaded political context, meant that these comments about the 'tendency' of reading sparked controversy. Even relatively progressive educational programmes in the period, such as those proposed by the Edgeworths in *Practical Education* (1798), were marked by the imperative of censorship: 'Few books', they claimed, 'can safely be given to children without the previous use of the pen, the pencil, and the scissars [sic].'[63] Reviewers that were charitable towards Godwin's descriptions of 'the true mode of reading' elsewhere in *The Enquirer* were thus critical of his recommendation of unrestricted childhood reading. 'Books are, in effect, companions', wrote one; 'and parents might almost as safely trust their children to gather up any straggler whom they may find in the streets for an associate, as, before their judgement is in some degree matured, to read any book that falls in their way.'[64] The comparison between this picture of naive socialisation and Priestley's imagery of warfare is instructive: in both scenarios the reader is vulnerable to harm, but the import of the vulnerability differs. The former account stipulates that external protection is required while the reader's judgement is immature, whereas the latter presents dangerous situations as necessary to the judgement's maturation, a process which strengthens ability and imparts skill. Godwin, like Priestley, believed that exposure to a broad range of reading matter trained the mind in its most vital task, discernment.

Godwin's advocacy of reading exposure in *The Enquirer* was not limited to the terms of rational discernment, however; he also developed Watts's instructions about sympathetic investment, the means by which a reader may 'enter in' to another's thought-world. This principle is clearly seen in the essay 'Of an Early Taste for Reading', which describes the powerful imaginative hold of certain texts in positive terms: 'When I read Thomson, I become Thomson; when I read Milton I become Milton', he asserts. 'I find myself a sort of intellectual camelion [sic], assuming the colour of the substances on which I rest.[65] Somewhat counter-intuitively, the critically active reader must begin by suspending their faculties and submitting to the whims of their material, almost to the extent of self-effacement. A good reader must 'become the creature of his author'; he 'bends with all his caprices, [and] sympathises with all his sensations'.[66] Reading is imagined as a temporary possession, by which the reader becomes assimilated into the world of the book. Godwin argued elsewhere in *The Enquirer* that a good author will 'pour their whole soul into mine [. . .] raise my ambition, expand my faculties, invigorate my resolutions, and seem to double my existence'.[67] In *Deloraine* and *St Leon* he depicted the advantages of sharing this immersive reading experience with a friend or family member: '[It] makes the proposition, the fact, or the sentiment, leap as it were from the insensible page, and become impregnate with life'; participants share 'modes of apprehending and judging'.[68]

The idea that reading in this way might 'expand' or 'double' the reader indicates the developmental purpose for which Godwin intended it. He believed that the faculty of sympathy was vital to intellectual life and that imaginatively invested reading was the key means of giving it exercise. It is '[t]his mode of reading, upon which we depend for the consummation of our improvement', Godwin claimed; by practising imaginative empathy from an early age, the reader would learn to sympathise with the situations and viewpoints of others, and thus expand their range of understanding.[69] As indicated by his phrase '*intellectual* camelion', he saw this as integral to the mind's task of judgement: feeling was essential to reason, not separable from it. Indeed, it is this immersive reading habit that has produced Godwin's 'man of talent' described at the beginning of the 'Early Taste for Reading' essay, an idealised enquirer who possesses great analytic and creative powers. Godwin's choice of Milton and Thomson as his example authors for this imaginative activity is not incidental, either; he considered poetry, drama and prose narrative especially important vehicles for the exercise of sympathy and, consequently, integral to the moral life.

Godwin continued to build upon this principle of mental exposure in later writings on education. In his 'Letter of Advice' it grounds instructions for reading several books simultaneously:

> [The student] should compare one authority with another, and not put himself under the guidance of any. This is the difference I make between reading and study. He that confines himself to one book at a time, may be amused, but is no student.[70]

This comment betrays the darker view of the mind that fuelled Godwin's recommendation of extensive reading. Readers have a tendency to be undiscerning and superficial: their judgements are easily clouded by immediate textual authority, so they need to be reminded not to entrust themselves to any single viewpoint or source. These dangers even led Godwin to make stipulations about the reader's physical environment. His 'Letter of Advice' argued that readers should be 'surrounded' with books, so that they 'sit in some measure in the middle of a library'; similarly, in a letter to Percy Shelley from 1812, he claimed that a 'true' reader should be 'surrounded with a sort of intrenchment [sic] and breastwork of books'. This environment was important because it reminded readers that they were engaged in dialogue, the material objects symbolising a circle of conversation.[71] In other words, it encouraged them to stay focused on the ends for which such intellectual exposure was intended: independent critical development. Godwin's military language, 'intrenchment and breastwork' (modes of fortification), makes this a hostile setting by positioning the mind in danger of attack. Surrounding oneself with a variety of books and engaging with them simultaneously provided a sort of mental barricade, defending the mind from assaults of error, partiality and passivity.

This sort of reading was accordingly an important statement of distinction for Godwin. It was a sign that the reader had resisted the intellectual vices of their age. Such conviction is evident in his 'Letter of Advice' comment about 'the difference [. . .] between reading and study'. Like Watts, he was presenting the activity of reading as fundamentally unprofitable when uncoupled from 'meditation, or study', and he offers simultaneous reading as an indication that this mistake has been avoided. In a similar vein the letter to Percy Shelley associates the reading of one book at a time with the ultimate cliché of superficial readership, 'boarding-school misses'. To read several books at once, Godwin implies, is to separate oneself from immature, amusement-driven readers, who have no interest in the life of the mind.[72]

Godwin also connected this extensive and varied reading regime to religious scepticism, and in this respect he departed from the advice and practice of his academy days. After the collapse of his faith in revealed religion Godwin resisted the interpretive authority that his educators had endowed upon the Christian scriptures, arguing that they should be read in the same manner as any other book. As Isabel Rivers points out, the pedagogical methods of dissenting academies were based upon theological assumptions about the scriptures' epistemic authority (the 'perfection of scripture as a Christian's *only* rule of faith and practice').[73] Thus, while Isaac Watts recommended that students 'Deal freely with every Author you read', he added that 'I would be understood to speak only of human Authors, not of the sacred and inspired Writings.'[74] As a young man Godwin felt this assumption of authority keenly, and his eventual response was to attempt to erase it. He reflected upon his education with frustration in 1818, writing of the Bible that:

> happy shall that man be, who comes to its examination and study with a firm and impartial mind, and not, as I did in my early acquaintance with its contents, with a mind overlaid with religious awe, and tutored beforehand as to what spirit it was to be read with, what I must look for and what I must find it, what set of feelings, arising in its perusal, I must instantly check, and what set of feelings I must cherish with fervour and devotion.[75]

Godwin was aligning his experience with that of his eponymous protagonist in *Mandeville* (1817) – a character whose environmental conditioning predisposes him to superstitious 'tingling and horror' upon his reading of religious texts – thus contrasting the restrictions of his childhood reading practice with the ideal of free enquiry upheld by dissenting educational theory. He drew from a key element of the Doddridge-Watts tradition – its mixture of confidence in the mind's discriminating powers and fear of its susceptibility to prejudice – and used it to undermine that tradition's confessional basis.

Godwin's recommendation of 'free', wide-ranging reading practice was thus conceived as a disciplined regime of intentional exposure that roused the mind's capacity for independent judgement and offset its potential for uncritical dependence upon external authorities. He underscored this regime's temporal requirements, arguing that reading must be frequent and regular from the earliest age in order to habituate 'enquiry'. Several *Enquirer* essays, especially 'Of the Sources of Genius' and 'Of an Early Taste for Reading', use familiar agricultural imagery to urge teachers to prescribe methodical reading for the young. Just as Watts had cautioned that 'infinite errors will overspread the mind, which [. . .] lies without any cultivation', Godwin justified quotidian discipline with a warning:

> [The child's] mind must not be suffered to lie idle. The preceptor in this respect is like the incloser of uncultivated land; his first crops are not valued for their intrinsic excellence; they are sown that the land may be brought into order.[76]

The sheer fact of regular reading prepares the ground for intellectual life; it is an essential part of mental cultivation, whatever the initial ability of the student. In an essay 'Of the Study of the Classics' Godwin particularly recommends that this programme include ancient languages – a key aspect of genteel education that was increasingly coming under fire in proposals for educational reform – on the premise that they deflect 'habits of inattention and irresolution' by inducing 'discipline of mind'.[77]

Through all these instructions Godwin was rechannelling the dissenting association of reading and labour towards a specific contemporary issue. Watts had resisted the general idea that intellectual ability could develop untutored, instructing would-be readers to 'Presume not too much upon a bright genius'. Later in the century the concept of 'original genius' gained traction in some writings on education, partly inspired by Edward Young's 'Conjectures On Original Composition' (1759) and William Duff's 'Essay on Original

Genius' (1767). In *The Enquirer* Godwin attacked belief in innate, natural genius explicitly as a rival educational trend; 'Of Learning', in particular, laments the state of students who have not 'engaged in any methodical and persevering course of reading' due to the hands-off approach of their tutors. '[L]earning is the ally, not the adversary of genius', he claimed. While children bring certain dispositions with them into the world, true genius is always generated subsequent to birth through structured immersion in the habits of enquiry.[78] For Godwin, an early routine of reading was essential for the creation of critical health.

Godwin addressed this issue of innate intellectual tendencies in both *The Enquirer* and *Thoughts on Man*, a continuity which suggests it troubled him throughout his career. In both collections he acknowledged permanent and innate differences in children at birth and yet simultaneously contended that education was the most powerful influence upon every mind.[79] His reading advice distils this uneasy combination of nature and nurture: recommendations for exposure express confidence in the mind's innate propensity to reason, judge and identify truth, yet the context of disciplined routine in which this exposure is conceived suggests that these propensities needed to be instilled from outside – indeed, it suggests that the young tend to forget or rebel against them. Agricultural imagery expresses this tension well, as crop growth is both a power or potential innate to the seeds and a condition that the farmer must labour towards. 'Of An Early Taste for Reading' thus describes the promise of talent in children as an 'embryon seed' which should be cherished carefully lest it 'suffer an untimely blight'.[80] Godwin theorised the dark side of the mind more explicitly in *Thoughts on Man*, devoting an essay to what he called the principle of 'innate rebelliousness' and arguing that 'It is the business of education to tame the wild ass, the restive and rebellious principle, in our nature.'[81] Viewed in this context, his instructions for reading routine express fear of intellectual corruption in equal measure to faith in intellectual potential.

Godwin became increasingly preoccupied with reading in relation to time as his career progressed. In *Thoughts on Man* he explored the life of the mind from various different temporal perspectives, most notably in 'Of the Duration of Human Life', 'Of Human Vegetation' and 'Of Leisure'. 'Of the Duration of Human Life' addresses the importance of using time effectively: Godwin details the ideal work patterns of a scholar, describing how temporal windows of mental efficiency should be exploited but not exhausted. Like Watts, he recommended strategies that would maximise temporal opportunities and exercise judgement to the greatest degree. Godwin focuses this issue through both quotidian rhythm and, in more zoomed-out perspective, lifespan: he recommends rereading books in old age, for example, because 'The same words and phrases suggest [. . .] a new train of ideas.'[82] In his essay 'Of Human Vegetation' he claimed that this focus on mental activity was only part of the story, however. He even quoted and critiqued his own account of 'the man of talent' in *The Enquirer*, claiming that he had overlooked the pervasive presence and multiple uses of mental indolence. He went on to distinguish between four mental states that together constituted the sum total of intellectual life, and recommended reading to the state of most heightened attention rather than the partial 'mental indolence' that one experiences, for example, while lying in bed. He did, however, make a distinction between the demands of 'books of instruction' and 'books of amusement', noting that partial intellectual passivity was a great source of pleasure to readers of fiction and spectators of theatre.[83] The basis of both essays is Godwin's contention that the ideal enquirer 'disposes of his hours much in the same manner, as the commander of a company of men whom it is his business to train in the discipline of war'.[84] Rather than a casual or haphazard occupation, reading is cast as an integral part of a military strategy.

Godwin's warfare imagery reflected his belief that disciplined, intentional reading practice was something that needed to be campaigned for in current society. Industrialisation, standardised time measurement and an ever-expanding literary marketplace meant that the concept of leisure – including leisure reading – had developed something like its modern sense during his lifetime. Godwin's attack upon the idea of reading solely for entertainment reflects this, and in a later essay 'On Leisure' he argued explicitly that the category of leisure time was just as much involved in the intellectual warfare of life as the time of business.[85] Reading in leisure hours was thus infinitely distinct from reading *for* leisure. These claims echo his previous contrast between the strategic bookishness of the 'true' reader and the entertainment-driven schoolgirl in his letter to Shelley; his 'true mode of reading' was methodical and industrious.[86] And indeed, the meticulous routine of reading, writing and conversation recorded in Godwin's fifty-year diary shows that he lived up to his own ideal.

A diligent routine of reading and an extensive reading scope were not enough on their own, however. For Godwin, as for Watts, 'true' reading necessarily involved specific skills of critical engagement. These skills marked the crucial difference between discipline and subjection in a reader, as his *Enquirer* essay 'Of Learning' makes clear:

> The discipline of mind here described is of inestimable value. He that is not initiated in the practice of close investigation, is constantly exposed to the danger of being deceived. His opinions have no standard; but are entirely at the mercy of his age, his country, the books he chances to read, or the company he happens to frequent. His mind is a wilderness.[87]

Like Price, Godwin assumed that intellectual independence was achieved through discipline, but he specified this discipline by making a particular sort of reading fundamental it. The reader that doesn't habituate 'close investigation' will remain dependent upon their cultural, social and historical circumstances, at the mercy of time and chance. Like Watts's undisciplined reader, their mind is unfruitful as a consequence, 'a wilderness'.

'Of Learning' exploits the familiar comparison of reading and digestion in order to argue that this sort of 'close investigation' is the only worthwhile reading practice. Godwin presents books as objects of dense 'nutriment' and argues that 'the true mode of reading' is the mode that processes them effectively, turning them to profit. He refutes the claim that avid reading overloads the mind with the thoughts of others and 'prevents its digesting them'. '[I]f the systems we read, were always to remain in masses upon the mind, unconcocted and unaltered, undoubtedly in that case they would only deform it'; the true reader, however, will 'mix', 'dissect' and 'sift' a work's contents, 'repassing in his thoughts the notions of which it consists'. Godwin claims that it is only through this processing activity that the reader's material is 'render[ed] his own', echoing Watts's alliance of textual digestion and independent possession of ideas.[88]

This essay further specifies 'the true mode of reading' as a two-edged process, which involves the dismantling and remaking of texts:

> if we read in a just spirit, perhaps we cannot read too much: in other words, if we mix our own reflections with what we read; if we dissect the ideas and arguments of our author; if, by having recourse to all subsidiary means, we endeavour to clear the recollection of him in our minds; if we compare part with part, detect his errors, new model his systems, adopt so much of him as is excellent, and explain within ourselves the reason of our disapprobation as to what is otherwise. A judicious reader will have a greater number of ideas that are his own passing through his mind, than of ideas presented to him by his author. He sifts his merits, and bolts his arguments.[89]

As the digestion imagery suggests, skilled reading is partly a process of breaking down: the reader must 'dissect', 'compare part with part', 'sift' and 'bolt' (used in the now uncommon sense of examining or separating by sifting, as through a bolting-cloth). Dissecting a text in this manner allows the reader to better grasp the structure and argument of their text, to ward off their own propensity to erroneous judgement, and to develop a healthy critical posture. Yet Godwin also allies this deconstructive scrutiny to a creative process. Readers must 'new model' the text, adopting its worthy elements and combining them with their own ideas to form new material. He weaves the activities of dismantling and remaking together so tightly that they seem hard to distinguish from each other in this extract, the structure of his description echoing the integrative reading process that he recommends. The point of such reading is to bring the ideas of the author into such intimate intercourse with those of the reader that, much like in the digestive process, they would be broken down in order to be remade and assimilated.

Elsewhere Godwin recommended various practical aids to this task of critical engagement, which built in many respects upon *The Improvement of the Mind*. As discussed above, he believed that reading several works simultaneously was crucial. Of equal importance was to 'Learn to read slow', as his 'Letter of Advice' instructs.[90] This theme was expounded upon with most zeal in his essay 'Of the Duration of Human Life' in *Thoughts on Man*:

> Be earnest in your application, but let your march be vigilant and slow. There is a doggrel couplet which I have met with in a book on elocution:
>   Learn to speak slow: all other graces
>   Will follow in their proper places.
>
> I could wish to recommend a similar process to the student in the course of his reading. [. . .] Nothing is more easy than to gabble through a work replete with the profoundest elements of thinking, and to carry away almost nothing, when we have finished.
>
> The book does not even deserve to be read, which does not impose upon us the duty of frequent pauses, much reflecting and inward debate, or require that we should often go back, compare one observation and statement with another, and does not call upon us to combine and knit together the *disjecta membra*.
>
> It is an observation which has often been repeated, that, when we come to read an excellent author a second and a third time, we find in him a multitude of things, that we did not in the slightest degree perceive in a first reading. A careful first reading would have a tendency in a considerable degree to anticipate this following crop.[91]

This essay unites slow reading with critical activity. The process does not seem to be necessarily linear – Godwin suggests that readers must pause, backtrack and tease apart premises and statements in order to unfold the work's scope within their mind. Slow reading creates the space and time necessary for dismembering ('compare one observation and statement with another') and remodelling ('combine and knit together the *disjecta membra*'). His advice resonates with the self-consciously temporal aspect of much Romantic-period literary practice and criticism, a feature which many recent studies highlight. Jonathan Sachs, for example, shows how poetic investment in the concept of slow time created 'new forms of literary experience by deploying a particular temporal framework to generate modes of attentiveness and habits of reading that counter the market's relentless generativity'.[92] Godwin's attempt to habituate slow reading participates in this movement, as does his ascription of pace-setting to good books and not only to good readers (for more on this, see Chapter 4). The particular mode of attentiveness he promotes, however, is funded by an older eighteenth-century tradition of 'Care and close Study' associated with the pedagogical legacies of Doddridge and Watts. '[C]onsult the Page again and again, and meditate on it, at successive Seasons', wrote Watts. 'A Student should labour by all proper methods to acquire a steady fixation of thought.'[93]

Godwin's diary suggests that he practiced this kind of concentrated, non-linear reading himself. Entries show that he often did not read through works systematically; he dwelt closely upon a cluster of pages at a time, particularly when consulting works of philosophy or history. His diary entries for July 1794, for instance, record 'Hume on Tragedy, 10 pp', 'Hume, Standard of Taste, 24 pp', and 'Hume, Phil. Sects, p. 12', rendering the question 'When did Godwin read Hume?' far from straightforward to answer. Godwin also appears to distinguish between two kinds of reading in his diary, using 'cala' to indicate his perusal through a text in a more piecemeal fashion ('*ca et la*').[94] These habits perhaps reflected his belief that, rather than racing through one book at a time, readers should focus upon specific sections of various books and bring them into conversation with their own thoughts. This was one way of avoiding the tendency to 'gabble' through books and leave them empty-handed.

Above all, Godwin argued that the practice of writing enabled 'true' reading. Doddridge had advised the student 'to read with a Pen in his Hand' and Watts had recommended that readers marked, summarised and rewrote passages. Following their lead, Godwin recommended specific practices of notation in his letter to Martin:

> I have practiced a manner [of reading] from my youth, to which in a considerable degree I ascribe my improvement, such as it is. This is, always to read with a pen in my hand, & to put down in the fewest words that can be made to convey a full & perspicuous meaning, such leading points of the author as strike me when they occur, points that I most wish to remember, & upon which his way of thinking principally turns; as well as such thoughts, properly my own, as suggest themselves in the perusal. This takes very little paper, frequently not above three or four pages, half the size I am now writing, for each author. [. . .] It must be of a sort that can be taken in almost at a glance, & consulted & reconsulted with facility.[95]

Here the assembly of one's own written materials is an essential part of textual processing. It enables readers to judge independently and remember these judgements when they revisit the text in the future, thus carving out and refining their private judgement ('thoughts, properly my own'). Yet Godwin went further than this; he expanded upon the role of writing to a greater degree than Watts, insisting that more formal composition was integral to the proper process of reading. He had already observed in 'Of Learning' that 'the industry which books demand, is of the same species as the industry requisite for the development of our own reflections; the study of other men's writings, is strikingly analogous to the invention and arrangement of our own'.[96] Later, he would argue in his letter to Shelley that to read well 'I must place myself in the situation of a man making a book, rather than reading books.'[97] 'True reading' might foster the critical industry essential to writing skills, but from another perspective the reader must assume the position of an author to recruit this kind of industry in the first place. It was this relationship that Godwin summarised in his letter to Martin:

> The great art perhaps of profitable reading is to have the mind, not passive, but active & at work during the whole sitting, composing, if I may so express it, for itself, even while studying the compositions of another. He that would read to purpose, should spend half as much time in writing compositions of his own, as in reading.[98]

Reading and composition were mutually reinforcing, for Godwin, their integration and collaboration essential to the formation of an autonomous critical posture. Any practice that alienated the two was therefore not 'profitable' or 'to purpose'.

Thoughts on Man reflects this growing investment in books and book-writing, for in it Godwin positioned textual production as the reader's ultimate goal or end more overtly than he had done before. 'The man who does not speak, is an unfledged thinker; and the man that does not write, is but half an investigator', he claimed in an essay 'Of Intellectual Abortion'.[99] This essay laments the fate of minds that enjoy 'the richest soil' and yet fall prey to 'indolence and irresolution', writing nothing in return. Their ideas and plans terminate in 'miscarriage' because

> They skim away from one flower in the parterre of literature to another, like the bee, without, like the bee, gathering sweetness from each, to increase the public stock, and enrich the magazine of public thought.[100]

Evoking Seneca's much-appropriated image of the bee, Godwin contrasts half-committed readers with a neoclassical scholarly ideal: unlike those who harvest and reproduce truth, virtue and knowledge for the benefit of society, they flit aimlessly from flower to flower, contributing nothing. The reader who actively commits their responses to paper, however, he aligns with a long-running heritage of productive enquirers, scholarly harvesters whose activity benefits the public realm. Unproductive reading did not merit the name, for Godwin; he believed that the making of minds was completed by the making of texts.

The marriage of reading and writing thus became the major skill of 'true reading' in Godwin's estimation. This preoccupation was a departure from the reading advice of Watts and Doddridge, which ultimately considered reading's end-goal as the personal knowledge of God-given truth; Godwin shifted the perspective more absolutely onto the process of knowledge exchange, or literary activity, itself. He constructed the textually productive reader as 'the genuine hero' in *Thoughts on Man*, a traveller who battled his way through a literary landscape against temptations to indolence and passivity:

> The man who merely wanders through the fields of knowledge in search of its gayest flowers and of whatever will afford him the most enviable amusement, will necessarily return home at night with a very slender collection. He that shall apply himself with self-denial and an unshrinking resolution to the improvement of his mind, will unquestionably be found more fortunate in the end. He is not deterred by the gulphs [sic] that yawn beneath his feet, or the mountains that may oppose themselves to his progress. He knows that the adventurer of timid mind, and that is infirm of purpose, will never make himself master of those points which it would be most honourable to him to subdue. But he who undertakes to commit to writing the result of his researches, and to communicate his discoveries to mankind, is the genuine hero.[101]

Once again, his argument clearly echoes Watts:

> In the pursuit of every valuable subject of knowledge keep the end always in your eye, and be not diverted from it by every pretty trifle you meet with in the way. Some persons have such a wandering genius, that they are ready to pursue every incident, theme or occasional idea, till they have lost sight of their original subject [. . .] like a man who is sent in quest of some great treasure, but he steps aside to gather every flower he finds, or stands still to dig up every shining pebble he meets with in his way, till the treasure is forgotten and never found.[102]

Both writers positioned the reader as a pilgrim along the lines of Bunyan's *Pilgrim's Progress*, arguing that a focus upon the end-goal of reading, the celestial city of knowledge, would enable them to withstand temptations of idleness and superficiality. Godwin thus associated his productive reader with a holy quest, distinguishing their journey from the profane loitering of inferior readers. Here the parallel ends, however. The goal for Watts's traveller was to find the kingdom of heaven, emphasised here by the allusion to Jesus's parable of the treasure in Matthew 13: 44; for Godwin, the reader's goal was not a body of treasure, as it were, but the journey itself. He modified the reading advice of his dissenting education to prioritise individual creative assertion, making the 'genuine hero' the reader who conquered the literary landscape through an active contribution to it.

This formal process of writing mattered so much to Godwin because it was, in his estimation, intimately linked to the production of sound judgement in society. His reading advice participates in a growing emphasis upon the uses of writing in his social theory: successive editions of *Political Justice* in the 1790s increasingly urged the communication of knowledge to be practised explicitly amid a current climate of repression and timidity, and his novels across the following decades upheld the centrality of written 'confession' to social advancement.[103] There is a sense in which this is optimistic, an attempt to inspire writer-readers who would foster an environment of free communication. But there is a sinister backdrop to that attempt: for Godwin, it also counteracts the mind's fundamental tendencies toward passivity, dependence and superficiality. His directions for making writing integral to reading signal his fear of these aspects of the mind, just like his instructions for ensuring the reader's exposure to variety and his insistence upon regularity and structure of reading practice. These habits of reading were conceived as remedies for social ills, emancipatory disciplines that enabled and enhanced the autonomous movement of the mind and its receptivity to truth.

Godwin's reading advice, then, like his literary criticism and depictions of fictional readers, was animated by live debates and unanswered questions about the mind as a medium of knowledge. What factors determine the apprehension of truth in the mind; to what degree; and in what circumstances? Godwin's insistence upon writing's role in cultivating the enquiring disposition provides a clue to the way in which he navigated this territory. The following chapters show that he explicitly addressed these questions about the mind and its mediation in his writings about the book as an object. In doing so he intervened in heated controversies about the social role and significance of print technology.

Notes

1. *The Enquirer*, p. 237.
2. Godwin to Percy Shelley, 10 December 1812, in 'Godwin/Shelley Correspondence', *CNM*, vol. 1, p. 81.
3. Adrian Johns, *The Nature of the Book: Print and Knowledge in the Making* (Chicago: Chicago University Press, 1998), p. 384.
4. See, for example, Lily Gurton-Wachter, *Watchwords: Romanticism and the Poetics of Attention* (Stanford: Stanford University Press, 2016); Deidre Lynch, *Loving Literature: A Cultural History* (Chicago: University of Chicago Press, 2015), pp. 153, 166–79.
5. Marilyn Butler, 'Introductory Essay' in *Burke, Paine, Godwin, and the Revolution Controversy* (Cambridge: Cambridge University Press, 1984), p. 12.
6. See, for example, Richard De Ritter, *Imagining Women Readers, 1789–1820: Well-Regulated Minds* (Manchester: Manchester University Press, 2015), p. 91; Susan Manly, 'William Godwin's "School of Morality"', *The Wordsworth Circle* 43.3 (2012): 135–42; Matthew Grenby, *The Child Reader, 1700–1840* (Cambridge: Cambridge University Press, 2011), p. 244; Robert Anderson, 'Godwin Disguised: Politics in the Juvenile Library', in *Godwinian Moments: From the Enlightenment to Romanticism*, ed. Robert Maniquis and Victoria Myers (Toronto: University of Toronto Press, 2011), pp. 125–46; Alan Richardson, *Literature, Education and Romanticism: Reading as Social Practice, 1780–1832* (Cambridge: Cambridge University Press, 1994), p. 127. Julie Carlson registers the equivocality of Godwin's principle of freedom in childhood reading: *England's First Family of Writers: Mary Wollstonecraft, William Godwin, Mary Shelley* (Baltimore: Johns Hopkins University Press, 2007), p. 217.
7. *The Enquirer*, p. 88. For a summary of approaches to childhood in this period see Robin Jarvis, *The Romantic Period: The Intellectual and Cultural Context of English Literature 1789–1830* (Harlow: Longman, 2004), pp. 94–5.
8. See the editor's introduction to Godwin, 'Letter of Advice to a Young American, on the course of studies it might be most advantageous for

him to pursue', *PPW*, vol. 5, pp. 318–38 (pp. 318–19), and references to Joseph Vallence Bevan in *DWG* throughout 1818.
9. *The Enquirer*, p. 78.
10. On dissenting academies see 'Dissenting Academies Online', *The Dissenting Academies Project*, The Queen Mary Centre for Religion and Literature in English, Queen Mary University of London. Available at <www.qmulreligionandliterature.co.uk/research/the-dissenting-academies-project> (last accessed 29 September 2020); predecessors to this project include Irene Parker, *Dissenting Academies in England: Their Rise and Progress and Their Place among the Educational Systems of the Country* (Cambridge: Cambridge University Press, 1914); H. McLachlan, *English Education Under the Test Acts: Being the History of the Non-Conformist Academies 1662–1820* (Manchester: Manchester University Press, 1931); Joe W. Ashley Smith, *The Birth of Modern Education: The Contribution of the Dissenting Academies, 1660–1800* (London: Independent Press, 1954).
11. Studies that register this influence upon Godwin include Pamela Clemit, 'Godwin's Educational Theory: "The Enquirer"', *Enlightenment and Dissent* 12 (1993): 3–11; Burton Ralph Pollin, *Education and Enlightenment in the Works of William Godwin* (New York: Las Americas, 1962), especially Chapters 1 and 2 on the concepts of rationality and perfectibility. On the wider connotations of 'free enquiry' in eighteenth-century culture, see Peter N. Miller, '"Free Thinking" and "Freedom of Thought" in Eighteenth-Century Britain', *The Historical Journal* 36.3 (1993): 599–617.
12. Quoted in Daniel E. White, *Early Romanticism and Religious Dissent* (Cambridge: Cambridge University Press, 2006), p. 10.
13. See Isabel Rivers, *Reason, Grace, and Sentiment: a Study of the Language of Religion and Ethics in England, 1660–1780*, vol. 1 (Cambridge: Cambridge University Press, 1991), and more generally, Michael Watts, *The Dissenters: Vol. 1: From the Reformation to the French Revolution* (Oxford: Clarendon, 1978) and *Vol. 2: The Expansion of Evangelical Nonconformity* (Oxford: Clarendon, 1995). On the rationalist strains of dissent and their legacy see Mark Philp, 'Rational Religion and Political Radicalism in the 1790s', *Enlightenment and Dissent* 4 (1985): 35–46 (esp. p. 36); *Enlightenment and Religion: Rational Dissent in Eighteenth-Century Britain*, ed. Knud Haakonssen (Cambridge: Cambridge University Press, 1996); Alan P. F. Sell, *Philosophy, Dissent and Nonconformity, 1689–1920* (Cambridge: James Clarke, 2004).
14. Much greater detail can be found in Rivers, *Reason, Grace, and Sentiment*, pp. 168–204.

15. Tessa Whitehouse, *The Textual Culture of English Protestant Dissent, 1720–1800* (Oxford: Oxford University Press, 2015), p. 17.
16. Richard Price, *Observations on the Importance of the American Revolution, and the Means of Making It a Benefit to the World* (Cambridge: Cambridge University Press, 2013), p. 51.
17. Philip Doddridge, *The Correspondence and Diary of Philip Doddridge, D.D. Illustrative of Various Particulars in His Life Hitherto Unknown; with Notices of Many of His Contemporaries, and a Sketch of the Ecclesiastical History of the Times in Which He Lived*, ed. John Doddridge Humphreys, 5 vols (London: Henry Colburn and Richard Bentley, 1830), vol. 1, pp. 198, 156.
18. See John Milton, *Areopagitica; A Speech of Mr. John Milton For the Liberty of Unlicenc'd Printing, To the Parliament of England*, in *Complete Prose Works of John Milton*, ed. Ernest Sirluck, 8 vols (New Haven: Yale University Press, 1959), vol. 2, pp. 480–570. For more information about Jennings's teaching, see 'Dissenting Education and the Legacy of John Jennings, c.1720–c.1729 (2nd edn)', ed. Tessa Whitehouse, *The Dissenting Academies Project*, Queen Mary University of London. Available at <www.qmulreligionandliterature.co.uk/online-publications/dissenting-education> (last accessed 29 September 2020); and Mark Burden, 'Jennings, John', in *A Biographical Dictionary of Tutors at the Dissenters' Private Academies, 1660–1729* (London: Dr Williams's Centre for Dissenting Studies, 2013), pp. 294–300.
19. See Doddridge, *Correspondence and Diary*, p. 464.
20. Samuel Palmer, *A Defence of the Dissenters Education in Their Private Academies: In Answer to Mr. W–Y's Disingenuous and Unchristian Reflections upon 'Em. In a Letter to a Noble Lord* (London: printed and are to be sold by A. Baldwin, 1703), pp. 15–16.
21. See Doddridge, *A Course of Lectures on the Principal Subjects in Pneumatology, Ethics, and Divinity: With References to the Most Considerable Authors on Each Subject* (London: J. Buckland et al., 1763). For a thorough explication of Doddridge's teaching see Isabel Rivers, *The Defence of Truth through the Knowledge of Error: Philip Doddridge's Academy Lectures* (London: Dr Williams's Trust, 2003). See also her discussion of Doddridge in 'Dissenting and Methodist Books of Practical Divinity', *Books and Their Readers in Eighteenth-Century England*, ed. Isabel Rivers (Leicester: Leicester University Press, 1982), pp. 136–8; *Reason, Grace, and Sentiment*, vol. 1, ch. 4; 'Doddridge, Philip (1702–1751)', *Oxford Dictionary of National Biography* (Oxford University Press Online, 2004).
22. Rivers, *The Defence of Truth*, pp. 18, 31.
23. Doddridge, *Correspondence and Diary*, vol. 4, p. 493 (emphasis original).

24. Doddridge, *Correspondence and Diary*, vol. 1, p. 97.
25. Ibid. p. 459.
26. Job Orton, *Memoirs of the Life, Character and Writings of the Late Reverend Philip Doddridge, D.D. Of Northampton* (Salop: printed by J. Cotton and J. Eddowes; and sold by J. Buckland, in Pater-Noster-Row, London, 1766), p. 16.
27. Ibid. p. 124.
28. Ibid. p. 125.
29. See Arthur Davis, *Isaac Watts: His Life and Work* (London: Independent Press, 1948), p. 100, and Whitehouse, *Textual Culture*. Notably the posthumous volume of Watt's *Improvement* was heavily edited by Doddridge and David Jennings.
30. '[T]he providence of God has brought printing into the world' – see Watts, 'A Discourse on the Education of Children and Youth', in *The Works of the Late Reverend and Learned Isaac Watts, D.D [. . .]*, vol. 5, pp. 359–408 (p. 372). Cf. Godwin, *Political Justice*, p. 141; *Political Justice: Variants*, pp. 138–9; *Thoughts on Man*, p. 248.
31. Watts, *The Improvement of the Mind*, in *The Works of the Late Reverend and Learned Isaac Watts, D.D [. . .]*, vol. 5, pp. 185–358 (p. 195).
32. Watts, *Improvement of the Mind*, p. 209.
33. Ibid. p. 67 (emphasis mine).
34. Ibid. pp. 185–8.
35. Ibid. p. 185.
36. Ibid. p. 188; cf. Watts, *Logick; Or, the Right Use of Reason in the Inquiry After Truth*, in *The Works of the Late Reverend and Learned Isaac Watts, D.D [. . .]*, vol. 5, pp. 1–184 (p. 162).
37. E.g. Watts, *Improvement of the Mind*, p. 195.
38. Ibid. p. 259; pp. 205–6.
39. Ibid. p. 208.
40. Ibid. p. 201.
41. See Gigante, *Taste: A Literary History*, p. 21 and *passim*.
42. Watts, *Improvement of the Mind*, p. 209.
43. Ibid. pp. 76, 198, 206, 211.
44. For a detailed account of commonplace book usage in the eighteenth century see David Allan, *Commonplace Books and Reading in Georgian England* (Cambridge: Cambridge University Press, 2010). Allan locates the decline of the commonplace book during Godwin's lifetime, a context which perhaps contributes to his insistence upon writing's alliance with reading (see Allan, *Commonplace Books*, pp. 261–3 and my discussion of Godwin below). Heather Jackson's study of marginalia specifies the 1830s and 40s as the period when '[t]he annotating reader went into retreat': see Heather J. Jackson,

Romantic Readers: The Evidence of Marginalia (New Haven: Yale University Press, 2005).
45. Watts, *Improvement of the Mind*, pp. 206–8 (p. 208).
46. Price, *Observations on the Importance of the American Revolution*, pp. 51–2 (emphasis original).
47. Rivers, *Reason, Grace, and Sentiment*, vol. 1, p. 204.
48. Edmund Burke, *Reflections on the French Revolution in France*, ed. Conor Cruise O'Brien (London: Penguin, 1986), p. 95.
49. See Rivers, *Defence of Truth*; eventually the lectures were used as inter-denominational ammunition during the early nineteenth century, when tense relations between evangelicals and liberals erupted into heated debates about the nature of Christian knowledge. On those debates more generally, see Watts, *The Dissenters*, vol. 2.
50. Samuel Johnson, 'Life of Watts', in *The Works of Samuel Johnson, LL.D.: Together with His Life, and Notes on His Lives of the Poets*, ed. John Hawkins, 11 vols (Cambridge: Cambridge University Press, 2011), vol. 4, pp. 179–88 (p. 186). See Davis, *Isaac Watts*, p. 88.
51. See 18 April 1792 in *DWG*.
52. Godwin, 'An Account of the Seminary That Will Be Opened on Monday the Fourth Day of August, at Epsom in Surrey, for the Instruction of Twelve Pupils in the Greek, Latin, French, and English Languages', *PPW*, vol. 5, pp. 9–10, 20.
53. Godwin, 'Autobiographical Fragments and Reflections', *CNM*, vol. 1, pp. 39–66 (p. 42). Cf. McLachlan, *English Education*, pp. 117–25.
54. *The Enquirer*, p. 85 (emphasis mine).
55. Ibid. p. 95. Cf. Isaac Watts, *Logick*, p. 1: 'Reason is the glory of human nature, and one of the chief eminencies whereby we are raised above our fellow-creatures the brutes in this lower world' (Watts's footnote defines *reason* as 'all the intellectual powers of man').
56. *The Enquirer*, p. 95.
57. Ibid. pp. 135–6; see Milton, *Areopagitica*, pp. 493, 569: 'this project of licencing crept out of the *Inquisition*'; 'this *authentic* Spanish policy of licensing books' (emphasis original).
58. *The Enquirer*, pp. 142, 143.
59. 'Considerations on Lord Grenville's and Mr Pitt's Bills', p. 155. Cf. Godwin's discussion of national education in *Political Justice*, p. 357.
60. Joseph Priestley, *Miscellaneous Observations Relating to Education: More Especially as It Respects the Conduct of the Mind* (London: J. Johnson, 1778), p. 59.
61. *The Enquirer*, pp. 138, 141. See Inchbald's very similar comments about disposition in relation to novel-reading: 'To the Artist', *The Artist*, No. XIV, Saturday, 13 June 1807.
62. *The Enquirer*, pp. 237–8.

63. Maria Edgeworth and Richard Lovell Edgeworth, *Practical Education* (London: J. Johnson, 1798), vol. 1, p. 322.
64. [William Enfield], 'Review of "The Enquirer"', *Monthly Review* 23 (1797): 291–302 (p. 294).
65. *The Enquirer*, p. 96.
66. Ibid.
67. Ibid. pp. 140–1; for the idea of reading as 'benign possession' in this period more generally, see Jackson, *Romantic Readers*, pp. 296–7.
68. *Deloraine*, pp. 236, 173 (see also pp. 16–23); *St Leon*, pp. 43–5. *Fleetwood*'s scene of marital reading is more compromised by domestic disharmony (pp. 198–201).
69. *The Enquirer*, p. 96.
70. 'Letter of Advice to a Young American', pp. 327–8.
71. Ibid.; Godwin to Percy Shelley, 10 December 1812, in 'Godwin/Shelley Correspondence', p. 81. For an insightful discussion of this 'simultaneous' reading advice in light of theories of sociality, see Julie Carlson, *England's First Family of Writers*, pp. 80–1. On the place and practice of conversation in dissenting and radical circles during this period, see John Mee, *Conversable Worlds: Literature, Contention, and Community, 1762 to 1830* (Oxford: Oxford University Press, 2011).
72. 'Letter of Advice to a Young American', p. 328; Godwin to Percy Shelley, 10 December 1812, in 'Godwin/Shelley Correspondence', p. 81.
73. Rivers, *The Defence of Truth*, p. 18.
74. Watts *Improvement of the Mind*, p. 207; see Rivers, *Defence of Truth*, p. 18. Dissenting rhetoric often appears to conflict with educational practice in this regard; Joseph Priestley, for example, preached that 'You, my brethren, have no interest whatever in the support of christianity, if it be false [. . .] we, therefore, as dissenters, shall be absolutely inexcusable, if we be not friends to free inquiry in its utmost extent, and if we do not give the most unbounded scope to the use of our reason in matters of religion'. *The Importance and Extent of Free Inquiry in Matters of Religion: A Sermon* [. . .] (Birmingham: printed by M. Swinney; for J. Johnson, no. 72. St. Paul's Churchyard, London, 1785), p. 24.
75. 'Of Religion', *PPW*, vol. 7, pp. 59–74 (p. 72).
76. *The Enquirer*, p. 85.
77. Ibid. pp. 103, 105.
78. Ibid. pp. 231, 238. See also the *Enquirer* essay 'Of the Sources of Genius', pp. 87–94, and the *Thoughts on Man* essay 'Of the Distribution of Talents', pp. 48–67. For the theological background of ideas about original genius, see D. W. Odell, 'The Argument of Young's "Conjectures on Original Composition"', *Studies in Philology* 78.1 (1981): 87–106.

79. See *The Enquirer*, pp. 87–94, 231, 238, and *Thoughts on Man*, pp. 48–67.
80. *The Enquirer*, p. 97.
81. *Thoughts on Man*, p. 100.
82. Ibid. pp. 110–18. Godwin revisited these comments on rereading in a fictional conversation between Deloraine and his first wife (*Deloraine*, p. 28).
83. Ibid. pp. 119–28 (pp. 123–4); cf. p. 133 (in the essay 'Of Leisure').
84. Ibid. p. 117.
85. Ibid. p. 133.
86. Godwin to Percy Shelley, 10 December 1812, in 'Godwin/Shelley Correspondence', p. 81. For more on Godwin's idea of leisure see Robert Anderson, 'Godwin, Keats and Productive Leisure', *The Wordsworth Circle* 33.1 (2002): 10–13.
87. *The Enquirer*, p. 103.
88. *The Enquirer*, pp. 233–7. Cf. Watts, *Improvement of the Mind*, p. 201.
89. Ibid. p. 237.
90. 'Letter of Advice to a Young American', p. 328.
91. *Thoughts on Man*, p. 115.
92. Sachs, *The Poetics of Decline in British Romanticism* (Cambridge: Cambridge University Press, 2018), p. 8. See also Lynch, *Loving Literature*, pp. 166–79.
93. Watts, *Improvement of the Mind*, pp. 198, 261.
94. See editors' introduction to *DWG* (Oxford: Oxford Digital Library, 2010). Available at <http://godwindiary.bodleian.ox.ac.uk> (last accessed 24 May 2018).
95. Godwin to Marmaduke Martin, 10 February 1798, *LWG*, vol. 2, pp. 9–10.
96. *The Enquirer*, p. 237.
97. Godwin to Percy Shelley, 10 December 1812, in 'Godwin/Shelley Correspondence', p. 81.
98. Godwin to Marmaduke Martin, 10 February 1798, *LWG*, vol. 2, p. 10.
99. *Thoughts on Man*, p. 41; *The Enquirer*, pp. 232–3.
100. *Thoughts on Man*, p. 73.
101. Ibid. p. 74; cf. p. 225.
102. Watts, *Improvement of the Mind*, p. 257.
103. *Political Justice: Variants*, p. 163; see Pamela Clemit, 'Self-Analysis as Social Critique: The Autobiographical Writings of Godwin and Rousseau', *Romanticism* 11 (2005): 161–80.

Chapter 4

Truth and Social Media: Books and Intellectual Regulation

In 1796, John Thelwall published an acerbic summary of William Godwin's authorial strategy. '[N]othing is perhaps more remarkable' he wrote, 'than that [he] should at once recommend the most extensive plan of freedom and innovation ever diffused by any writer in the English language, and reprobate every measure from which even the most moderate reform can rationally be expected.'[1] By identifying 'measure' as the sticking point, Thelwall was not only responding to Godwin's criticism of his own involvement in the cultural apparatus of political radicalism; he was also pinpointing an internal conflict that would pervade Godwin's entire corpus. The fact of truth's 'irresistible advance', throughout his writings, is flanked by anxious assessments of the means of this advance, from reading habits and texts to the substance of the mind itself. He was persistently troubled by the particular ways in which truth could be apprehended by the mind and thus realised as human knowledge.[2]

This problem is brought into sharp focus by Godwin's writing about the media of social interaction. *Political Justice* (1793), for example, includes a description of a hypothetical situation in which truth spreads throughout society. This happens through the activities of a chosen few, who acquire and communicate knowledge with ease:

> Let us imagine to ourselves a number of individuals, who, having first stored their minds with reading and reflection, proceed afterwards in candid and unreserved conversation to compare their ideas [. . .] We shall then have an idea of knowledge as perpetually gaining ground, unaccompanied with peril in the means of its diffusion. Reason will spread itself, and not a brute and unintelligent sympathy.[3]

Framed as it is by the language of imagination, this idealised picture of reading and speaking collides with a litany of warnings and qualifications concerning how it should be achieved in the here-and-now. In the text surrounding this extract and throughout the treatise as a whole, it is the 'peril' that looms large: written and spoken words are untrustworthy vessels, hindering truth's apprehension by the contexts of production and reception that they necessarily involve, amounting, in Angela Esterhammer's terms, to a wholesale 'suspicion of speech acts'.[4] Hard on the heels of its publication Godwin made such mediatory problems the overt theme and structural logic of *Caleb Williams* (1794), which set the trend for his later novels by figuring a world in which truth is eclipsed by a storm of communal bias, personal passion and manipulative rhetoric. Ensuing editions of *Political Justice* (1796, 1798) preserved the original version's strange duality, however. The advance of truth remained Godwin's rallying cry, yet he was simultaneously preoccupied with its dark counterpart, the 'peril in the means of its diffusion'.

Godwin's direct discussions of text and speech illuminate what was felt to be at stake – for him and for others – in their operation and associated perils. 'Of Revolutions' in *Political Justice* (1793–8), 'Of Learning' in *The Enquirer* (1797) and 'Of Belief' in *Thoughts on Man* (1831) all assess the printed codex as a 'means of diffusion' and contrast its social work to that of conversation. The comments they contain have sometimes been recruited as evidence for a change in direction, according to which Godwin's enthusiasm for the conversational culture of London's radical intellectuals in *Political Justice* gave way to his (perhaps less sanguine) investment in books.[5] But in fact they betray more continuity of thought than discontinuity, for they are fundamentally united by a regulative concern. Godwin contends that book-reading and conversation, properly conceived, should work in harmony to balance the speed of intellectual exchange, giving them complementary temporal roles in the social pursuit of knowledge. As Christina Lupton has observed, Godwin endowed the codex with temporal significance in his writing, using it to articulate his progressivist stance towards futurity.[6] His assessments of media technology are best situated in an enduring vision of intellectual 'economy' – which could be retarded or animated by reading or speaking respectively – and they expose the connections he made between these temporal states and the postures or textures of mind that characterised its participants.

Godwin was anxiously preoccupied by these temporal dynamics of knowledge exchange, however, even as he consistently propounded a communicative ideal. The roles he assigned to reading and conversation were ambiguous and qualified, raising questions about sources of epistemic authority: his descriptions hinge upon an uncertainty concerning which factors determine the knowing process and to what degree. At times truth is at the mercy of its mediation, and at others mediatory channels are subservient to truth as a self-sufficient, self-manifesting force. Ultimately, Godwin probed a question that had confronted writers and philosophers throughout the previous century: to what extent is truth dependent upon the activities, structures and mediation of social groups, and to what extent is it external to them? It was rooted in a twofold conception of truth that was resonant throughout the previous century's writing about media technology, including David Hume's 'Of Essay Writing' (1742), Samuel Johnson's 'On Studies' (1753) and Isaac Watts's *Improvement of the Mind* (1741, 1751). The conflicted ways in which dissenting thinkers, in particular, navigated the problem of truth's apprehension, left a conceptual legacy that fuelled Godwin's clashes with fellow political radicals such as Thelwall later in the century. This legacy was not simply a problem, but also became a literary tool by which Godwin invested reformatory hopes in his media environment. His writing unearths the vibrant alethic dialogue of his time and shows important ways in which it shaped public expressions of the book's role in British society.

Media and Temporality

The most consistent feature of the book-object in Godwin's writing is its tendency to slow intellectual exchange. In 'Of Revolutions' its social role is presented in terms that initially appear deprecatory:

> Books have by their very nature but a limited operation; though, on account of their permanence, their methodical disquisition, and their easiness of access, they are entitled to the foremost place. But their efficacy ought not to engross our confidence. The number of those by whom reading is neglected is exceedingly great. Books to those by whom they are read have a sort of constitutional coldness. We review the arguments of an 'insolent innovator' with sullenness, and are unwilling to stretch our

minds to take in all their force. It is with difficulty that we obtain the courage of striking into untrodden paths, and questioning tenets that have been generally received. But conversation accustoms us to hear a variety of sentiments, obliges us to exercise patience and attention, and gives freedom and elasticity to our mental disquisitions. A thinking man, if he will recollect his intellectual history, will find that he has derived inestimable advantage from the stimulus and surprise of colloquial suggestions; and, if he review the history of literature, will perceive that minds of great acuteness and ability have commonly existed in a cluster.[7]

The 'very nature' of books here is 'methodical', 'limited' and 'cold'; they impose restrictions and difficulties upon readers that conversational exchanges do not. A book's 'efficacy' as a vector is undermined by its rigid and uncompromising 'constitution', thus apparently counteracting the very mental flexibility (or 'elasticity') which features in *Political Justice* as the gateway to social justice and human achievement. Conversation is the inverse, an activity defined by its promotion of 'freedom and elasticity'. Its expansive and enabling effects seem to position it as unquestionably superior: it stretches, releases and strikes out into 'untrodden paths', whereas book-reading limits, chills and discourages fresh enquiry. A manuscript draft of this passage takes the contrast further:

> Every man, that will recollect the history of literature, will perceive that great intellectual penetration has commonly existed in a cluster. What is elicited in the commerce of mutual friendship, in the actual contact of mind with mind, is incomparably more excellent than what we draw from the shelves of a library. It is by an experimental acquaintance with the sallies of mind, by that observation which resolves the compound, knowledge, into its constituent parts, by the sympathy that participates in friendly commerce [sic] the vigour of the inventor, that men are taught to feel the practicability of wisdom, are excited to generous emulation, and led forward by gradual steps to the summit of excellence. It is with difficulty that we obtain the courage of striking into untrodden paths, and questioning tenets that have been generally received; but example infuses into the mind both enterprise and firmness. We often read the arguments of an 'insolent innovator' with sullenness, and are unwilling to stretch our minds to take in all their force. But conversation obliges us to exercise a polite attention [. . .]. – Familiar discussion therefore is an object next in importance to that of laying open our ideas to general examination, giving permanence to their form, and inviting public attention to the important topics to which they may relate, through the medium of the press.[8]

Here conversational friendship facilitates a kind of mental 'commerce' that book-reading inhibits. The sympathy generated by 'actual contact of mind with mind' mobilises a joint venture in the realm of thought; a deleted word in Godwin's manuscript reveals that 'friendly commerce' was originally 'friendly shares', underscoring the nature of conversation as mutual participation in an intellectual economy.[9] A book is thus not simply a sluggish or less effective medium of truth, but is a disruption of this interpersonal circulation – by blocking the 'actual contact of mind with mind', it stands in the way of truth's direct apprehension.

At the same time as he identifies this reticence in the book-form, however, Godwin takes for granted that it does not detract from the book's 'foremost place' in intellectual life. His manuscript draft likewise places familiar discussion as 'an object *next* in importance' to that of the dissemination and scrutiny of printed works. In fact, they earn this place precisely because they are stiff and stubborn; they foster habits of discipline that are necessary for mental independence, the 'courage of striking into untrodden paths'. This idea had surfaced in the preface to the first edition of *Political Justice*, which claimed that a book was 'by its very nature an appeal to men of study and reflexion'.[10] While conversation features in this passage as an essential lubricant for the mind, therefore, the 'methodical' pace of book-reading is implicitly presented as a stabilising counterbalance to its colloquial freedom.

The surrounding context makes it explicit that such slowness was indeed conceived as an advantage: as suggested by the chapter's title, 'Of Revolutions', Godwin's assessment of media was part of an argument about the appropriate means of political reform. Shortly before the quoted passage he had launched a criticism along temporal lines of the activities of radical organisations, such as the London Corresponding Society, whose exploitation of large-scale oral appeal he deemed unconducive to private judgement. 'Instead of informing the understanding of the hearer by a slow and regular progression, the orator must beware of detail, must render everything rapid', he complained. 'Truth can scarcely be acquired' in this context; participants neglect 'laborious enquiry' and instead bend to superficial rhetoric. In this critique, which Godwin reiterated in his 'Considerations on Lord Grenville's and Mr Pitt's Bills' (1795), heat accompanies rapidity as a hallmark of unreflective exchange – the 'cauldron of civil contention simmers' – indicating that his ascription of 'constitutional coldness' to the codex was in part a counter-discourse to the dangers of oratorical enthusiasm. This context, explored in greater detail below, explains his emphasis upon both the slowness of books and the merits of small-group conversation among friends (as opposed to that of larger meetings or formal associations). For Godwin, a certain kind of conversation worked in harmony with book-reading as a remedy for rash conviction; together they shaped the enquiring mind and regulated its intellectual pace.[11]

Godwin restated this approach to book-reading in his *Enquirer* essay 'Of Learning', which uses the idea of the book's 'methodical industry' to argue for the importance of reading in early education. He elaborates upon the properties of the book at length, arguing that stately, moderate speed is something the printed codex 'imposes upon' its reader:

> Books undertake to treat of a subject regularly; to unfold it part by part till the whole is surveyed; they are entirely at our devotion, and may be turned backward and forward as we please; it is their express purpose to omit nothing that is essential to a complete delineation. They are written in tranquility, and in the bosom of meditation: they are revised again and again; their obscurities removed, and their defects supplied. Conversation on the other hand is fortuitous and runs wild; the life's blood of truth is filtrated and diluted, till much of its essence is gone. The intellect that depends upon conversation for nutriment, may be compared to the man who should prefer the precarious existence of a beggar, to the possession of a regular and substantial income.[12]

Here books order their readers: they encourage them to explore a subject regularly, 'to unfold it part by part', a process of intellection that mirrors the turning pages. Evoking Milton's *Areopagitica*, which his diary suggests he consulted during *The Enquirer*'s composition, Godwin argues that books have a concentrated potency that renders them more intellectually nutritious than the spoken word. A book, for Milton, is 'the *pretious* [sic] life-blood of a master spirit, imbalm'd and treasur'd up', 'preserv[ing] as in a violl the purest efficacie and extraction of that living intellect that bred them'.[13] Godwin contrasts this vision of the book to the qualities of conversation, which dilutes truth rather than distilling it. He also reworks the commerical conceit of *Political Justice* to claim that books establish a reliable system of profit. Books, he suggests, counteract a tendency towards hastiness and disorder. Their dense, 'methodical' nature works to secure and stabilise ideas precipitated by conversation, and in doing so respects the very nature ('life's blood') of truth.

In fact, despite its emphasis on method and regularity, this passage highlights the disruptive properties that Godwin ascribed to book-reading: books lend themselves to being 'turned backward and forward as we please', resisting the incessant linear flow of conversation and creating a space of concentrated reflection. Godwin frames this as a rebuttal to the contention that books could impede education by clogging up the mind: 'We have been told, that a persevering habit of reading [...] overloads the intellect with the notions of others.'[14] His response in 'Of Learning' is to theorise the book's intrusive nature as an aid to intellectual health. He describes reading as a process by which the mind 'collate[s] itself with other minds', a verb that suggests thickening or fusion rather than flow but which has positive connotations. It denotes the arena of 'actual contact' that in *Political Justice* was reserved for familiar discussion. Books stop readers in their tracks, Godwin argues, and the pause is enriching rather than inhibiting.

This positive conception of the book's disruptive nature resurfaced many years later in Godwin's essay 'Of the Durability of Human Achievements and Productions' in *Thoughts on Man*. As he interrogated the book-object's capacity for historical preservation (books 'embalm' bodies of human achievement), Godwin presented book-reading as an activity that weighs an accumulated legacy of understanding against the current intellectual moment.[15] Although the essays in this collection reflect several interests that matured after his 1790s work, as a whole they sustain the temporal concern with media that emerged in *Political Justice* and *The Enquirer*. In particular, his essay 'Of Belief' is concerned with the power of conversational speed; it depicts the sudden conviction elicited by speech as a kind of intellectual ambush and contrasts it with the effects of book-reading:

> [I]nestimable as is the benefit we derive from books, there is something more searching and soul-stirring in the impulse of oral communication. We cannot shut our ears, as we shut our books; we cannot escape from the appeal of the man who addresses us with the earnest speech and living conviction. [...] Sudden and irresistible conviction is chiefly the offspring of living speech. We may arm ourselves against the arguments of

an author; but the strength of reasoning in him who addresses us, takes us at unawares. It is in the reciprocation of answer and rejoinder that the power of conversation specially lies. A book is an abstraction. It is but imperfectly that we feel, that a real man addresses us in it, and that what he delivers is the entire and deep-wrought sentiment of a being of flesh and blood like ourselves, a being who claims our attention, and is entitled to our deference. The living human voice, with a countenance and manner corresponding, constrains us to weigh what is said, shoots through us like a stroke of electricity, will not away from our memory, and haunts our very dreams. It is by means of this peculiarity in the nature of mind, that it has been often observed that there is from time to time an Augustan age in the intellect of nations, that men of superior powers shock with each other, and that light is struck by the collision, which most probably no one of these men would have given birth to, if they had not been thrown into mutual society and communion. And even so, on a narrower scale, he that would aspire to do the most of which his faculties are susceptible, should seek the intercourse of his fellows, that his powers may be strengthened, and he may be kept free from that torpor and indolence of soul, which, without external excitement, are ever apt to take possession of us.[16]

This essay continues Godwin's evaluation of the human voice and the printed page in relation to time. Discussion instigates speed – it stirs, shoots and excites – whereas the book's abstract nature contributes to sluggishness or 'torpor'. Conversation is again the realm of 'actual contact' through which the exchange of knowledge most naturally occurs, but Godwin is ambivalent about its merits. Speech 'takes us at unawares' in contrast to the book's less immediate effect. From this angle, 'Of Belief' affirms *The Enquirer*'s presentation of books as objects that 'force us to reflect' rather than manipulating belief. Godwin was reiterating his argument that books bring pockets of order to bear against the dispersed energy of conversation; that they promote a regular, orderly, contemplative mode of intellectual life.[17]

What emerges from this continuity in Godwin's discussion of media technology – his focus upon flow, speed and regulation – is a wider concern with an ideal of intellectual commerce. He insistently promoted a specific version of community, one in which reading, speaking and writing played different but equally important roles. This is signalled by Godwin's repetition of terms such as 'cluster', 'collate' and 'communion', which he uses to stress the necessity of fellowship or participation in an economy of knowledge. It is the hinge upon which his judgements turn: in *Thoughts on Man*, conversation's positive, energising role depends upon the fact that it induces 'reciprocation', 'communion' and 'intercourse' among its participants in a way that books cannot. *The Enquirer* denounces educational reliance upon conversation by comparing it to beggarly means and describing book-reading, in contrast, as a regular system of profit. Comments in *Political Justice* are concerned with easing an imagined flow of knowledge: books tend to disrupt or stall intellectual exchange, which has positive functions, but also creates the need for the mobilising force of conversation, properly conceived.

Godwin was using an idiom familiar to eighteenth-century readers. A shared language of movement, speed and regulation had been used by writers and philosophers throughout the century to discuss the exchange of knowledge and its social ramifications – they assumed, in Robin Valenza's words, an 'economic model of knowledge generation and transmission'.[18] He perhaps drew most from David Hume, whose work distilled an interest in the social nature of knowledge among Scottish intelligentsia and exploited a shared language of intellectual flow or exchange in the process. Hume's scepticism may have been unusual for his time, but as Fred Parker and others have shown, his work exemplifies the ways in which implicit ambivalence towards the nature of knowledge was frequently translated into confidence, or perhaps ideological investment, in particular forms of textual dissemination during the eighteenth century.[19] 'Of Essay Writing' (1742), for example – which is indebted to Joseph Addison's vision for *The Spectator* (1711–12) – describes a harmonious society as one in which 'every one displays his Thoughts and Observations in the best Manner he is able, and mutually gives and receives Information, as well as Pleasure'. Economic language is the extended conceit; Hume argues for the importance of initiating and maintaining 'Commerce', 'Correspondence' or 'Balance of Trade' between the Men of Letters and the Men of the World, between realms of books and of speech.[20] As his focus upon the role of the learned essayist suggests, however, such discourse about intellectual commerce was developing in conjunction with concerns about the kinds of people, institutions or channels that regulated the system. As theories of knowledge were increasingly embedded in theories of sociality, the scope and means of sociality became a locus for philosophical and political anxiety.

These regulatory concerns about the mediation of knowledge found potent expression in Samuel Johnson's essay 'On Studies' (1753), which explores the difficulty encountered by the public intellectual or 'man of letters' in his stewardship of the intellectual economy. Taking its cue from Bacon's famous aphorism – 'Reading maketh a Full Man; Conference a Ready Man; And Writing an Exact Man' – it articulates how practices of reading, speaking and writing should be used to facilitate an ordered flow of knowledge, yet also places them in a context of innate tendency towards disorder, disproportion and confusion.[21] Johnson extols the importance of books against the accusation that they are 'useless lumber', yet also warns against the dangers of book-learning: scholars easily become 'overloaded', 'entangled' and inflexible, thus ineffective at communicating knowledge to the wider community. Conversation develops bookreaders into 'ready', adaptable and effective communicators, yet it easily engenders sophism, 'inaccuracy' and 'confusion'. This leads Johnson to posit the stabilising role of writing, something that fixes, contracts and scrutinises what conversation diffuses. His emphasis upon the ways in which different communicative forms counteract or balance each other finds more than an echo in Godwin's essay 'Of Learning'.

Johnson finishes, however, by acknowledging the immense difficulty of holding these activities in harmony. He claims that 'To read, write, and converse in due proportions is [. . .] the business of a man of letters', yet he considers the conditions or opportunities that enable these proportions to be exceedingly rare. His closing remark encapsulates the consequent ambivalence of the man of letters' mediatory task: 'it is, however, reasonable, to have perfection in our eye; that we may always advance towards it, though we know it never can be reached'. Society's intellectual economy always relies upon compromised communication, Johnson implies, a falling-short of 'due proportions'. Nevertheless, progress towards perfection is possible – indeed, it is the human experience. Both Hume and Johnson assume, although they express it in different ways, that knowledge exists as a force or movement independent of the knower, while their work remains ambiguous about the extent to which the media of social interaction have power over it.

Godwin's assesments of media technology feature this inherited discourse of intellectual economy in a way that brings its ambivlance concerning regulative authority to the foreground. As he describes their social roles, reading and conversation disturb and encroach upon one another; both appear full of inherent dangers to truth's progress, yet the very properties that cause this jeopardy are deemed essential for balancing the other's defects. Conversation 'runs wild' into hasty conviction or shallow chatter, yet these problems of fluidity are necessary for dislodging the prejudice, torpor and seclusion that book-reading promotes. Books are slow, difficult and disengaging, yet these things counteract the facile slipperiness of the spoken word. In his reading advice the two activities were imagined in such intimate relations that they often overlapped: Godwin prescribed methods of conversational reading, for example, by which numerous texts were brought into a circle of dialogue and the reader's written responses enlisted them in a network of critical exchange.

Godwin's specification of different kinds of conversation further complicate these relations. As we have seen, he recommended oral discussion on the basis that it kept the participant free from 'torpor and indolence of soul'; like many moral and educational theorists, he placed great value upon the sympathy generated by face-to-face contact. Human presence acts as a mental stimulus by which imaginative empathy develops, a faculty involved in many aspects of the understanding. Yet Godwin's depiction of conversation as an instigating force was also a response to a different sort of conversation – an inhibited and unfruitful sort associated with contemporary culture. As Jon Mee has shown, Godwin wrote from a position of critique that considered mainstream conversational culture to be artificial and unhelpfully restrained by custom. The dissenting ideal of conversational candour – which Godwin sometimes calls 'sincerity' or 'frankness' – was about clearing away these cultural blockages to allow for truth to be clearly sought after and apprehended.[22] Godwin argued in *Political Justice* that 'dictates of worldly prudence and custom' and 'artificial delicacy' had produced an intellectual economy in which 'everything is disfigured and distorted', yet he maintained that if candid intellectual enquiry were to be pursued, 'Conversation would speedily exchange its present character of listlessness and insignificance, for a Roman boldness and fervour.'[23] As indicated by his reference to classical republican culture, this argument was inherently political. Godwin understood political institutions to be detrimental to such revitalised exchanges of ideas: 'Whenever government assumes to deliver us from the trouble of thinking for ourselves, the only consequences it produces are those of torpor and imbecility.'[24] Awareness of these political dimensions was heightened during the 1790s when Pitt's government cracked down upon radical activity by introducing new measures of censorship and restrictions upon meetings.

Godwin qualified this ideal of conversational inhibition throughout his work, however, careful to distinguish it from the kind of unrestraint that he associated with political societies and public oratory.[25] Immediately after extolling the consequences of allowing truth 'a plain and direct appeal' to human understanding by removing the 'obstacles' to its discussion in cultural life, he adds:

> But these consequences are the property only of independent and impartial discussion. If once the unambitious and candid circles of enquiring men be swallowed up in the insatiate gulf of noisy assemblies, the opportunity of improvement is instantly annihilated. The happy varieties of sentiment which so eminently contribute to intellectual acuteness are lost.[26]

This distinction draws attention to the difficult balance that Godwin attempts to negotiate: conversation must remain 'independent' and 'impartial', yet its very benefits have been described as arising from its co-opting nature, its powerful current of sympathetic stimulation. Sheer numbers become the decisive factor, explaining Godwin's assertion in *Political Justice* that 'Discussion perhaps never exists with so much vigour and utility as in the conversation of two persons. It may be carried on with advantage in small and friendly societies.'[27] The unruly potential of speech must be harnessed by a small group limit, a non-institutional context, and the practice of book-reading, which stabilises and enriches conversational enquiry.

Godwin's assessments of different kinds of reading matter complicate this picture still further. Ephemeral printed forms are associated with the promiscuous immediacy of speech, a criticism which becomes a plot device in *Caleb Williams* (1794) and *Deloraine* (1833). In both novels, handbills and newspapers exchange complicated truths for reductive and incendiary opinions. Godwin was tapping into a widespread contemporary awareness of the temporal implications of ephemeral print; as Mark Turner records, newspapers and periodicals encoded a particular sort of time in the social imagination, 'in a period in which temporal shifts and disruptions were a sign of its modernity'.[28] In 1814 the French philosopher Benjamin Constant spelled out the relevance of these temporal shifts to political fears:

> All enlightened men seemed to be convinced that complete freedom and exemption from any form of censorship should be granted to longer works. Because writing them requires time, purchasing them requires affluence, and reading them requires attention, they are not able to produce the reaction in the populace that one fears of works of greater rapidity and violence. But pamphlets, and handbills, and newspapers, are produced quickly, you can buy them for little, and because their effect is immediate, they are believed to be more dangerous.[29]

Constant describes a common connection between ephemeral print and the 'rapidity and violence' of the mob in the minds of the educated classes. Godwin's depictions of handbills and newspapers in his novels appear to fall in with this view: they are inflammatory and manipulative, media which rush past the truth and hunt down the innocent.[30]

In fact, despite Godwin's generalised claims about the slowness of books in his theoretical works, certain 'books of narrative and romance' also become a source of impetuous speed in *Caleb Williams*. Caleb's childhood books are described in terms of the hastiness instigated by speech and ephemeral print: 'I could not rest', he records, 'I panted for the unravelling of an adventure.' They shape him into an impetuous and irresolute character, whose actions are driven by 'unremarked and involuntary sympathy'. These were dangerous effects that Godwin clearly did not attribute to his own novels, the express purpose of which he described as the instigation of 'moral and political enquiry'.[31] Other sorts of books have different effects upon his protagonist. Godwin added an episode to the second edition of the novel, in which Caleb's chance encounter with a dictionary prompts him to embark upon a careful study of language. This sort of reading marries both 'industry and recreation', channelling his mind in a healthier direction, but it is soon disrupted by Falkland's pursuit.[32]

Godwin's correspondence reveals a similarly conflicted assessment of epistolary writing. An exchange in November 1795 with Thomas Wedgwood, pioneer of early photography and son of the potter Josiah

Wedgwood, is illustrative. Godwin made an irritable remark concerning the need to clarify the content of his previous letter: 'Do you not feel how very inadequately epistolary communication supplies the place of oral discussion?' This prompted Wedgwood to respond that 'on some accounts I prefer writing to conversation. But this preference is owing entirely to my want of a prompt & clear expression of my thoughts, which exercise alone can supply.'[33] Godwin's rejoinder reveals the centrality of the temporal to his thinking:

> Your preference of correspondence to conversation seems to be founded in part in suggestions of vanity. How intolerably creeping & tedious is this interchange? I am not inclined to doubt that my time is well spent in your society; but, in writing thus, I comply with my feelings, & run counter to the bias of my judgment. I believe correspondence ought scarcely in any case to be admitted, but when the parties are at a distance from each other.[34]

Godwin assumes here that letters are intended as conversational substitutes, and on these grounds dismisses them as unsatisfactory. The merits of conversation stem from the stimulating effect of personal presence, from the immediate 'reciprocation of answer and rejoinder', which is precluded by the 'intolerably creeping & tedious' breaks between letters. Epistolary exchange thus occupies an uncertain territory between the personal force of speech and rigidity of books, yet participates in the temporal dynamics of neither medium.[35]

Even reading spaces both enable and jeopardise the knowledge economy in Godwin's work. A letter of 1805 to his acquaintance Joseph Planta, principal librarian at the British Museum, contends that public reading rooms can diffuse one's mental powers, and thus counteract the beneficial fixity of books:

> But it is impossible for me to express, or for any person who has never been engaged in a work of patient & unintermitted investigation fully to conceive, the disadvantages that must attend an examination of authorities & documents in a public Reading Room. For this purpose passages must not only be read with a deep & concentrated attention, but the writer must also reason, weigh, & make inferences, as he reads. But a public Reading Room, however decorously ~~managed~~ conducted, must be attended with infinite distractions to ~~such a writer~~ a person so employed. The majority of the frequenters of such a room will always be

persons who read more from a spirit of vague curiosity, & that they may spend their time agreeably to themselves, than from any other motive.³⁶

The scholar's activity here combines all the crucial elements of reading ('deep & concentrated attention'), conversation ('reason, weigh, & make inferences') and writing ('engaged in an elaborate work'), yet it is fundamentally undermined by the public nature of the reading room. The presence of other readers distracts the mind and promotes 'a spirit of vague curiosity', the antithesis of the concentrated attention that books require. It was a critique that would resurface in Thomas Carlyle's famous complaints about the Museum library in the 1830s, leading to the establishment of the London Library in 1841. Godwin had already expressed similar ideas in the preface to his *Life of Chaucer* (1803), claiming that the Museum's refusal to allow him to borrow books and consult them in his 'own chamber' was 'productive of great loss of time and many disadvantages'.³⁷

If public libraries detract from the beneficial qualities of book-reading, however, private libraries concentrate them into vices. In *Fleetwood* (1805), the protagonist's personal 'reading closet' becomes a symbol of the character distortion engendered by bookish isolation. Ruffigny, a family friend and paternal figure, warns Fleetwood about his need to maintain a balance between private book-reading and social interaction:

> The furniture of these shelves constitutes an elaborate and invaluable commentary; but the objects beyond those windows, and the circles and communities of my contemporaries, are the text to which that commentary relates.

Yet the reading space that Fleetwood frequented in his ancestral home has already proved too powerful:

> [H]ere it had ever since been my custom to retire with some favourite author, when I wished to feel my mind in its most happy state [. . .] I entered it now, after a twelvemonth's absence, with a full recollection of all the castles which I had sat there are builded in the air, the odes, the tragedies, and heroic poems which, in the days of visionary childhood, upon that spot I had sketched and imagined. [. . .] how unalterably it had fixed its hold upon me as my favourite retreat.³⁸

The 'hold' of this particular reading space reflects and precipitates Fleetwood's stubborn, antisocial adherence to his feelings, a character flaw that was fostered by his education: undisciplined, isolated reading habits lead him to privilege his sentiment above every other social demand, including relational responsibilities. His wife's unknowing appropriation of the reading space is doubly poignant, a threat to his material memories and his mental habits of castle-building, and it triggers a sequence of jealousy and passion.[39] In what spatial context is truth best pursued? Godwin presents an ambiguous answer, a Johnsonian balancing act of public and private environments, of the sociality of books and people.

Truth thus emerges from Godwin's work hampered by regulative problems, which are found both in the means of exchange and the environments in which those exchanges occur. Behind all of these factors, however, is the movement of truth itself. Godwin's wariness about the speed instigated by ephemeral print and oral appeal, for example, was not a response to immediacy per se, but involved the belief that this velocity did not correlate with truth's own progress. Describing the work of a beneficial book in 'Considerations', he argued that

> If it undermine the received system, it will undermine it gradually and insensibly; it will merely fall in with that gradual principle of decay and renovation, which is perpetually at work in every part of the universe.[40]

A truly revolutionary book, here, is not one that incites sudden action, but one that colludes in the organic advance of truth among society as a whole, 'that gradual principle of decay and renovation'. Godwin thus references an intellectual tempo that transcends the dynamics of reading or speaking, a spirit of change that is everywhere 'perpetually at work'. This principle leads him to claim that 'Reform must come [. . .] if we endeavour to keep it out too long, it will overwhelm us.'[41]

It is important to recognise that the expression of this 'gradual principle' was integral to Godwin's immediate political aims in 'Considerations'. The pamphlet was designed to contribute to public debate about proposed legislation to limit the activities of radical societies by making their meetings illegal and by censoring the press (the 'Gagging Acts' of 1795). Godwin wanted to make his own position clear, and it involved sharp critiques of both government officials and radical activists. By presenting truth as a self-manifesting force, he downplayed his radicalism and distanced himself from the political activism that was causing establishment alarm, casting himself as a non-threatening gradualist. His depictions of oratory as a precipitate force reflect this strategy: 'It is not [...] in crowded audiences, that truth is successfully investigated', Godwin claims, here establishing his break with Thelwall. At the same time, the 'gradual principle' allowed Godwin to justify his reformist credentials to radicals: their hopes and desires were vindicated because 'Reform *must* come'. By casting books as naturally reformatory objects, he presented the literary world of which he was a part as innately allied to the radical cause.[42] In other words, by defending the social work of books according to the 'gradual principle', Godwin was appealing to a higher authority in order to deflect hostility from both poles of the debate. It was a political strategy that shaped much of his work in the 1790s, including his revisions to *Political Justice* throughout the decade.

Yet Godwin's description of the gradual principle also exposes an unstable relationship between truth and media that transcends this immediate context. Throughout 'Considerations' the cultural apparatus of print seems to threaten or confuse the force of truth, rather than simply 'fall in' with it as Godwin claims. An abstract version of the printing press is presented in competing terms to the 'gradual principle', as a transcendent force that cannot be withstood once set into motion. Godwin even uses a quote from the gospel of Luke to position it as the Messianic cornerstone, 'against which whosoever stumbles, shall be broken'. Crucially, as 'Considerations' involves a plea for the freedom of the press, both this power of print and its associated 'principle' of renovation appear at the mercy of human arbitration. 'Lord Grenville's bill is probably the most atrocious', he writes, 'because writing and the publication of science, [...] of all imaginable things, [are] the most essential to the welfare of mankind.' According to this argument, the bill places at risk 'all that is dignified, all that is ennobling'. Godwin thus frequently appeals to a version of truth which is an unstoppable force, yet apparently considers it jeopardised from all sides by society's mediatory structures – by the cultural apparatus that orchestrates both the printed and the spoken word. Truth's apprehension, Godwin acknowledges, is 'a delicate and awful task'.[43]

Godwin had already personified the vulnerability of this 'gradual principle' in the character of Clare in *Caleb Williams*. This novel delineates a dramatic battle for psychological ownership, fuelled by both eloquent oral appeals and inflammatory printed matter. Yet these intense exchanges are held in sober contrast to Clare, whose 'unreserved' conversation 'flowed with [. . .] ease', whose 'frankness' was 'tranquil' and measured. Most significantly, his public speaking was orderly and appropriate: 'Every word was impressed with its true value, and none was brought forward with disproportioned and elaborate emphasis.'[44] Clare embodies the intellectual benefits of speech, for Godwin, which obtained only insofar as it respected the proportioned advance of truth itself, something that freely 'flowed' and yet retained a 'mild', stately caution. Clare is an authoritative figure while he lives, deeply respected by all, and Falkland listens with tears to his parting admonition. Yet he dies early, and his advice is ignored. The rest of the novel is a riotous distortion of the 'true value' that he represents: print, speech and even physical appearances are vehicles of deception, passion and confusion. Caleb describes how he is 'hurried along I do not know how', subject to 'uncontrollable enthusiasm', 'irresistible force' and 'rapidity'. He is overtaken by the contagious warmth associated with political associations in Godwin's *Enquiry* and 'Considerations', confessing, 'I had no time to cool or to deliberate.'[45]

Truth and Dissent

For the novel's first readers, Clare's exemplary qualities had a further layer of significance. Terms such as 'frankness', 'flow' and 'unreserve' were watchwords of dissenting educational culture and testify to the fact that Godwin's concern about mediatory authority was an inherited one. As Chapter 3 explored, the Jennings-Doddridge tradition of dissenting academies upheld an ideal of 'free enquiry', which referenced a perceived need to liberate intellectual exchange within society and which also promoted teaching methods that prioritised the process of 'enquiry' over and above its specific propositional content or doctrine. At the same time, this principle encapsulated the twofold alethic understanding that was emergent in dissenting culture. In some contexts, truth was understood as an objective body of knowledge, accessed progressively by humankind to the extent that they engaged in this 'free enquiry'. Truth was commonly described as self-evident to the impartial enquirer, because human rationality was a God-given resource and truth itself was divine revelation. Joseph Priestley reflected this when he claimed that 'Truth will always have an infinite advantage over error, if free scope be given to inquiry.'[46] Belief in this advantage became the overt justification for theories of intellectual and moral perfectibility, and fuelled the vibrancy and confidence of dissenting academy life. Because its apprehension was, in part, a soteriological issue, presenting it as naturally self-manifesting was profoundly consequential for theological doctrine and had obvious implications for the growth of universalism.[47] Truth was presented as both a fixed ideal and an unstoppable movement, and this depiction undergirded a general optimism in the human condition.

This confidence, however, was held alongside sharp critiques of forces deemed to constrain or distort truth's apprehension. Dissenting communities were keenly aware of their marginalised social status and often characterised mainstream culture in terms of superficiality or prejudice, an environment in which the flow of truth was either dispersed by triviality or blocked by closed-mindedness.[48] There were also theological disagreements over the extent to which human sin had noetic implications. Professions of truth as self-evident thus collided with images of a society in which truth was jeopardised, thwarted, elusive. The ideal of 'candour' or 'frankness' in sociable exchange reflects these concerns, evoking a context in which Priestley's 'free scope' was hard to come by. Indeed, figures including Priestley and Horne Tooke began to give language itself a formative role in belief, sometimes complicating the dissenting emphasis upon 'pure' (*im*mediate) communication. Another version of truth was being addressed, one increasingly bound to the processes and means of its discovery.

This double vision of truth – at once self-evident and elusive, self-sufficient and dependent – was clearly illustrated by the scrutiny with which this educational tradition approached media technology. A good example is Isaac Watts's *Improvement of the Mind* (1741), a treatise that sprung from the Jennings-Doddridge community yet enjoyed influence far beyond. The work upholds intellectual enquiry as a spiritual ideal, yet is dedicated to scrutinising the dangers of different communicative means, and advising the reader as to how their involvement with such means should be conducted. Book-reading is a case in point: while Watts evokes the familiar connection between print technology and spiritual-intellectual progress, and epitomises the central place given to reading in the sociable ideals of his dissenting culture, the task seems problematic from the outset. After wading through decisions about what is necessary to read in the first place, Watts considers how the reader's enquiry is threatened by the book's own form. Its 'bulk' or weighty nature can promote uncritical assent, on the one hand, leading to over-reliance upon an author's opinions and thus a 'dogmatical spirit'; yet on the other, it can discourage investigation entirely, leading weaker readers to 'hover always on the surface of things' and remain irresolute. Both dangers involve superficiality, by which the book's literal surfaces engender surface-level thinking. To illustrate their social ramifications, an example is given:

> *Subito* is carried away by title pages, so that he ventures to pronounce upon a large octavo at once, and to recommend it wonderfully when he had read half the preface. [. . .] But *Subito* changes his opinion of men and books and things so often, that no body regards him.[49]

Subito represents the person, or rather imagined social type, who tries to short-cut knowledge by speeding up the labour of intellectual enquiry. His name references a musical term, familiar to Watts the hymnodist, meaning 'sudden'; it denotes temporal disruption and contrasts with the language of order, regularity and tranquillity that characterises the instructions of the treatise at large. Significantly, *Subito*'s haste is connected to his status as a fickle, insubstantial conversationalist. His lack of reading discipline means that he thins and diffuses the flow of truth, rendering him a chatterer of no service to the knowledge economy at large. Ironically, for Watts, the book's 'bulk' can starve intellectual life; a large volume can promote hasty, lightweight thinking. He argues that this danger must be counteracted by rigorous reading habits, about which he goes into great detail.

What was at stake in such instructions about the pursuit of knowledge was regulative authority: the degree of epistemological weight one should ascribe to mediatory forms as opposed to truth itself. Watts's assessments of media draw attention to a latent ambiguity in dissenting thought over the degree to which individual effort, media environment or the supposed power of truth itself was decisive in engendering belief. For those who held a theological doctrine of revelation that enabled them to have confidence in truth's divinely ordained tenacity, the implications of this internal tension were kept at bay. Yet the approach laid foundations for a different counterculture at the turn of the century, which came to fruition in dissenting-educated thinkers such as Godwin. He inherited, on the one hand, a version of truth as an unstoppable force pertaining to salvific ends, and on the other, a version that was subordinate to the contemporary social environment, human faculties and the very stuff and substance of mediatory channels.

As cultural historians have documented, this dissenting 'dream of intellectual flow without collision' assumed controversial political dimensions in late eighteenth-century London.[50] Its ethos and rhetoric informed the activities of many reformist organisations – most prominently the Revolution Society, the Society for Constitutional Information and the London Corresponding Society – which faced criticism not only from mainstream conservatives, but from equally radical thinkers such as Godwin himself. The emotive speeches of their mass-meetings were a key point of contention for both sides: Burke famously sneered that they contained 'nothing of politics but the passions they excite', and Godwin likewise denounced them as inimical to 'Sober inquiry' on the grounds that their 'oratorical seasoning is an appeal to the passions'.[51] This shared ground of critique draws attention to a notable feature of the radical societies: they were, on the whole, less cautious about media form than many dissenting predecessors, less qualified in their faith in the efficacy of print and speech towards the dissemination of truth, despite the ongoing suspicion of sociocultural authority that they had inherited. Jon Mee terms this tendency 'print magic', 'a form of magical thinking [that] assumed a power in the medium regardless of causative relations'.[52] This context inflected Godwin's portrayal of the book as a difficult and demanding means of knowledge. By emphasising the 'peril' in equal measure to the 'magic' of media technology, his writing distils the epistemological tension that shaped ways of imagining social change in radical communities.

Godwin's assessments of reading and speaking, then, with their fraught dynamics of speed, weight and temperature, reflect and negotiate an authority problem of his educational inheritance. He retained the double vision of truth that pervaded dissenting culture, and remained sensitised to a language that evaluated means and methods of socialisation in terms of temporal dynamic. He appropriated this language to negotiate contemporary debates about the nature of sociopolitical reform, critiquing radical societies in the 1790s by positioning them at the extreme ends of scales measuring heat and cold, rapidity and stasis. On a more fundamental level, however, his discourse gestured to a conceptual ambiguity concerning how this intellectual system was regulated. Truth's innate authority had to be asserted in order to theorise perfectibility, yet in order to diagnose the noetic ills of society its means of apprehension were endowed with great, often terrible, power.

This becomes even more explicit when one considers Godwin's direct descriptions of 'truth'. Throughout the 1790s he presented it as a force self-sufficient enough to make independent progress: in 1793 'truth is omnipotent', in 1795 truth is a 'resistless tide', and in 1797 'Truth is powerful, and, [will] make good her possession.' The revised editions of *Political Justice* all continue to place hope for social reform in the 'value and energy of truth' itself.[53] Yet alongside this portrayal is a vulnerable, dependent version of truth. The same pages that proclaim truth's omnipotence contend that 'if there be such a thing as truth, it must infallibly be struck out by the collision of mind with mind'. A later manuscript note confirms this idea, remarking that 'Truth, [. . .] arises from the relative character & disposition of two persons or things, the speaker & the hearer, the words uttered, & the temper of him by whom the words are received.'[54] Godwin makes an uneasy combination of the two versions in his 1797 essay 'Of Scepticism', in which he argues that the sceptical empiricist 'is the genuine friend of truth'. Truth here is a self-evident body like the sun: 'The sceptic makes bare his own bosom to receive the beams of truth.' Yet it is also a means of direction or discovery, like the wind: the sceptic 'always holds himself ready for the gale of truth, and spreads his canvas that he may feel its lightest breath. His voyage of discovery is never finished. His views perpetually vary, yet perpetually improve.'[55] The friction between these concepts of truth is encapsulated by a comment in *Political Justice*:

> The great cause of humanity, which is now pleading in the face of the universe, has but two enemies; those friends of antiquity, and those friends of innovation, who, impatient of suspense, are inclined violently to interrupt the calm, the incessant, the rapid and auspicious progress

> which thought and reflection appear to be making in the world. Happy would it be for mankind if those persons who interest themselves most zealously in these great questions would confine their exertions to the diffusing, in every possible mode, a spirit of enquiry [. . .]![56]

The movement of truth here is calm and gradual, yet rapid and incessant; it naturally manifests its progress through thought and reflection, yet is reliant upon the exertions and zeal of certain proponents; it is the unassailable *telos* of humanity and yet is threatened both by those who conserve tradition and those who instigate change. The language of 'diffusing' and 'spreading' that Godwin frequently uses to describe truth's advance suggests an intangible and uncontrollable force, yet truth also appears dependent, chaotic and material, 'struck out' by a process of collision. From this mixed portrayal flows the mixed instructions that Godwin gives to his readers: while he urges them to have serene confidence in truth's authority, he also confronts them with qualified and often conservative social advice. Truth's nature as a progressive force is constantly weighed against the contention that it must be properly stewarded by the structures and channels of society. It is both an assumption (transcending the activities of knowledge exchange) and a conclusion (produced solely by their proper enactment).

Godwin's concerns about mediatory regulation thus feature a bifurcated concept of truth, which was one major legacy of dissenting educational culture. In the process they betray a broader philosophical development, an alethic cross-current in British empiricism that was integral to much Romantic-period writing. As Tim Milnes has shown, Coleridge, Keats and Shelley all exploited a recognised 'tension between truth as ideal and truth as dialogue'. They explored, in implicit and explicit ways, what it meant to be committed to truth as an intersubjective reality: something that was constituted by subjects in dialogue and yet, at the same time, was a presupposed condition that enabled and limited this dialogic activity.[57] Godwin's work recruits the same ambivalence, probing the extent to which truth is dependent upon the activities, structures and tools of social groups, and the extent to which it is external to them. Indeed, the tension was perhaps especially poignant for an ex-nonconformist minister like Godwin, who was tied to his inheritance closely enough to define truth as a forceful, teleological ideal, yet secularised enough to abandon belief in its personal divine origin and emphasise its provisional, dependent nature at any given time.

The quotation from *Political Justice* at the beginning of this chapter suggests that Godwin's full response to this conceptual tension involved a leap of faith. 'Let us imagine to ourselves', it begins, presenting his ideal of intellectual community in terms of an imaginative summons by which the reader is exhorted to anticipate something as yet unrealised. The following sentences reiterate this summons, beginning with 'let us suppose', linking imagination to assumption. Godwin's group of imagined 'enquirers' read and speak in such a manner that true knowledge naturally gains ground: 'Reason will spread *itself*'. And the ideal that they encapsulate should stimulate real attempts to 'bring [truth] into daily use', Godwin argues. This effort will inevitably gain social momentum: 'the beauty of the spectacle will soon render the example contagious'.[58]

Such recruitment of readerly imagination features across Godwin's corpus, undergirding both fiction and philosophy, educational and historical commentary. It is more than a rhetorical flourish. It is a literary strategy that trades upon competing perspectives on truth – a sustained appeal for faith in truth's authoritative bearing and an invitation to initiate its realisation. The final words of Godwin's last philosophical work reaffirm its centrality to his thought. After describing the wonderful capacities of human nature, and the heights to which it has soared at various points in history, *Thoughts on Man* concludes:

> And it is but just, that those by whom these things are fairly considered, should anticipate the progress of our nature, and believe that human understanding and human virtue will hereafter accomplish such things as the heart of man has never yet been daring enough to conceive.[59]

This closing sentence entices the reader into an imaginative task: to consider, anticipate and believe. Godwin echoes Dugald Stewart's 1792 claim that belief in societal improvement 'realizes the event which it leads us to anticipate',[60] arguing that conviction in truth and its progress is necessary for the task of its discovery. *Thoughts on Man* thus ends by evoking its 'very nature' as a book-object, according to Godwin. Its inherently demanding, disruptive form lends itself to this imaginative pursuit, in which the paused mind 'strikes out' beyond the confines of its usual channels.

We have seen that Godwin's assessments of reading and speaking reflect an historical moment in which the social operation of media was highly politicised. The spatial and temporal dynamics of intellectual life were debated as matters of controversy, and Godwin's appropriation of the discourse of regulation was in part an attempt to publicly negotiate his own position as a gradualist reformer. Yet his contribution also shows that these debates were conditioned and enlivened by a context of philosophical turbulence. Godwin recruited the media environment of Romantic-period London in order to 'anticipate the progress of our nature' – to invest in truth's ideal while simultaneously grappling with the problems of its apprehension, the 'peril in the means of its diffusion'. His writing thus exposes an alliance between the period's literary consciousness of media technology and the shifting alethic commitments of its writers.

Despite these tensions, Godwin continued to give the book 'the foremost place' in his evaluations of media, and *Political Justice* indicates that from the beginning of his career he linked this position to 'its permanence'. His essay 'Of the Durability of Human Achievements and Productions' in *Thoughts on Man* revisited that idea through its description of printed volumes 'embalmed in collections', presenting the book-object as not simply a temporal regulator, but a temporal survivor. The following chapter argues that Godwin increasingly wrote about books in this way. His essays from the first decade of the nineteenth century explicitly presented books as objects that enabled the minds of their authors to escape the power of death. This strategy was one of the most interesting and powerful contributions to debates about social and cultural progress in Romantic-period Britain.

Notes

1. John Thelwall, *The Tribune*, vol. 2 (London: Symonds, Ridgway, and Smith, 1796), p. vii. In its immediate context, Thelwall's complaint responds to 'Considerations on Lord Grenville's and Mr Pitt's Bills' (1795), in which Godwin condemns both the legislative proposals of government and the activities of London's politically radical societies, such as the London Corresponding Society, which such legislation was designed to censor. For Godwin's disagreement with Thelwall, see Mark Philp, 'Godwin, Thelwall, and the Means of Progress', and

Jon Mee, '"The Press and Danger of the Crowd": Godwin, Thelwall, and the Counter-Public Sphere', both in *Godwinian Moments: From the Enlightenment to Romanticism*, ed. Robert Maniquis and Victoria Myers (Toronto: University of Toronto Press, 2011).
2. For 'irresistible advance' see *Political Justice: Variants*, p. 138. As this sentence implies, I use *knowledge* to denote human apprehension of *truth* (the concept of which this chapter investigates).
3. *Political Justice*, p. 121. Retained in all subsequent editions.
4. Esterhammer, 'Godwin's Suspicion of Speech Acts', *Studies in Romanticism* 39.4 (2000): 553–78.
5. See, for example, Julie Carlson, *England's First Family of Writers: Mary Wollstonecraft, William Godwin, Mary Shelley* (Baltimore: Johns Hopkins University Press, 2007), pp. 77–9; Mee, *Conversable Worlds, Literature, Contention, and Community, 1762 to 1830* (Oxford: Oxford University Press), p. 148. Other works that assume this shift include: Garrett A. Sullivan, '"A Story to Be Hastily Gobbled Up": "Caleb Williams" and Print Culture', *Studies in Romanticism* 32.3 (1993), 323–37; Kristen Leaver, 'Pursuing Conversations: "Caleb Williams" and the Romantic Construction of the Reader', *Studies in Romanticism* 33.4 (1994), 589–610; Gillian Russell and Clara Tuite, 'Introducing Romantic Sociability', in *Romantic Sociability: Social Networks and Literary Culture in Britain, 1770–1840* (Cambridge: Cambridge University Press, 2002), pp. 1–23 (p. 16).
6. Lupton, *Reading and the Making of Time* (Baltimore: Johns Hopkins University Press, 2018), pp. 122–52.
7. *Political Justice*, p. 121 (kept in all subsequent editions).
8. *Political Justice: Variants*, pp. 151–2.
9. Ibid. p. 151.
10. *Political Justice*, p. v.
11. *Political Justice: Variants*, pp. 144, 143; 'Considerations on Lord Grenville's and Mr Pitt's Bills', p. 133. For Godwin's specific conversational ideal and for more on political dissent in the 1790s, see discussion below.
12. *The Enquirer*, p. 237.
13. See 3 June 1796 in *DWG*. Milton, *Areopagitica*, pp. 492–3.
14. *The Enquirer*, p. 233. Cf. Carla Hesse, 'Books in Time', in *The Future of the Book*, ed. Geoffrey Nunberg (Berkeley and Los Angeles: University of California Press, 1996), p. 27.
15. *Thoughts on Man*, p. 88.
16. Ibid. pp. 176–7.
17. *The Enquirer*, p. 96.
18. Robin Valenza, *Literature, Language, and the Rise of the Intellectual Disciplines in Britain, 1680–1820* (Cambridge: Cambridge University

Press, 2009), p. 13. See also Christopher J. Berry, *The Idea of Commercial Society in the Scottish Enlightenment* (Edinburgh: Edinburgh University Press, 2013); Stephen Copley, 'Commerce, Conversation and Politeness in the Early Eighteenth-Century Periodical', *British Journal for Eighteenth-Century Studies* 18 (1995): 63–77.

19. Fred Parker, *Scepticism and Literature: An Essay on Pope, Hume, Sterne, and Johnson* (Oxford: Oxford University Press, 2003); Cf. Timothy Milnes, 'Trusting Experiments: Sociability and Transcendence in the Familiar Essay', *Romantic Circles: Praxis Series*, 2017, <https://www.rc.umd.edu/praxis/prose/praxis.2016.prose.milnes.html> (last accessed 24 May 2018).
20. Hume, 'Of Essay Writing', *Essays, Moral and Political*, vol. 2 (Edinburgh: A. Kincaid, 1742), pp. 1–8.
21. Samuel Johnson, 'On Studies' [originally untitled], *The Adventurer* 85 (28 August 1753): 85–90; for the original aphorism see Francis Bacon, *Essayes or Counsels, Civill and Morall* (London: John Haviland, 1632), pp. 293–4. Cf. Robert DeMaria, *Samuel Johnson and the Life of Reading* (Baltimore: Johns Hopkins University Press, 1997).
22. See Mee, *Conversable Worlds*, pp. 137–67; the dissenting backdrop to this ideal is outlined in Tessa Whitehouse, *The Textual Culture of English Protestant Dissent, 1720–1800* (Oxford: Oxford University Press, 2015), and D. O. Thomas, *The Honest Mind: the Thought and Work of Richard Price* (Oxford: Clarendon Press, 1977). For differences in conversation culture between provincial and urban dissenters, see Anne Janowitz, 'Amiable and Radical Sociability: Anna Barbauld's "free Familiar Conversation"', in *Romantic Sociability: Social Networks and Literary Culture in Britain, 1770–1840*, ed. Gillian Russell and Clara Tuite (Cambridge: Cambridge University Press, 2002), pp. 62–81. For the theory of conversation more generally in this period, see Peter Burke, *The Art of Conversation* (Cambridge: Polity, 1993) and Katie Halsey and Jane Slinn (eds), *The Concept and Practice of Conversation in the Long Eighteenth Century, 1688–1848* (Newcastle: Cambridge Scholars Publishing, 2008).
23. *Political Justice: Variants*, pp. 161–2.
24. *Political Justice*, pp. 320–1.
25. For positive aspects of public speaking in Godwin's work, see Victoria Myers, 'William Godwin and the "Ars Rhetorica"', *Studies in Romanticism* 41.3 (2002), 415–44.
26. *Political Justice*, p. 122.
27. Ibid. p. 121.
28. Mark Turner, 'Time, Periodicals, and Literary Studies', *Victorian Periodicals Review* 39.4 (2006): 309–16 (p. 312), and 'Periodical Time in the Nineteenth Century', *Media History* 8.2 (2002): 183–96.

29. Benjamin Constant, *De La Liberte Des Brouchures, Des Pamphlets et Des Journaux* (Paris: Chez H Nicolle, a la Librairie Stereotype, 1814), quoted in translation by Carla Hesse in 'Books in Time', p. 27.
30. *Political Justice*, p. 123. Cf. Garrett A. Sullivan, '"Caleb Williams" and Print Culture', pp. 332–3.
31. *Caleb Williams*, pp. 280, 121. 'Letter to the Editor of the *British Critic*', 7 June 1795, *LWG*, vol. 1, p. 117.
32. *Caleb Williams*, p. 328.
33. To Thomas Wedgwood, 7 November 1795, *LWG*, vol. 1, p. 132, and p. 135 n.7.
34. To Thomas Wedgwood, 10 November 1795, *LWG*, vol. 1, p. 134.
35. For an overview of Godwin's ambivalent relationship to letters, see Pamela Clemit, 'Holding Proteus: William Godwin in his Letters', in *Repossessing the Romantic Past*, ed. Heather Glen and Paul Hamilton (Cambridge: Cambridge University Press, 2006), pp. 98–115 (especially pp. 100–1). Cf. Judith Barbour, '"Obliged to Make This Sort of Deposit of Our Minds": William Godwin and the Sociable Contract of Writing', in *Romantic Sociability: Social Networks and Literary Culture in Britain, 1770–1840*, ed. Gillian Russell and Clara Tuite (Cambridge: Cambridge University Press, 2002), pp. 166–85.
36. Godwin to Joseph Planta, 12 June 1805, *LWG*, vol. 2, pp. 354–6 (p. 355).
37. Preface to *Life of Geoffrey Chaucer, the early English poet: including memoirs of his near friend and kinsman, John of Gaunt, Duke of Lancaster: with sketches of the manners, opinions, arts and literature of England in the fourteenth century*, 2 vols (London: Richard Phillips, 1803), vol. 1, p. xvi. The letter to Planta was written during Godwin's research for his *History of the Commonwealth of England; from its commencement, to the restoration of Charles the Second*, 4 vols (London: Henry Colburn, 1824–8).
38. *Fleetwood*, pp. 69, 194.
39. Ibid. p. 194.
40. 'Considerations on Lord Grenville's and Mr Pitt's Bills', p. 141.
41. Ibid. p. 159.
42. For more on this see Paul Keen, *The Crisis of Literature in the 1790s: Print Culture and the Public Sphere* (Cambridge: Cambridge University Press, 1999).
43. 'Considerations on Lord Grenville's and Mr Pitt's Bills', pp. 159, 145–6, 131–2.
44. *Caleb Williams*, pp. 23–5.
45. Ibid. pp. 107, 117, 145, 249.
46. Joseph Priestley, *The Importance and Extent of Free Enquiry in Matters of Religion*, p. 18. The same view lies behind Blake's famous line, 'Truth can never be told so as to be understood, and not be believ'd'. See *The Marriage*

of Heaven and Hell in *William Blake's Writings*, ed. G. E. Bentley, Jr, vol. 1 (Oxford: Clarendon Press, 1978), pp. 74–99 (p. 84).
47. See e.g. Passmore, *The Perfectibility of Man*, 3rd edn (Indianapolis: Liberty Fund, 2000), p. 330.
48. Whitehouse, *Textual Culture*, pp. 22–3, 54.
49. Watts, *The Improvement of the Mind*, pp. 190–1.
50. Quotation from Mee, *Conversable Worlds*, p. 167. Studies of politically radical cultures and their relationship to media include Mee, *Print, Publicity and Radicalism in the 1790s: The Laurel of Liberty* (Cambridge: Cambridge University Press, 2016); Kevin Gilmartin, *Print Politics: The Press and Radical Opposition in Early Nineteenth-Century England* (Cambridge: Cambridge University Press, 1996); Stephen Behrendt, *Romanticism, Radicalism, and the Press* (Detroit: Wayne State University Press, 1997); Andrew McCann, *Cultural Politics in the 1790s: Literature, Radicalism and the Public Sphere* (Basingstoke: Palgrave, 1999), and McCann, 'William Godwin and the Pathological Public Sphere: Theorizing Communicative Action in the 1790s', *Prose Studies* 18.3 (1995): 199–222; John Barrell, *The Spirit of Despotism: Invasions of Privacy in the 1790s* (Oxford: Oxford University Press, 2006).
51. Burke, *Reflections on the French Revolution in France*, ed. Conor Cruise O'Brien (London: Penguin, 1986), p. 94; Godwin, 'Considerations on Lord Grenville's and Mr Pitt's Bills', p. 133.
52. Mee, *Print, Publicity and Radicalism in the 1790s*, pp. 1, 8–9.
53. Ibid. p. 159; *Political Justice*, p. 120; *The Enquirer*, p. 143; *Political Justice: Variants*, pp. 156–7. Godwin's own timeline of his 'Philosophical Principles' lists under 1778 the conviction 'That truth is immutable and independent'. See the transcription in Mark Philp, 'Introduction' to *PPW*, p. 17.
54. *Political Justice*, p. 15; 'Notes on the biographical sketch of William Godwin inserted in the "Monthly Mirror", Jan. & Feb. 1805', MS. Abinger c. 31, fol. 117. The transcription is Clemit's in 'Self-Analysis as Social Critique: The Autobiographical Writings of Godwin and Rousseau', *Romanticism* 11 (2005): 161–80 (p. 174).
55. 'Of Scepticism', p. 309.
56. *Political Justice*, p. 127.
57. Timothy Milnes, *The Truth About Romanticism: Pragmatism and Idealism in Keats, Shelley, Coleridge* (Cambridge: Cambridge University Press, 2010), *passim* (quotation from p. 82).
58. *Political Justice*, pp. 121–2.
59. *Thoughts on Man*, p. 292. Cf. 'Reply to Parr', pp. 207–8.
60. Stewart, *Elements of the Philosophy of the Human Mind*, in *The Collected Works of Dugald Stewart*, ed. Sir William Hamilton (London: Thoemmes Press, 1994), p. 247.

Chapter 5

Books, Bodies and Monuments: Print and Perfectibility

In 1809 William Godwin published his *Essay on Sepulchres*, a proposal for a system of national monuments that would commemorate writers rather than fighters. He justified this arrangement by describing authors as persons who were not truly dead:

> Military and naval achievements are of temporary operation: the victories of Cimon and Scipio are passed away; these great heroes have dwindled into a name; but whole Plato, and Xenophon, and Virgil have descended to us, undefaced, undismembered, and complete. I can dwell upon them for days and for weeks: I am acquainted with their peculiarities; their inmost thoughts are familiar to me; they appear before me with all the attributes of individuality; I can ruminate upon their lessons and sentiments at leisure, till my whole soul is lighted up with the spirit of these authors.[1]

Such dismissal of military claims to historical tenacity was a bold move, especially as it appeared during Britain's long and expensive conflict in Europe (1803–15). Even more striking, however, are the terms in which Godwin makes his counterclaim for literary achievement. The classical authors he mentions should be commemorated, not because they are in danger of being forgotten, but because they remain cultural participants. They deliver 'lessons', exchange 'sentiments' and contribute towards social enlightenment. Unlike the wounded heroes of the military they remain 'whole' and 'undismembered', present to the living in corporeal terms. And indeed, they are not just survivors but regenerators: as *un*defaced and *un*dismembered they actively counteract the dissolution that time entails.

At first sight this does not seem unusual. Recent scholarship underscores the temporal bearings of Romantic-period claims to literary value and canonisation, linking them to the social anxieties attendant on commercialisation: 'concerns with immortality', Jonathan Sachs writes, 'come to have new significance in the face of the seeming ephemerality of so many products of the press'. The backdrop to this trend is a dominant cultural narrative about the decline of literature – in its quality, its social status, and the calibre of its audiences – against which certain forms and uses of literature are upheld as tokens of resistance.[2] The Godwin of 'Essay of Sepulchres' has often been interpreted as a participant in this trend, who draws from prevalent tropes of authorial 'remains' and immortality to make claims about literary tradition and national identity which, if they don't exactly temper his radical progressivist outlook, at least naturalise it by means of a seemingly conservative sensibility.[3]

This chapter modifies that view by exposing a neglected dimension of Godwin's nineteenth-century writings: they persistently recruit the material properties of books in order to advocate belief in necessary intellectual improvement on local, national and global scales. Godwin's public disagreement with Malthus epitomises the pressure that he faced throughout his career to justify his belief in the innate perfectibility of human nature and society. He exploited familiar cultural images that represented books as bodies and monuments and subverted them in order to refute salient narratives of decline, and he did so increasingly as the nineteenth century progressed. Initially through literary biography and subsequently through his *Essay on Sepulchres* (1809) and manuscript essay 'On Death' (1810), Godwin rewrote Sir Thomas Browne's ideas about bodily resurrection in order to argue that the book embodied a mind, which functioned as an ongoing member of intellectual community and had the potential to instigate social change. 'On Death' is in many ways the climax to this argument, for it claims that books do not simply perpetuate human minds but transform them into something that transcends mortal limitations and, ultimately, regenerates human nature. In making this case Godwin was fleshing out a contention of several late eighteenth-century philosophers, notably Dugald Stewart, that print technology constituted an essential change in the human conditon. This is confirmed by his final essay collection *Thoughts on Man* (1831), which claims the printed codex as both the guarantee and the structuring force of a universal process of intellectual transposition.

Recovering this account is important because it shows us that properties attributed to books as material media played crucial and conflicting roles in the arguments about social and cultural futurity that animated Romantic-period Britain. In a time of civil unrest, economic anxiety and historical self-consciousness, Godwin's work encapsulated the significance of media technology for debates about societal decline and progress, and exposed its ties to a radical intellectual tradition. This contentious process of figuration, moreover, illuminates for the present day an oft-neglected dimension of media history, which underlay what Andrew Piper describes as 'the naturalization of the book in the nineteenth century'.[4] As Adrian Johns has shown, book history to date has involved active cultural processes through which it became accepted and assumed that properties of credibility and fixity were intrinsic to print. Godwin's writing highlights one such cultural process: it shows us that the object-status of the book was imagined and reflected upon in Romantic literature in ways that made it essential to understandings of the memory, authenticity and perpetuation of British society.

Bodies and Literary Lives

Godwin was one of the first writers to theorise the social power of biography. He began to do so at the turn of the nineteenth century, just as literary biography was developing into an independent and highly popular genre that was aiding the development of a national literary canon and the concept of literary celebrity.[5] Capitalising on this growing cultural interest in relations between texts and lives, Godwin blurred the boundary between authors, their works and their biographies, using this elision to argue that printed books could become living participants in a universal process of social reform. He described his literary biographies as works that mediated personal presence, in part through their very materiality: a good biography embodied a mind, he argued, which functioned as on ongoing member of intellectual community and thus had the power to instigate social change. As he reflected in a biography of 1815, 'I never felt within me the power to disjoin a great author from his work.'[6]

Godwin articulated this conviction in germinal form in 1798 through his *Memoirs of the Author of A Vindication of the Rights of Woman*, a biography of his late wife Mary Wollstonecraft. The *Memoirs* prioritise the intellectual dimensions of Wollstonecraft's life: Godwin references his interest in the 'features of her mind' and the growth of 'her understanding', and he ends the first edition with the reflection, 'I believe I have put down the leading traits of her intellectual character.' He also repeatedly presents this mind in embodied terms. He describes his biographical task as a compilation of Wollstonecraft's 'materials', recounts her physical demise in detail, and even transcribes her gravestone into the text: 'HERE LIES MARY'.[7] In his preface, Godwin highlights the connection that he envisaged between this materialised mind created through biography and his project to instigate social reform. He anticipates that 'The justice which is thus done to the illustrious dead, converts into the fairest source of animation and encouragement to those who would follow them into the same carreer [*sic*].' He owns himself convinced that,

> the more fully we are presented with the picture and story of such persons as the subject of the following narrative, the more generally we shall feel in ourselves an attachment to their fate, and a sympathy in their excellencies. There are not many individuals with whose character the public welfare and improvement are more intimately connected, than the author of A Vindication of the Rights of Woman.[8]

Drawing from the essay 'Of History and Romance' that he drafted the previous year, Godwin links vivid characterisation to the recruitment of moral sense and the instigation of intellectual enquiry. He assumes that Wollstonecraft's 'picture and story' will incite sympathetic attachment in its readers, a process which will produce, in turn, 'public welfare and improvement'. The biography, in other words – the textual rendering of Wollstonecraft's 'character' – will enable readers to apprehend and benefit from the 'excellencies' of her life, including her efforts towards social reform. There is, moreover, a second aspect to this sort of textual life. By replacing her name with that of her printed works ('the author of A Vindication', as in the title of the *Memoirs*), Godwin presents Wollstonecraft's own authorial achievements as a form of embodiment. His publication of her edited posthumous works alongside the biography reinforces such a conception. By means of the texts written by and about her, he implies, Wollstonecraft herself will be present to readers and continue her impact upon the minds and hearts of members of society.[9]

Somewhat ironically, this association of print with personal knowledge became the focal point of the harsh reviews that the *Memoirs* received. One writer for the *Anti-Jacobin Review* mocked Godwin for 'Thinking her whoredoms were not known enough, | Till fairly printed off in black and white', connecting his textual dissemination of Wollstonecraft's life to a scandalous, rather than inspirational, form of personal knowledge.[10] The poem exposes a gendered aspect to the idea of literary intimacy in this period through its exploitation of the familiar connection between women writers and sexual laxity. Yet it also highlights more generally how contentious the concept of personal knowledge through print had become at the turn of the century. By bringing the relationship between intimacy and publicity under scrutiny, printed biographies or 'lives' unearthed disagreements on a philosophical level about the relationship between attachment and judgement. Once 'printed off in black and white', Wollstonecraft's social deviancy was construed as a force of moral corruption by critics of the *Memoirs*, rather than a stimulus to intellectual enquiry. Her written life was thus found offensive rather than inspiring.

Despite this hostile reaction, Godwin continued to develop the link his *Memoirs* established between authorial embodiment and social reform. It became explicit in 1803 through his *Life of Geoffrey Chaucer*. In the preface to this work, Godwin described the biographer as a necromancer:

> It was my wish [. . .] to carry the workings of fancy and the spirit of philosophy into the investigation of ages past. I was anxious to rescue for a moment the illustrious dead from the jaws of the grave, to make them pass in review before me, to question their spirits and record their answers. I wished to make myself their master of the ceremonies, to introduce my reader to their familiar speech, and to enable him to feel for the instant as if he had lived with Chaucer.[11]

Here the biography is imagined as a site of personal presence. The biographer obtains personal knowledge of his subject, embodies this in textual form, and thus connects the reader's life to Chaucer's life. It is an image of sociability, according to which the reader gains access to the 'familiar speech' of former times. This counteracts one of the key effects of human death, the separation of past generations from present ones: the reader feels 'as if *he had* lived with Chaucer' because he can still form attachments and exchange ideas with him. Echoing the language of his *Memoirs*, Godwin states his desire to 'do justice to' the person of Chaucer, presenting his *Life* as a locus for the spread of knowledge between past and present communities.[12]

Once again, Godwin made the mind central to this picture. Chaucer must be resurrected intellectually, he claimed, if he was to be brought to 'full and complete life':

> The full and complete life of a poet would include an extensive survey of the manners, the opinions, the arts and the literature, of the age in which the poet lived. This is the only way in which we can become truly acquainted with the history of his mind, and the causes which made him what he was.[13]

Godwin argues that to truly know Chaucer, one must investigate 'the history of his mind'. This involves looking beyond the literary works that he produced, and beyond bare historical facts and dates, to his formative environment – to the intellectual and literary tenor of fourteenth-century England. This is an important object for Godwin because, as the preface makes clear elsewhere, Chaucer is a representative figure for the nation's intellectual improvement at large: 'No one man in the history of human intellect ever did more, than was effected by the single mind of Chaucer.'[14] By presenting Chaucer's intellectual life to a new generation of readers, the biography extends its power into the contemporary social world.

This approach to literary biography attracted ridicule, particularly from those sympathetic to the British antiquarian movement. Walter Scott produced a scathing account for the *Edinburgh Review*: 'The authenticated passages of Chaucer's life may be comprised in half a dozen pages; and behold two voluminous quartos!'[15] Scott's assessment hinges upon a disagreement with Godwin over the nature and bounds of Chaucer's life, which for Scott was lost amid digression and speculation. His reference to 'authenticated passages' reveals the importance of documentation to his conception of historiography; this was a priority that had been precipitated among antiquarians in part by the ballad collections of Thomas Percy and Joseph Ritson (and which always contained a measure of ambivalence in its definition or modes of authenticity, as many note).[16] What to Godwin contains the very essence of Chaucer's life – 'the causes which made him what he was' – are to Scott extraneous and spurious matters, and the work is dismissed as a history 'not so much of what Chaucer actually did *do*, as of what he and all his contemporaries *might, could, would,* or *should have done*'. Rather insightfully, Scott links this dynamic to Godwin's novel-writing:

> [Chaucer's] biographer might with equal plausibility have grafted upon his story a supposed attempt to escape, and given us a Newgate calendar chapter from the horrors of Caleb Williams, or the langours of St Leon.

This comment unintentionally reinforces the connection that Godwin himself had made between history and romance in 1797. The things that diminished the *Life of Chaucer* for Scott – cultural commentary, imaginative speculation, intellectual context – were the very things that, for Godwin, brought Chaucer to life.[17]

Godwin's correspondence surrounding the production of his *Life of Chaucer* reveals a more complex picture of the sort of life that he imagined his work to embody or to mediate, however. The *Life*'s preface briefly references a disagreement with his publisher, Richard Phillips: Godwin recalls that in the midst of his composition, when 'I saw my materials growing under my hand', Phillips assured him that the work would not be commercially viable beyond the two quarto volumes they had originally settled upon.[18] Disputes of this nature were common, especially as the price of paper had dramatically increased during the Napoleonic Wars.[19] Godwin suggests that he submitted rather peacefully to the decision to retain these limits, but personal correspondence shows otherwise. He had passionately argued against it, using graphic corporeal imagery to make a case for the *Life*'s social significance and thus special treatment:

> I have thought a thousand times, since our conversation of Tuesday, with great earnestness & anxiety, of this unhappy question that has arisen about the Chaucer. [. . .]
>
>   What horrible confusion! What monstrous disproportion! What an entire dislocation of all the members of a well-arranged work!

A thousand times I have said to myself, I will give up the point. Yet, why should I ruin the best book I ever undertook? Why should I be myself the man to put an extinguisher over my literary character? I am now in the best & maturest part of my existence; I have taken incredible pains in collecting & arranging the materials of this book: must all this be made a sacrifice to *erroneous* calculations? [. . .]

The public is not so blind & stupid as you imagine. They will see the ridiculousness of a book pretending to be a standard-book & then changing its plan in the middle; & will despise the author as he ought to be despised. The main characteristics of the great literary works of man, beyond all flights of genius & original sallies of thought, are the proportion of parts & the symmetry of a whole.

You are most fundamentally mistaken in your *pecuniary calculation*. Two volumes patched up in the manner you recommend will sell perhaps better in the first month: fools will not know the difference: but in a very short time the men of sense & taste will be heard, & the book will be consigned to contempt & oblivion. With what face shall a work claim to be regarded as a standard-work, thus crampt, & cribbed, & mangled in its most essential members; a figure with a well looking head and trunk, but shrivelled & blasted in its lower extremities? [. . .]

I conclude with urging again upon your consideration, that there are books of genius, & there are books that are otherwise. If you think my book is of the vulgar & every day class, you do well in your present proposition. But, if it is in its constituent nature what I suppose we both hope it is, you do not act the part of a bookseller (understanding by a bookseller a man dealing in books, & capable of feeling his true interests, even when the case should not be of the sort that every day brings before him), but of a murderer & a suicide in one.[20]

Godwin was making an argument about the principles of book production: he claimed that formal dimensions should be subordinate to content, rather than the other way around, describing this relation as 'true proportion'. He had made a similar move during the previous year, accusing Phillips of a 'shabby mode of printing' and arguing that a higher aesthetic standard of production 'best brings out an author's meaning' – in short, Godwin felt that business thrift was threatening both the form and content of his literary work.[21] This subsequent letter makes the argument intensely personal, envisaging the work curtailed to two volumes as a tortured, abortive form: 'crampt & cribbed, & mangled in its most essential members; [. . .] a well looking head and trunk, but shrivelled & blasted in its lower extremities'. Evoking

Psalm 139 – 'Thine eyes did see my substance, yet being unperfect; and in thy book all my members were written' – Godwin contrasts the care of divine synthesis to this enforced 'dislocation of [. . .] members', presenting Phillips's requirement as a destructive act. The accusation of murder echoes Milton's anthropomorphism in *Areopagitica*, according to which 'hee who destroyes a good Booke, [. . .] kills the Image of God, as it were in the eye'. Godwin associates Phillips with political censorship, positioning his demands as oppressive, unreasonable and damaging to national intellectual life.[22]

Given the argument about necromancy in Godwin's preface to the *Life*, one might associate the identity of this mangled book-body with Chaucer himself. Godwin refers to the dispute as a question about 'the Chaucer', a shorthand reference to the title which tacitly elides his textual subject with the book's material dimensions. It is Chaucer whose 'face' will be mismatched by a 'monstrous' body; it is Chaucer's life at stake should Phillips choose to become 'a murderer'. However, Godwin also claims that the book's unsuitable proportions will maim '*my* literary character'. Just as the work itself will be considered repulsive for 'changing its plan in the middle', its author will be despised as someone who falls short in the middle of his career: 'I am now in the best & maturest part of *my* existence'. The victim of the murder is also Godwin, 'shrivelled and blasted' in the climax of his authorial efforts. But he goes even further, aligning his vocation with 'the great literary works of man' and casting himself as representative. Just as his preface to the *Life* would make Chaucer a synecdoche for national intellectual pursuit, Godwin's letter conflates his own work with cultural work more generally, presenting Phillips's proposal as an injury against all 'books of genius'.

Godwin's letter, then, associates the material dimensions of his book with various vitalities: that of its textual subject, his own authorial person, and the mind of a collective ideal, Man. He claims that the *Life of Chaucer* is valuable for 'its constituent nature', a suggestive phrase that refers to a physical collection of pages, an embodied subject, an invested author, and the shared essence of all 'books of genius'. Godwin's writings in and about literary biography expose his view that several kinds of life could intersect in a book, contributing to the social good. They also indicate that the material form of the book was integral to this imagined process.

Ironically, even though Godwin submitted to Phillips's two-volume limit, most reviews of the *Life of Chaucer* considered it too long. Godwin hinted at plans for a third, supplementary volume, yet never managed to expand it, and its second edition was issued with only minor revisions.[23] His conception of the book's inherent vitality, however, was developed and enriched over the ensuing years to form an ambitious defence of the role of the printed codex in society's progress towards intellectual perfection.

Monuments and Literary Death

As the first decade of the nineteenth century drew to a close, Godwin wrote two essays that addressed the subject of death. This was a time during which he also showed renewed interest in the power of the printed word, persistently probing in his writings 'the degree to which books are dead or alive', in Julie Carlson's words. This dual interest in lifespans and books, Carlson suggests, was precipitated by Godwin's disintegrating social network and his newly hostile encounters with the print market, which entailed stark financial and emotional challenges.[24] We might add to this the death of several reformist acquaintances: Thomas Holcroft, Thomas Paine and the publisher Joseph Johnson all died in 1809, and Godwin wrote Johnson's obituary notice for the *Morning Chronicle*. Evidence suggests that Godwin also believed his own death was imminent.[25] Yet this interest in the relationship between books and death was not simply a reaction to immediate circumstances; it was the outworking of a long-standing belief in the ability of books to generate social reform. Throughout his educational, historiographical and biographical writings to date, Godwin had been developing the idea that books could mediate personal encounters and thus be considered in themselves active agents of intellectual improvement.

Essay on Sepulchres, as its subtitle explains, is 'a proposal for erecting some memorial of the illustrious dead in all ages on the spot where their remains have been interred'. In order to understand the nature and purpose of this scheme, we must understand the view of death that Godwin sets out in the *Essay*'s opening pages. Death is depicted here first and foremost as a problem for the mind. It is at its most devastating, Godwin argues, in the loss that it entails for the intellectual progress of human societies. 'It is impossible to calculate how much of good perishes, when a great and excellent man dies', he exclaims. 'It is owing to this [...] that the world for ever is, and in some degree for ever must be, in its infancy.' In other words, when a 'great' person perishes, all their advances in moral and political thought are lost, their contribution to social good ceases, and this stalls the improvement of the world at large. Referring back to this concept of infancy later in the essay, Godwin writes that 'The world is much like a school; [...] the studies that are entered on, and the instruction that is given, are perpetually beginning.'[26] It is as though society is subject to a constant haemorrhage of mind, by which collective striving towards truth and justice is thwarted.

In addressing this topic, Godwin was responding to the criticism that his public statement of belief in human perfectibility had received over the past years. He had been accused of whitewashing reality in *Political Justice*, which had finished by painting a picture of futurity in which evil and mortality would be surpassed as the human mind improved. Perhaps the most infamous of these attacks was from Thomas Robert Malthus, whose *Essay on the Principle of Population* (1798) argued that misery, vice and death were necessary to the survival of the species because they kept population size and food supply in equilibrium. Malthus contended that the burden of proof lay with those who advocated mass perfectibility. Comparing Godwin to a writer who claims he will necessarily become an ostrich over time, he insisted that evidence of the allegedly impending transformation should be supplied before belief was warranted: 'And till the probability of so wonderful a conversion can be shewn, it is surely lost time and lost eloquence to expatiate on the happiness of man in such a state.'[27] Godwin had responded in his 'Reply to the attacks of Dr. Parr' (1801), but he continued to feel the pressure of the challenge, eventually publishing a book-length reply to Malthus entitled *Of Population* (1820). *Essay on Sepulchres* appeared between these two ripostes and formed part of their justification of his confidence in intellectual progress. He used it to address the problem of death directly, and in order to do so he conceded that it was indeed *the* major setback for human perfectibility. It rendered human societies like infant schools, which constantly lost their most advanced members and constantly gained new, ignorant ones. But there was, he claimed, a solution.

Godwin hints at this solution from the beginning of *Essay on Sepulchres* when he observes that minds are not wholly lost through death. He identifies a material aspect to intellect and claims that a remnant of this has posthumous existence. Although he confesses himself 'more inclined to the opinion of the immaterialists; than of the materialists' when it comes to defining the nature of thought itself, he considers it important that 'my acquaintance with the thoughts and the virtues of my friend, has been made through my eyes and my ears'. Knowledge is embodied, and to love someone's intellect is to love their whole person. Such love spills over into the objects and places associated with them, and these gain, he argues, 'an empire over my mind'. He was drawing from a growing interest in the ability of memory to forge connections between places, objects and persons, prominent in the literary work of Robert Southey and William Wordsworth, among others – the latter's own 'Essay on Epitaphs' was published in 1810.[28] Godwin argues that it is not only unavoidable, but reasonable to become attached to the physical spot of a friend's interment, because this 'is our only reality'. It is the material locus through which we recall 'the thoughts and the virtues' of the deceased person; through tangible places of mourning, the living can reclaim something of the dead.[29]

This insistence on the material embeddedness of knowledge leads Godwin to present an initial critique of the commemorative practices of current society. He argues that British citizens do not make the most of the real intellectual solidity of dead persons available to them, and thus they miss an opportunity to counteract some of the social loss inflicted by death. 'We remarked some way back, that "the world was for ever in its infancy"', Godwin recalls; 'It is indeed so: we cut ourselves off from the inheritance of our ancestors.' He implies that his readers deliberately neglect the material reality of dead minds. He argues later that the British inhabit an 'old country', its soil literally composed of the remains of great thinkers and thus full of sites of potential knowledge recovery, but they spurn its advantages: 'They do not husband their inheritance.'[30] What Godwin intends by husbandry at this stage remains mysterious, but he clearly suggests that British society does nothing to prevent a process of *dis*membering: the material parts of dead minds are being forgotten, left to dissolve into oblivion.

These observations about the nature of death pave the way to Godwin's infamous solution: a national effort to memorialise the greatest minds. He exhorts his readers to 'seize on what we can. Let us mark the spot [. . .] let us visit their tombs; let us indulge all the reality we can now have, of a sort of conference with these men.'[31] Dead people can continue as social beings, for Godwin – they can still participate in intellectual life – yet this only happens when the living 'seize' upon something of their material remains. The appeal is later rendered as a demand:

> I wish to live in intercourse with the Illustrious Dead of All Ages. I demand the friendship of Zoroaster. [. . .] I would say, with Ezekiel, the Hebrew, in his Vision, 'Let these dry bones live!' Let them not live merely in cold generalities and idle homilies of morality; but let them live, as my friends, my philosophers, my instructors, and my guides! I would say with the moralist of old, 'Let me act, as I would wish to have acted, if Socrates or Cato were the spectators of what I did!' And I am not satisfied only to call them up by a strong effort of the imagination, but I would have them, and men like them, 'around my path, and around my bed,' and not allow myself to hold a more frequent intercourse with the living than with the good departed.[32]

The idea of conversing with the dead through tokens of remembrance was commonplace, but Godwin redirects it into unusually literal territory. The materiality of commemorative monuments is his great preoccupation in the *Essay*; he does not allow his readers to settle for an 'effort of the imagination' alone but locates the reality of dead thinkers in their remaining 'solidity', the *hic jacet* of a sepulchre.[33] Considering how busts or portraits can bring historical figures to life in the mind of their contemplators, he elevates tombs to a higher level, arguing that 'the dust that is covered by his tomb, is simply and literally *the great man himself*'.[34] It is a physical reality that works in partnership with a psychological reality – the imaginative nature of man, who is 'a creature "looking before and after"' – and creates a real meeting of past and present minds. Godwin asks of the dead, 'Had their thoughts less of sinew and substance [. . .] than ours?', encapsulating the strange alliance of material and immaterial that he propounds. Intellectual exchange is incarnated, given 'sinew and substance', through the monument itself. Godwin's sepulchres are the loci of material-spiritual encounters, sites that foster appropriate sentiment towards 'Illustrious' thinkers and thus embody real relationships.[35] In this manner they counteract the loss to collective intellectual improvement that death entails.

Before investigating these curious suggestions in depth, it is important to note Godwin's emphasis upon location: *Essay on Sepulchres* is an argument about a nation. He describes the proposal as 'a scheme for Great Britain', although he hopes that leaders of other countries will follow the British example. Godwin proposes that a map be produced of the British Isles in its tomb-studded aspect, alongside a 'Catalogue' or directory of those interred in its soil – a literary-cartographical project that resonated in Leigh Hunt's later essay 'The World of Books' (1833).[36] Forging a link between national thinkers and the earth upon which they trod, Godwin positions his countrymen as inheritors of a starkly material legacy. They are unified not simply around a land mass, but a land 'of the most admirable fertility'; a land in which the material remains of the 'Illustrious Dead' are 'fruitful of sentiments and virtues' that 'elevate [man] to a God'.[37] Godwin presents the British nation as the collective heir of an inheritance of intellectual production, and proclaims a message of unity around this shared past. Citizens of the present day 'do not husband their inheritance', he argues, because they do not understand how integral it is to their national make-up. And of course, this British heritage includes writers from ancient Greece and Rome – Godwin lists Shakespeare and Milton in the same line as Plato and Virgil – which advocates the importance of living British thinkers by giving them an ancient lineage, and subtly aligns them with an idealised republican past.[38]

All this seems rather a departure from the Godwin of *Political Justice*, who had argued fiercely against the prejudicial sentiment engendered by national governments. The *Monthly Review* certainly felt so, commending *Essay on Sepulchres* for being 'more in the style of *antient piety* than of *modern philosophy*'.[39] Godwin's exhortation that British readers should 'husband their inheritance' seems especially Burkean, perhaps part of the wider 'reconceptualization of the literary past as a form of collective cultural patrimony' that Philip Connell identifies as a salient feature of society in this period.[40] Yet Godwin's concern with monuments to the intellect is also subversive of his immediate political context. He wrote during a time of unprecedented investment in military monuments, which had been precipitated by the Napoleonic wars and particularly by the death of Nelson in 1805. His *Essay* challenges the idea that British military victories were fundamental to the nation's identity – and more broadly, challenges those that defined the essence of British nationhood in terms of a tradition of physical prowess or Protestant loyalty in distinction from Catholic Europe.[41] 'Military and naval achievements are of temporary operation', he argues, 'but whole Plato, and Xenophon, and Virgil have descended to us, undefaced, undismembered, and complete.' He evokes the literal dismembering of Nelson, who had lost his arm at the Battle of Santa Cruz de Teneriffe, implying that books have greater resilience and worth than the battle heroes of popular commemoration. Hazlitt would later mirror this idea in his essay 'On Thought and Action' (1821) – 'poets are a longer-lived race than heroes [. . .] They survive more entire in their thoughts and acts' – yet in his schema the literary life complemented the life of military or political action, rather than superceding it.[42] Godwin uses his picture of literary survival to urge the cultivation of a radically alternative national identity, one constituted solely by a legacy of intellectual achievement.

Godwin's intellectual monuments are in fact presented as a usurpation of national cultural memory as it stands. He proposes that his directory of monuments should replace the 'Catalogue of Gentlemen's Seats' that were commonly included in travellers' guides.[43] Visionary thinkers and writers should become the national landmarks, he implies, rather than the landed estates of noble families. He constructs a vision of the British nation that is marked (literally) by intellectual merit, embodied by symbols of the virtues of the mind, rather than of aristocratic authority or political power. Throughout the essay Godwin attacks cultural links between monuments and wealth, explicitly rejecting the ornamental style of burial associated with those in sociopolitical power. The erection and maintenance of tombs at Westminster Abbey, he contends, have no correlation to genuine merit, only to fortune. The sepulchre of his proposal, by contrast, is 'A very slight and cheap memorial, a white cross of wood'; he will 'leave the rest to the mind of the spectator'.[44] Perhaps Godwin's appeal to private subscription for the financing of his project was also a response to the contention over the funding of Westminster Abbey's literary 'pantheon', a suggestion that those with the means to patronise commemorative schemes should disown private interests and devote themselves instead to this public ideal.[45]

Contemporary reviews show that no one was really sure what Godwin's concrete objective was in his *Essay on Sepulchres*. Some directly assessed the shortcomings of his monument scheme – why wood, if the monuments were supposed to endure? – others understood it 'rather as a play of genius than as a serious proposal'.[46] Yet whatever his intentions were concerning the memorials, it is clear that Godwin invited his readers to use them as a way of thinking about books. While at one point in the essay books work in tandem with monuments – reading an author's work in a particular location helps to bring the text to life – at many other points books are clearly positioned as monumental materials themselves. Great thinkers 'are still with us in their stories, in their words, in their writings'; a deceased friend can survive only 'in his memory, and his works'.[47] As seen in the quotation that opened this chapter, Godwin sometimes collapses this concept of book-monument with that of book-body: 'whole Plato' have survived, like preserved bodies.[48] Godwin's use of negatives – 'undefaced, undismembered' – evokes an image of time as a brutaliser, destroying faces and limbs, and yet simultaneously asserts that this process is defied by the book form. His reference to battle injury implies that these particular books have emerged victorious from a process of intellectual warfare. He echoes the language of his letter to Phillips, which had lamented the 'entire dislocation of all the members' of his work, and connects the idea to that of survival through history. A good book is here a re-membering of its author.

In fact, from the start Godwin applies this principle to *Essay on Sepulchres* itself as a book-object. In his preface, anticipating the question 'If your proposal is impracticable, why then is it published?', he uses the same language that appears later to describe the sentiment produced by monument contemplation. The book is not to be 'considered as complete' in itself, but will work in partnership with the 'intellectual eye', resulting in an 'elevation of mind'. There is something in the very act of reading *Essay on Sepulchres*, Godwin suggests, which makes the project it describes 'a reality':

> For just so much time as any one shall spend in reading and meditating on the suggestions of these pages, provided it be done in a serious frame, the project is a reality, and is as if it were executed.[49]

This conditional clause – 'provided it be done in a serious frame' – echoes that of his later instructions for visiting book-monuments. Locating the presence of the Illustrious Dead 'in their stories, in their words, in their writings', Godwin describes these materials as 'their place, [. . .] where, *if* we dwell in a composed and a quiet spirit, we shall not fail to be conscious of their presence'.⁵⁰ Books and monuments are conflated in this self-referential turn. Both are presented as the material loci of immaterial presence, and thus as potential sites of relationship, attachment and personal knowledge.

This assimilation of monuments and books is reinforced by Godwin's intriguing comment about literary characters. 'Yet to an imaginary person I do not refuse the semblance of a tomb', he states, observing that 'I should be delighted to visit the spot where Cervantes imagined Don Quixote to be buried, or the fabulous tomb of Clarissa Harlowe.'⁵¹ At first glance this seems to undermine his previous insistence upon the importance of physical remains ('the dust that is covered by his tomb, is simply and literally *the great man himself*'). Yet if we imagine books as such physical remains, as Godwin encourages us to do, it is easier to understand how this material potency might function as a monument to a character as much as to an author. Godwin's own fictional characters use the language of 'monument' to frame their projected legacy; St Leon and Mandeville both describe themselves in such terms.⁵² In the manuscript ending of *Caleb Williams*, the protagonist declares: 'I am a stone – a GRAVE-STONE! – an obelisk to tell you, HERE LIES WHAT WAS ONCE A MAN!'⁵³ This conflation of subject and sepulchre is important, for it reflects Godwin's interest in the ways in which materialisation made voices durable. He changed the ending of *Caleb Williams* because it appeared too bleak to his reformist contemporaries, but Caleb's turning to stone in the original version articulates this monumentalising vision in germinal form. Just as he printed Wollstonecraft's grave into her biography, Godwin's monumental presentation of his fictional characters was a gesture of faith in reform. He was embodying the subject, marking the site of its presence, that the reader might be moved towards 'a sort of conference with these men'. This concern with materialised voices was profoundly influential – resonating, for example, in the eerily self-reflexive narration of Mary Shelley's *The Last Man* (1826).

Key to understanding Godwin's concept of the book in his *Essay on Sepulchres* is an explicitly secular version of immortality. The essay was partly a riposte to the conclusions of Sir Thomas Browne's *Hydriotaphia, Urne-Buriall, or, a Discourse of the Sepulchrall Urnes*

Lately Found in Norfolk (1658), which he read in 1804 and consulted again in 1808 about six months before he started writing the essay.[54] Browne describes the work of the archaeologist in terms not dissimilar from those Godwin uses to describe his sepulchre project: 'to preserve the living, and make the dead to live, to keep men out of their urns, [. . .] is not impertinent unto our profession'.[55] Browne argues, however, that monuments are ultimately a testament to human futility, which should prompt the living to invest in a Christian conception of afterlife:

> Pyramids, arches, obelisks, were but the irregularities of vain-glory, and wild enormities of ancient magnanimity. But the most magnanimous resolution rests in the Christian religion, which trampleth upon pride and sits on the neck of ambition, humbly pursuing that infallible perpetuity, unto which all others must diminish their diameters, and be poorly seen in angles of contingency. [. . .]
>
> To subsist in lasting monuments, to live in their productions, to exist in their names and predicament of chimeras, was large satisfaction unto old expectations, and made one part of their Elysiums. But all this is nothing in the metaphysicks of true belief. To live indeed, is to be again ourselves, which being not only an hope, but an evidence in noble believers, 'tis all one to lie in St Innocent's church-yard as in the sands of Egypt. Ready to be anything, in the ecstasy of being ever, and as content with six foot as the *moles* of Adrianus.[56]

For Browne, the ancients' hope that they might 'live in their productions' was a vain superstition that had been surpassed by 'the metaphysicks of true belief'. Browne's particular version of this 'metaphysicks', more explicit in his earlier *Religio Medici* (1643), was partly a contribution to debate about the nature of bodily resurrection, a topic that profoundly shaped philosophical and theological debates in seventeenth-century Europe. Browne argued that the body includes a physical element that survives apparent dissolution after death – Jon W. Thompson describes this as an 'imperceptible material seed' – and used this to argue that God, on the Last Day, will raise each person's body numerically the same as it was during life. Browne was defending the orthodox position, but departed from traditional scholastic views of substance in order to do so.[57]

In his *Essay* Godwin exploited the materiality of this view of resurrection in order to subvert it. Whereas Browne reflects on commemorative monuments in order to contend that they are unnecessary for achieving an enduring legacy – because the body will be resurrected through its 'material seed' – Godwin argues that the only subjects who survive are those commemorated in books, suggesting that books *are* in some sense the material seed: 'They are not dead. They are still with us in their stories, in their words, in their writings.' In Godwin's secular vision of the human race – that of perfectible beings, yet with no Christian resurrection awaiting them – hope for longevity lies precisely in what Browne dismisses as futile. In direct refutation of Browne, he asserts that the dead indeed 'subsist in lasting monuments' and 'live in their productions'.

This mattered for Godwin because the perspective taken by *Urne-Buriall* encapsulated what he considered to be one of the most pernicious aspects of Christian religion, its claim that complete improvement to moral and intellectual life would be achieved only after death. He reiterated this criticism in his manuscript essay 'Of Religion' (1818) and later in his final and unfinished work, *The Genius of Christianity Unveiled* (1836). For centuries, he argued, Christian emphasis upon the celestial realm had suppressed the true potential of the human mind to improve in the terrestrial, in part by causing believers to doubt the mind's capacities in the here-and-now. 'Christianity is the nightmare that has pressed down all [the mind's] exertions, and paralysed its articulations', he claimed.[58] *Essay on Sepulchres* laid the foundations for this argument by presenting perfectibility as an emphatically earthly reality, and claiming that books testify to the ongoing intellectual vitality that human persons can achieve. In this respect it is perhaps more radical than its critics have allowed it to be; it certainly seems ironic that it was praised it for its '*antient piety*'.

Godwin thus used his *Essay on Sepulchres* to claim that books represented and facilitated a process of universal intellectual progress: they preserved the best minds of the past (the 'Illustrious Dead') in order to nourish the minds of the living. Its argument owes a debt to Milton's *Areopagitica* (1644), seen most clearly in Godwin's depiction of books as objects containing a special sort of life, the best of which survive a process of intellectual warfare. Milton's famous argument against the licensing and censorship of the printing press involved the claim that 'a good Booke is the pretious [*sic*] life-blood of a master spirit, imbalm'd and treasur'd up on purpose to a life beyond life'. The value of these book-lives was associated, not simply with the personal merits of their authors, but with the universal power of truth and reason: great books contain 'the breath of reason it selfe, [. . .] an immortality rather than a life'.[59] This conception of certain books being inherently authoritative and vital undergirds Godwin's *Essay*, surfacing most noticeably in his claim that 'great' books always survive the challenges of time and changing fashion by a process of natural selection:

> It is with the memories of men, as it is with books. Those will always be the most numerous, which are of the freshest date. But this is all accident. The books and the memories of men in the eighteenth century, at present overrun our libraries, and clog up our faculties. But the time is hastening on, when this shall not longer be the case, when they shall be reduced to their true standard, and brought down to their genuine numbers. The tomb, the view of which awakens no sentiment, and that has no history annexed to it, must perish, and ought to perish. The description of the fate of mortal writings, so admirably given by Swift in his Dedication to Posterity, is not less applicable to the present subject.[60]

True to his dissenting background, Godwin assumes that truth has self-evident value and he uses this to argue that only 'Illustrious' minds survive through print in the long term. He evokes Milton's association of truth and life in order to envision a process by which, in spite of – or even because of – the contemporary proliferation of printed works, only the most able minds would survive and thrive in book-form across generations. The mere materiality of printed pages is not enough in itself; the tomb 'which awakens no sentiment' will perish.

This aspect of Godwin's *Essay on Sepulchres* at once echoes and subverts many of the jeremiads of modern print culture that featured in the writing of his time.[61] It was almost cliché to use the relentless generativity of the literary marketplace to argue that quality – of both books and readers – was being eclipsed by quantity; 'as their numbers increased, they sank still lower', Coleridge wrote of the book's social demise in *Biographia Literaria* (1817).[62] One gloomy satire for the *Monthly Expositor* summoned the contemporary print market as evidence to refute Godwin's particular belief in perfectibility, conjuring up a *Dunciad*-inspired image of 'scribblers who cannot write a verse' in order to show that 'the world degenerates from age to age'.⁶³ Godwin gestures to these ideas with his description of eighteenth-century books that 'overrun our libraries, and clog up our faculties', yet he resists the inference of degeneration that others were inclined to draw. He references the tradition of Scriblerian satire that resonated in many narratives of decline, naming in particular Swift's dedication to 'His Royal Highness Prince Posterity' in *A Tale of a Tub* (1704), which mocked the vast numbers of writers who claimed literary immortality in their prefaces and follows their works to their final uses in ovens, brothels and toilets: 'I inquired after them among readers and booksellers, but I inquired in vain; the memorial of them was lost among men, their place was no more to be found.'⁶⁴ Just as Swift identifies a body of intellectually vacuous works that forfeit memorialisation and become waste matter, Godwin's *Essay on Sepulchres* identifies a class of 'mortal writings' that lack the immaterial power required for longevity. Yet for Godwin this funds belief in natural literary selection: he uses Milton's alliance of truth and life to argue that book-monuments survive in their 'genuine numbers', that the earth will ultimately absorb the flood of unworthy modern print. In this way, he argues, books testify to the possibility and reality of intellectual progress – they are the foretaste of evidence for perfectibility that Malthus claimed was absent. They show the power of truth through 'Illustrious' minds, who have made and continue to make headway in the human struggle towards intellectual perfection.

The following year Godwin drafted an essay 'On Death' (1810) that refined this concept of the book-object's special kind of life. *Essay on Sepulchres* had considered books as modes of presence, by which dead minds were preserved and made manifest. 'On Death' developed this connection between books and social authority but from a contrary perspective – by exploring books as modes of absence. Unpublished to date, 'On Death' describes how a book can endow its author with a divine-like existence through its function as a distance medium. In other words, Godwin claims that books do something more than simply preserving or distilling great minds; they transform them, enabling them to transcend the limitations of human nature.⁶⁵

'On Death' evaluates the book-object in terms of disembodiment. Godwin begins by observing that bodily absence lent authority to ancient Eastern monarchs and argues that their practice was based upon an acute perception of the human heart: 'That which we clearly understand, & can define in all its bearings, we do not contemplate with reverence.' He then applies this principle to books, portraying 'the author & the friend' in sharp contrast to each other:

> The man that I admire most at a distance, if I fall into unrestrained & often intercourse with him, will lose much of my reverence. [. . .] I see he is a man, I perceive that in many ways he is ever such a one as myself, I find in him human infirmities, & know that he cannot always be great; my eye becomes fatigued with continually looking up; & having repeatedly contemplated him in his elevations, I come at last to survey him in his littlenesses. There is another thing beside this: if he is an author, & I take him in his works, I can never read him through – no, I can never read him through. Let us suppose that I am thoroughly master of his writings; yet he has written, it may be, only upon one, or upon two subjects; I cannot tell how he would have expressed himself, or how he thought, upon others. An author, when he purposes to write, retires himself into his treasury, and unlocks all his hoards. But he does not use them all: he selects only such as are to his present purpose. When he has composed a book, he closes the door of his sanctuary, & comes forth. It is perhaps a splendid assemblage of beauties that he exposes before me. But I cannot tell what there is still accumulated in the magazine he has quitted. It is for his unknown wealth, as I may say principally, that I worship him. I do not love to gauge the dimensions of his mind. I love to guess & wonder, & guess & wonder still. But, if I am his familiar acquaintance, I then can read him through. It is no longer in his power [. . .] to play the miser or the politician with me. He does not now bring forth a certain arrangement of magnificent materials, & close the door of the magazine upon all the rest. We talk on all subjects; I propose to him upon one occasion or another all questions, & he supplies to me with the frankness of a manly mind; I can almost tell what he thinks, & how he would express himself, on every subject. The differences between the author & the friend is nearly as great as between a scriptory evidencer or affidavit, where a man says just the things his judgment suggests & arranges them to his mind, & an evidencer, placed up in the witness box, who is questioned, & sifted, & exposed as a laughing-stock to all the bystanders.

Godwin argues here that the book has social authority – it provokes continuous intellectual pursuit and commands respect – because it represents something fundamentally absent, 'unknown wealth'. It is not only that the necessarily selective content trades upon such virtual capital; the book-object also holds its author forever out of reach, preventing any personal familiarity with readers. Face-to-face meetings promote frankness and friendship, but they confront the participants with 'human infirmities' and thus forfeit long-term reverence. In conversation the dimensions of the mind can be gauged. Authors are immune to such measurement, however, because their material works distance them from their audiences. Books represent what cannot be gauged, and thus possess that unfathomable element that Burke ascribed to the sublime. By the mystery of removal they endow the author with transcendent authority – 'I cannot read him through' – and thus keep the eyes 'continually looking up', elevated above the mortal realm. They exalt their authors into objects of 'worship', something beyond the human. Books thus function here as idols rather than monuments, for they represent and iconise sacred beings.

Godwin goes on to develop this idea of deification, arguing that books endow their authors with god-like attributes:

> [W]e studiously plant the inevitable season of death with exaggerated terrors, & render it formidable to our deluded imaginations. It is to destroy this view of the subject, that these pages are written: & I assert, in opposition to this statement, that <u>death is to the genuine votary of fame the hour of his triumph.</u> [. . .]
>
> Death is to the great man a real apotheosis. There is a deeper truth than the vulgar customarily imagine, in the Greek and Roman idea, that death turns a man into a God. It undoubtedly heaps upon him some of the characteristic privileges of a God. It renders him invisible, a being whose influence may powerfully be felt, but whose power no eye can see. It renders him incomprehensible, a being that discloses of himself as much as he thinks proper to disclose, but of whom no one knows more than he chooses to reveal, & whose secrets cannot be found out. It renders him impassible: we may conceive towards him any idle resentment; but all our wrath and all our artillery will be directed against him in vain. It clothes him with a character supernatural & divine: the man who speaks to us, & the man who from his closet addresses to us a letter, acts according to the known laws of the material universe: but the man who for a thousand years has ceased to occupy a place in any corner of the globe, & yet who exercises over us his omnipotence undiminished, is surely after a certain fashion a God. Let therefore him who aspires to be truly great, no longer look upon death with repugnance; let him think it his choicest & most unvalued privilege; let him regard it as that sacred & much desired moment, when he shall divest him of every thing extraneous, degrading & vulgar, when he shall become simply & entirely himself, & enter now & for ever into his genuine inheritance.

Godwin draws from the so-called incommunicable attributes traditionally ascribed to the Christian God and applies them to 'the author', a figure who becomes increasingly idealised as the essay progresses: omnipresent, inscrutable, impassible and consequently able to exercise a unique power over the minds of readers. The crucial point here is that it is *through books* that this author escapes 'the known laws of the material universe'. His capacity to contribute to the intellectual improvement of society is no longer confined to a mortal person, with all the spatial limits, emotional vulnerability and sheer ordinariness that it entails. Most significant perhaps is his escape from intellectual transparency and finitude. Through his upbringing and time at seminary, Godwin was familiar with the idea that God was sovereign over the creature-Creator knowledge encounter and thus known only insofar as he gives himself to be known; here the author likewise becomes 'a being that discloses of himself as much as he thinks proper to disclose'. For Godwin, the truly great obtain this divine prerogative of 'incomprehensibility' through the book-object, which endows them with authority over the knowing process. In other words, books transform dead human minds into quasi-divine minds that can direct and govern the intellectual pursuits of the living.

'On Death' thus seems to overturn many of Godwin's conclusions in *Essay on Sepulchres*. Rather than fleshing out authors, rendering them familiar, corporeal and accessible, books disembody and de-familiarise them. The value of particular locations in *Essay on Sepulchres* is replaced by an ideal of omnipresence; great authors are those who have 'ceased to occupy a place in any corner of the globe'. Whereas in *Essay on Sepulchres* books embody life, here books are death-objects, exploiting all the social advantages of personal absence and remove. In 1809 death was 'The greatest of earthly calamities', yet in 1810 death is 'that sacred & much desired moment'. Rather than depriving the earth of illustrious thinkers, death is 'the hour of [their] triumph', a 'privilege', for it invests them with a cultural power that is unfettered by material finitude. By embodying death, in a curious paradox, books overcome the terrors traditionally annexed to its power.

In an important respect, however, Godwin's essays are united. Both are anxious to show that books transpose authorial life into a higher plane of existence, and that they do this by virtue of their material form.

In both, books are a life-in-death, tokens of victory over the forces of loss and silence that human history entails. Both contend that the book is continually powerful: whether considered as a site of presence or absence, it renders death 'a real apotheosis' for the great thinker, rendering him 'simply & entirely himself'. *Essay on Sepulchres* is perhaps more in keeping with Godwin's previous work through its association of books with attachment, friendship and personal presence. It reads in some ways as the climax of his biographies of Wollstonecraft and Chaucer, for it is devoted to the fusion of books and lives. Yet 'On Death' brings to the foreground an alternative strand of thinking that had been present throughout all these works; the author's power as an ideal or an icon. Godwin's entire project in *Essay on Sepulchres*, indeed, was designed to refute what he describes as a modern tendency to consider the life of dead ancestors 'too poorly and literally'. It depends upon a 'spirit of propagation', a shared understanding of literature as an inheritance with transcendent value.[66]

Taken together, these essays are best understood as a belated expansion of the astonishing claims made about print technology by several prominent philosophers in the 1790s. In the first edition of *Political Justice* Godwin had already endorsed the Marquis de Condorcet's view that print technology and its liberation from political restriction were essential stages in the necessary development of all human societies:

> As to the progress of truth, it is not so precarious as its fearful friends may imagine. Mr. Condorcet has justly insinuated in the course of his argument, that 'in the invention of printing is contained the embryo, which in its maturity and vigour is destined to annihilate the slavery of the human race.' Books, if proper precautions be employed, cannot be destroyed. Knowledge cannot be extirpated.[67]

In Scotland, Dugald Stewart made similar arguments in his *Elements of the Philosophy of the Human Mind* (1792). Godwin's diary suggests he accessed this work through a review by Holcroft on 9 February 1793; he later met Stewart and conversed with him (certainly in 1816 and possibly earlier than this).[68] For Stewart, the invention of the printing press was an event which, 'independently of every other, is sufficient to change the whole course of human affairs', because it has 'render[ed] the condition of the human race *essentially different* from what it ever was'.⁶⁹ In other words, print technology had fundamentally altered the human condition in a way that guaranteed the perfectibility and improvement of societies across the globe. Like Condorcet, Stewart claimed that his society was only now entering the true age of print freedom, and the inherent potential ('embryo') that was there in the technology from its inception was finally being realised in the wake of an international sociopolitical revolution.

Malthus had referenced these claims about print technology at the very start of his *Essay on the Principle of Population*, noting that 'the extention of the art of printing' had coincided with a variety of other factors 'to lead many able men into the opinion, that we were touching on a period big with the most important changes, changes that would in some measure be decisive of the future fate of mankind'.⁷⁰ But he evokes the argument only to dismiss it in the light of his observations about population trajectory: of what account was the printing press when a necessarily expanding population faced a necessarily limited food supply? In his *Essay on Sepulchres* and essay 'On Death' Godwin reversed Malthus's logic, offering print technology as the key to an alternative futurity, a trajectory of re-generation that marks a qualitative difference in life as we know it. The book, specifically, becomes Stewart's essential difference in the course of human life and history: it renders death itself 'a real apotheosis' by structuring and guaranteeing a new form of life that is 'essentially different' from anything experienced before.

'On Death' was never published, but Godwin incorporated its argument into his later collection *Thoughts on Man* (1831). He wove its claims about divinity into the opening essay 'Of Body and Mind', which contends that 'the man of great literary and original endowments' achieves a god-like status, transcending the confines of his mortal body.⁷¹ In a discussion 'Of Imitation and Invention' Godwin connects this individual divinisation with the progress of the human mind at large. As he addresses the subject of death, he argues that an author's ability to transcend the grave is integral to the intellectual improvement of humankind:

> If, as the beast dies, so died man, then indeed we should be without hope. But it is his distinguishing faculty, that he can leave something behind, to testify that he has lived. And this is not only true of the pyramids of

> Egypt, and certain other works of human industry, that time seems to have no force to destroy. It is often true of a single sentence, a single word, which the multitudinous sea is incapable of washing away. [. . .] It is the characteristic of the mind and the heart of man, that they are progressive. One word, happily interposed, reaching to the inmost soul, may 'take away the heart of stone, and introduce a heart of flesh.' And, if an individual may be thus changed, then his children, and his connections, to the latest page of unborn history.[72]

The works of great writers, down to their individual sentences and words, are here summoned as evidence for the 'progressive' nature of the human mind over time. Their influence extends beyond individual readers to their families, friends and generations yet to come, rendering the entire manner of death ascibed to the human species qualitatively different from that of 'the beast'. This is so much the case that history itself is encompassed by the metaphor of the codex at the end of the passage ('latest page'). Godwin's closing plea in this essay is against 'Presumptuous innovators' who have adapted the writings of Chaucer and Spenser into modernised English: 'you may as well attempt to preserve the man when you have deprived him of all his members; as think to preserve the poet when you have taken away the words that he spoke'.[73] Echoing the corporeal language of his letter to Phillips almost twenty years earlier, Godwin figures the words of a great writer as his limbs. Only the reproduction of these same words can continue his presence among the living and render him a tangible, ongoing benefit to the minds and hearts of readers.

The essay in *Thoughts on Man* in which Godwin's previous claims about the properties of the book-object are most explicit, however, is 'On the Durability of Human Achievements and Productions'. The most astonishing and unique feature of human life, he argues, is 'the faculty we possess of giving a permanent record to our thoughts'. As he considers death's pervasive power, he claims that books are the only true survivors of history:

> Books have the advantage of all other productions of the human head or hand. Copies of them may be multiplied forever [. . .] The Iliad flourishes as green now, as on the day that Pisistratus is said first to have stamped upon it its present order. The songs of the Rhapsodists, the Scalds, and the Minstrels, which once seemed as fugitive as the breath of him who chaunted [sic] them, repose in libraries, and are embalmed in collections.[74]

The 'fugitive' nature of human life is counteracted, Godwin argues, by the printed book. He creates a sense of stasis – 'stamped', 'embalmed' – to represent the longevity enabled by the book-form, whose fixity and uniformity counteracts powers of loss and decay. Yet he also gives books vitality and agency, describing them as things that multiply and flourish like living organisms. The dead continue to sing and to speak, communicating with the living communities who preserve them. Like *Essay on Sepulchres*, this essay on durability upholds the book-form as the linchpin of long-term social progress, a site of re-membering that works against the tendency of human civilisation to function like a never-ending infant school. Its conclusion is that 'Knowledge, in its most considerable branches shall endure, as long as books shall exist to hand it down to successive generations.'[75]

It is clear that the material power of the printed codex was not, in Godwin's understanding, the only active cause of truth's social apprehension through print. As the other chapters of this book have shown, he argued in various ways throughout his corpus that readers must be of a certain kind; that literature itself may be more or less conducive to 'true enquiry' through its content and style; and that truth itself had an independent force or weight manifested (to some extent) through all these things. Godwin's concern with 'Illustrious' thinkers in his *Essay on Sepulchres* reflects some of these complications, for it involves two claims that sit uneasily alongside each other: that certain writers have historical traction due to the intrinsic value of their ideas, and that the vitality of these writers also depends upon the activity of readers, who have a duty to 'husband' their particular inheritance. The materiality of print was thus not sufficient for intellectual regeneration, in Godwin's estimation, but it was necessary. He assigned real power to media technology, a strategy which enabled him to write confidently about the reforming capacity of the printed codex.

In his nineteenth-century writings, then, Godwin described and figured the book as an object and ideal that not simply preserved but transformed the human mind. He formulated his ideas in contexts of personal and public loss, and during a period in which his central belief in the perfectible nature of human society was subject to intense criticism. Writing about the book was an attempt to engage and reshape the conversations about social futurity that were animating this period; in the face of new (and newly publicised) economic, religious and cultural uncertainty, Godwin confidently deployed the book-object as a form of redress and a symbol of hope. In short, Godwin's writing shows us how, in an age obsessed with diagnosing itself – the age of the spirit of the age, in J. S. Mill's estimation – media technology became a way to imagine and interpret the times.[76]

It is perhaps ironic that the end of Godwin's career coincided with the beginning of Thomas Carlyle's, for whom the entire cultural world, including printed literature, was degenerating under the influence of the mechanical: 'books are not only printed, but, in a great measure, written and sold, by machinery', he famously claimed in 'Signs of the Times' (1829).[77] For Godwin, the mechanisation of the press and the mass-trajectory of literary culture was instead a harbinger of increasing humanisation: 'By the easy multiplication of copies, and the cheapness of books, everyone has access to them. [. . .] By this art we seem to be secured against the future perishing of human improvement.' Print technology, he repeatedly argued, is 'that great engine for raising men to the dignity of gods'; 'that glorious instrument for advancing the march of human improvement'.[78] Such statements remind us, perhaps, that reflections on the significance of media technology and its uses have never been simply that. For centuries they have been bound up with other cultural shifts, including changing assumptions about the very nature and ends of human life.

Notes

1. *Essay on Sepulchres: or, a Proposal for Erecting some Memorial of the Illustrious Dead in All Ages on the Spot where their Remains have been Interred*, PPW, vol. 6, pp. 28–9.
2. Sachs, *The Poetics of Decline in British Romanticism* (Cambridge: Cambridge University Press, 2018), p. 88.
3. Useful accounts of 'Essay on Sepulchres' include: Mark Salber Phillips, *Society and Sentiment: Genres of Historical Writing in Britain, 1740–1820* (Princeton: Princeton University Press, 2000), pp. 322–41; Carlson, *England's First Family of Writers: Mary Wollstonecraft, William Godwin, Mary Shelley* (Baltimore: Johns Hopkins University Press, 2007), pp. 149–50, 166–8; Weston, 'History, Memory, and Moral Knowledge': William Godwin's "Essay on Sepulchres"', *The European Legacy* 14.6 (2009); Paul Westover, *Necromanticism: Traveling to Meet the Dead,*

1750–1860 (Basingstoke: Palgrave Macmillan, 2012), pp. 48–74; Lynch, *Loving Literature: A Cultural History* (Chicago: University of Chicago Press, 2015), pp. 220–2; David McAllister, *Imagining the Dead in British Literature and Culture, 1790–1848* (Basingstoke: Palgrave Macmillan, 2018), pp. 73–112.
4. Piper, *Dreaming in Books: The Making of the Bibliographic Imagination in the Romantic Age* (Chicago: University of Chicago Press, 2009), p. 13.
5. See Richard Altick, *Lives and Letters: The History of Literary Biography in England and America* (New York: Knopf, 1966); Annette Wheeler Cafarelli, *Prose in the Age of Poets: Romanticism and Biographical Narrative from Johnson to De Quincey* (Philadelphia: University of Pennsylvania Press, 1990); Bradley and Rawes, *Romantic Biography*, ed. Arthur Bradley and Alan Rawes (Aldershot; Ashgate: Routledge, 2003); Heather Jackson, 'What's Biography Got to Do with It?', *European Romantic Review* 22.3 (2011): 357–72 (especially pp. 357–64); Lynch, *Loving Literature*, p. 22.
6. *Lives of Edward and John Philips, Nephews and Pupils of Milton* (London: Longman, Hurst, Rees, Orme, and Brown, 1815), p. vi.
7. *Memoirs of the Author of A Vindication of the Rights of Woman*, CNM, vol. 1, pp. 85–142 (pp. 88, 127, 141, 139–40). For the corporeal aspect of this text, see Angela Monsam, 'Biography as Autopsy in William Godwin's "Memoirs of the Author of A Vindication of the Rights of Woman"', *Eighteenth Century Fiction* 21.1 (2008): 109–30.
8. *Memoirs of the Author of A Vindication of the Rights of Woman*, p. 87.
9. Tilottama Rajan explores Godwin's concept of personal 'tendency' in the *Memoirs* and posthumous works from a different critical perspective; see especially 'Framing the Corpus: Godwin's "Editing" of Wollstonecraft in 1798', *Studies in Romanticism* 39.4 (2000): 511–31.
10. [Sharpe], 'The Vision of Liberty: Written in the Manner of Spencer [sic]', *Anti-Jacobin Review and Magazine* 9.38 (August 1801): 515–20 (p. 518).
11. *Life of Geoffrey Chaucer*, vol. 1, p. xi.
12. Ibid. pp. vii–viii.
13. Ibid. p. viii.
14. Ibid. p. vii.
15. Sir Walter Scott, 'Review of Godwin's "Life of Chaucer"', *Edinburgh Review* 3 (January 1804): 437–52.
16. See, for example, McLane, *Balladeering, Minstrelsy, and the Making of British Romantic Poetry* (Cambridge: Cambridge University Press, 2008); Susan Manning, 'Antiquarianism, Balladry and the Rehabilitation of Romance', in *The Cambridge History of English Romantic Literature*, ed. James Chandler (Cambridge: Cambridge University

Press, 2009), pp. 45–70; Rosemary Sweet, *Antiquaries: the Discovery of the Past in Eighteenth-Century Britain* (London: Hambledon and London, 2003); Fielding, *Writing and Orality: Nationality, Culture, and Nineteenth-Century Scottish Fiction* (Oxford: Clarendon Press, 1996).
17. Godwin's response to Scott's review, a letter to the editor of the *Edinburgh Review*, survives only in part. See *LWG*, vol. 2, pp. 302–3. The extant section echoes the language of his letter to Phillips (see analysis below), claiming that the reviewer has 'confounded the two main orders of human minds, the man of genius, & the blockhead'.
18. *Life of Geoffrey Chaucer*, vol. 1, pp. xiii–xiv.
19. See Erikson, 'The Romantic-Era Book Trade', in *A Concise Companion to the Romantic Age*, ed. Jon Klancher (Oxford: Blackwell, 2009), p. 212.
20. Godwin to Richard Phillips, 31 March 1803, *LWG*, vol. 2, pp. 276–8 (emphasis original).
21. Godwin to Richard Phillips, 18 July 1802, 19 July 1802 and 21 July 1802, in *LWG*, vol. 2, pp. 252–6 (pp. 253, 255).
22. Milton, *Areopagitica*, p. 492.
23. For a summary of reviews, see Graham, *William Godwin Reviewed: A Reception History, 1783–1834* (New York: AMS Press, 2001), pp. 214–15, 221–2. For the projected 'future volume' see Godwin to Phillips, 5 April 1803, *LWG*, vol. 2, pp. 278–9. The original two quarto volumes were made four octavo for the second edition, but the text was not lengthened (see 17 February 1804 in *DWG*).
24. Carlson, *England's First Family of Writers*, pp. 78–80.
25. Obituary notice for Joseph Johnson, *Morning Chronicle*, 21 December 1809, p. 3 (published anonymously). Cf. Philp, 'Introduction' to *PPW*, pp. 23–4.
26. *Essay on Sepulchres*, pp. 8, 14.
27. Malthus, *An Essay on the Principle of Population, as it affects the future improvement of society, with remarks on the speculations of Mr. Godwin, M. Condorcet, and other writers* (London: J. Johnson, 1798), p. 10. See my Introduction for further detail about the Godwin-Malthus dispute.
28. See Philp, 'Introduction' to *PPW*, p. 23. Cf. Wordsworth, 'Essay on Epitaphs', in *The Prose Works of William Wordsworth*, ed. W. J. B. Owen and Jane Worthington Smyser (Oxford: Clarendon, 1974), vol. 2, pp. 43–119.
29. *Essay on Sepulchres*, pp. 8, 10.
30. Ibid. pp. 14, 19.
31. Ibid. p. 12.
32. Ibid. p. 22.

33. Ibid. p. 10.
34. Ibid. p. 20 (emphasis original).
35. Ibid. p. 23. On the connection between Godwin's *Essay on Sepulchres* and associationism, see Phillips, *Society and Sentiment*, pp. 322–41, and Rowland Weston, 'History, Memory, and Moral Knowledge', pp. 651–65.
36. *Essay on Sepulchres*, pp. 24, 29–30; cf. Hunt, *Essays and Sketches by Leigh Hunt*, ed. R. Brimley Johnson (Oxford, 1906), pp. 96–104. For more on *Essay on Sepulchres* and location, see Westover, 'William Godwin, Literary Tourism, and the Work of Necromanticism', *Studies in Romanticism* 48.2 (2009): 299–319, incorporated into *Necromanticism: Traveling to Meet the Dead*.
37. *Essay on Sepulchres*, pp. 18–19.
38. Godwin later summarised his idealised view of classical republicanism in a letter to Mary Shelley: 'The species has, I believe, for the last fifteen or eighteen hundred years, been grievously depressed below the standard which is set before us in the ancient republics of Greece and Rome' (transcribed in *PPW*, vol. 7, p. 79).
39. [Anon.], 'Review of "Essay on Sepulchres"', *Monthly Review* 61 (1810), Art. 44, p. 111.
40. Philip Connell, 'Bibliomania: Book Collecting, Cultural Politics, and the Rise of Literary Heritage in Romantic Britain', *Representations* 71 (Summer 2000): 24–47 (p. 30).
41. On the context of military monuments, see Alison Yarrington, 'Nelson the Citizen Hero: State and Public Patronage of Monumental Sculpture 1805–18', *Art History* 6.3 (September 1983): 315–29. On the formation of national identity in opposition to European powers in this period, see Linda Colley, *Britons: Forging the Nation, 1707–1837* (New Haven: Yale University Press, 1992).
42. Hazlitt, 'Of Thought and Action', in *Table Talk; or, Original Essays* (London: John Warren, 1821), p. 249.
43. *Essay on Sepulchres*, pp. 28–30.
44. Ibid. pp. 12–13, 7, 18.
45. See Philip Connell, 'Death and the Author: Westminster Abbey and the Meanings of the Literary Monument', *Eighteenth-Century Studies* 38.4 (2005): 557–85 (p. 563), and Matthew Craske, 'Westminster Abbey 1720–70: A Public Pantheon Built upon Private Interest', in *Pantheons: Transformations of a Monumental Idea*, ed. Richard Wrigley and Matthew Craske (Aldershot: Ashgate, 2004), pp. 57–79.
46. [Anon.], 'Review of "Essay on Sepulchres"', p. 111. For a summary of the reviews of Godwin's *Essay*, see Graham, *William Godwin Reviewed*, pp. 299–302.

47. *Essay on Sepulchres*, pp. 23, 8 (emphasis mine).
48. Ibid. pp. 28–9.
49. Ibid. pp. 5–6.
50. Ibid. p. 23.
51. Ibid. p. 24.
52. *St Leon*, p. 31; *Mandeville*, pp. 146, 217–18, 309.
53. *Caleb Williams*, p. 340.
54. See 17–19 April 1804 and 15–16 March 1808 in *DWG*. A copy of Browne's work was listed among Godwin's posthumous book sales: see Munby, 'The Catalogue of the Curious Library of that Very Eminent and Distinguished Author William Godwin (1836), compiled by Sotheby and Son', printed in *Sale Catalogues of Libraries of Eminent Persons*, ed. A. N. L. Munby, vol. 8 (London: Mansell with Sotheby Parke Bernet Publications, 1973), pp. 283–318.
55. Sir Thomas Browne, *Hydriotaphia, Urne-Buriall, or, a Discourse of the Sepulchrall Urnes Lately Found in Norfolk.* [. . .] (London: Hen. Brome, 1658), p. 5.
56. Browne, *Urne-Buriall*, pp. 82–4.
57. Thompson, 'Personal and Bodily Identity: The Metaphysics of Resurrection in 17th Century Philosophy', PhD thesis (Kings College London, 2019), pp. 79–81; see Browne, *Religio Medici and other works*, ed. L. C. Martin (Oxford: Oxford University Press, 1964), pp. 45–6.
58. *The Genius of Christianity Unveiled*, *PPW*, p. 199; see 'Of Religion', *PPW*, p. 67.
59. Milton, *Areopagitica*, pp. 492–3.
60. *Essay on Sepulchres*, p. 26.
61. On the ubiquity of corruption narratives in Romantic-period discussions of print see Sachs, *The Poetics of Decline*; McDowell, 'Towards a Genealogy of "Print Culture" and "Oral Tradition"', in *The Broadview Reader in Book History*, ed. Michelle Levy and Tom Mole (Peterborough, ON: Broadview, 2015), pp. 395–415; Piper, *Dreaming in Books*, pp. 5–6.
62. Coleridge, *The Major Works* (Oxford: Oxford University Press, 1985), p. 187.
63. [Anon.] A GODWINIAN, 'Modern Perfectibility', *The Scourge, or, Monthly Expositor of Imposture and Folly* 1 (June 1811): 463–6 (pp. 464–5, 463).
64. Jonathan Swift, *A Tale of a Tub: To which is added The Battle of the Books and the Mechanical Operation of the Spirit*, ed. A. C. Guthkelch and David Nichol Smith, 2nd edn (Oxford: Oxford University Press, 2014), pp. 34–5. Godwin further explored Swift's 'Dedication' and this quotation specifically in his essay 'On the Durability of Human Achievements and Productions' in *Thoughts on Man* in *PPW* (p. 83).

65. 'Untitled [Essay on Death]', 1810, Oxford, Bodleian Library, Abinger Collection, MS. Abinger c. 86, Fols. 36–9. Following quotations are from this source and transcriptions are my own. Godwin recorded the composition date of this essay as 6 October 1810 in *DWG*.
66. *Essay on Sepulchres*, pp. 6–7, 18. For more on the icon/friend dynamic in Godwin's work and its resonance, see Westover, 'William Godwin, Literary Tourism, and the Work of Necromanticism', p. 307, and Lynch, *Loving Literature*, pp. 35, 92.
67. *Political Justice*, p. 141; cf. Condorcet, *Sketch for a Historical Picture of the Progress of the Human Mind*, trans. June Barraclough (London: Weidenfeld & Nicolson, 1955), pp. 99–123.
68. See editor's notes on entry for Dugald Stewart in *DWG*.
69. Stewart, *Elements of the Philosophy of the Human Mind*, in *The Collected Works of Dugald Stewart*, ed. Sir William Hamilton (London: Thoemmes Press, 1994), p. 242 (emphasis mine).
70. Malthus, *An Essay on the Principle of Population*, pp. 1–2.
71. *Thoughts on Man*, pp. 46–7.
72. Ibid. pp. 149; 142–3.
73. Ibid. p. 150. Cf. *Lives of Edward and John Philips*, p. 325, in which an abridgement is described as akin to a 'naked skeleton', and the essay 'Of the Study of the Classics' in *The Enquirer*, which attacks both abridgements and translations as a 'waste of time' (pp. 100–1).
74. *Thoughts on Man*, pp. 80, 88.
75. Ibid. p. 90.
76. Mill, *The Spirit of the Age* (Chicago: University of Chicago Press, 1942), p. 1.
77. Carlyle, 'Signs of the Times', in *A Carlyle Reader*, ed. G. B. Tennyson (Cambridge: Cambridge University Press, 1984), p. 36.
78. *Political Justice*, p. 138; 'Considerations on Lord Grenville's and Mr Pitt's Bills', *PPW*, p. 155; *Thoughts on Man*, p. 248.

Bibliography

Primary Sources

[Anon.], 'Deloraine. By the Author of "Caleb Williams"', *Literary Gazette* 838 (1833): p. 81.

[Anon.] A GODWINIAN, 'Modern Perfectibility', *The Scourge, or, Monthly Expositor of Imposture and Folly* 1 (June 1811): 463–6.

[Anon.], 'Remarks on Mandeville', *Blackwood's Magazine* 2 (January 1818): 402–8.

[Anon.], 'Review of "Essay on Sepulchres"', *Monthly Review* 61 (1810), Art. 44, p. 111.

[Anon.], 'Review of "Life of Geoffrey Chaucer"', *Critical Review, or, Annals of Literature* 1.1 (January 1804): 60–5.

[Anon.], 'Review of Mandeville; A Tale of the Seventeenth Century by William Godwin', *The North-American Review and Miscellaneous Journal* 7.19 (1818): 92–105.

Aristotle, *Poetics*, trans. Malcom Heath (London: Penguin, 1996).

Bacon, Sir Francis, *Essayes or Counsels, Civill and Morall* (London: John Haviland, 1632).

Barbauld, Anna, *The British Novelists; with an Essay, and Prefaces Biographical and Critical, by Mrs. Barbauld. A New Edition*, 50 vols (London, York and Edinburgh: printed for F. C. and J. Rivington et al., 1820).

Blackstone, Sir William, *Commentaries On the Laws of England; 10th edition, with the last corrections of the author; additions by Richard Burn, LL.D. and continued to the present time by John Williams*, 4 vols (London: A. Strahan, T. Cadell and D. Prince, 1787).

Blake, William, *William Blake's Writings*, ed. G. E. Bentley, Jr, 2 vols (Oxford: Clarendon Press, 1978).

Browne, Sir Thomas, *Hydriotaphia, Urne-Buriall, or, a Discourse of the Sepulchrall Urnes Lately Found in Norfolk. Together with the Garden of Cyrus, or the Quincunciall, Lozenge, or Net-Work Plantations of the Ancients, Artificially, Naturally, Mystically Considered. With Sundry Observations* (London: Hen. Brome, 1658).

—, *Religio Medici and other works*, ed. L. C. Martin (Oxford: Oxford University Press, 1964).

[Bulwer-Lytton, Edward], 'Cloudesley, by the Author of Caleb Williams', *The New Monthly Magazine and Literary Journal* 28.109 (January 1830): 368–73.

Burke, Edmund, *Reflections on the French Revolution in France*, ed. Conor Cruise O'Brien (London: Penguin, 1986).

Carlyle, Thomas, 'Signs of the Times', in *A Carlyle Reader*, ed. G. B. Tennyson (Cambridge: Cambridge University Press, 1984), pp. 31–54.

Coleridge, Samuel Taylor, *The Major Works* (Oxford: Oxford University Press, 1985).

Condorcet, Antoine-Nicolas de, *Sketch for a Historical Picture of the Progress of the Human Mind*, trans. June Barraclough (London: Weidenfeld & Nicolson, 1955).

Constant, Benjamin, *De La Liberte Des Brouchures, Des Pamphlets et Des Journaux* (Paris: Chez H Nicolle, a la Librairie Stereotype, 1814).

Doddridge, Philip, *The Correspondence and Diary of Philip Doddridge, D.D. Illustrative of Various Particulars in His Life Hitherto Unknown; with Notices of Many of His Contemporaries, and a Sketch of the Ecclesiastical History of the Times in Which He Lived*, ed. John Doddridge Humphreys, 5 vols (London: Henry Colburn and Richard Bentley, 1830).

—, *A Course of Lectures on the Principal Subjects in Pneumatology, Ethics, and Divinity: With References to the Most Considerable Authors on Each Subject* (London: J. Buckland et al., 1763).

Edgeworth, Maria and Richard Lovell Edgeworth, *Practical Education* (London: J. Johnson, 1798).

[Enfield, William], 'Review of "The Enquirer"', *Monthly Review* 23 (1797): 291–302.

Godwin, William, *Collected Novels and Memoirs of William Godwin*, ed. Mark Philp, Pamela Clemit and Maurice Hindle, 8 vols (London: Pickering & Chatto, 1992).

—, *History of the Commonwealth of England; from its commencement, to the restoration of Charles the Second*, 4 vols (London: printed for Henry Colburn, 1824–8).

—, *Life of Geoffrey Chaucer, the early English poet: including memoirs of his near friend and kinsman, John of Gaunt, Duke of Lancaster: with sketches of the manners, opinions, arts and literature of England in the fourteenth century* (London: Richard Phillips, 1804).

—, *Lives of Edward and John Philips, Nephews and Pupils of Milton* (London: Printed for Longman, Hurst, Rees, Orme and Brown, 1815).

—, *Lives of the Necromancers: or, an account of the most eminent persons in successive ages, who have claimed for themselves, or to whom has been imputed by others, the exercise of magical power* (London: Frederick J. Mason, 1834).

—, 'Notes on the biographical sketch of William Godwin inserted in the "Monthly Mirror", Jan. & Feb. 1805', Oxford, Bodleian Library, Abinger Collection, MS. Abinger c. 31 Fol. 117.

—, Obituary notice of Joseph Johnson, *Morning Chronicle,* 21 December, 1809, p. 3.

—, 'On the Composition of History; An Occasional Reflection', n.d., Oxford, Bodleian Library, Abinger Collection, MS. Abinger c. 29 Fols. 5–16.

—, *Political and Philosophical Writings of William Godwin*, ed. Mark Philp, Pamela Clemit and Martin Fitzpatrick, 7 vols (London: Pickering & Chatto, 1993).

—, *The Diary of William Godwin*, ed. Victoria Myers, David O'Shaughnessy and Mark Philp (Oxford: Oxford Digital Library, 2010) <http://godwindiary.bodleian.ox.ac.uk> (last accessed 24 May 2018).

—, *The Letters of William Godwin*, ed. Pamela Clemit, 2 vols (Oxford: Oxford University Press, 2011).

—, 'Untitled [Essay on Death]', 1810, Oxford, Bodleian Library, Abinger Collection, MS. Abinger c. 86 Fols. 36–9.

—, 'Untitled [on Matter, Thought, Motion and Identity]', n.d., Oxford, Bodleian Library, Abinger Collection, MS. Abinger c. 36 Fol. 3.

Hartley, David, *Observations on Man: His Frame, His Duty, and His Expectations* (Cambridge: Cambridge University Press, 2013).

Hays, Mary, *The Correspondence (1779–1843) of Mary Hays, British Novelist*, ed. Marilyn L. Brooks (Lewiston, NY: Edwin Mellen Press, 2004).

—, *Memoirs of Emma Courtney*, ed. Marilyn L. Brooks (Peterborough, ON: Broadview, 2000).

Hazlitt, William, 'The Spirit of the Age', in *The Collected Works of William Hazlitt*, ed. A. R. Waller and Arnold Glover, vol. 4 (London: J. M. Dent & Co., 1902), pp. 185–368.

—, *Lectures on the English Comic Writers* (London: Taylor and Hessey, 1819).

—, *Table Talk; or, Original Essays* (London: John Warren, 1821).

Helvétius, Claude Adrien, *De L'Esprit: Or, Essays on the Mind, and Its Several Faculties* (London: Vernor, Hood and Sharpe, 1810).

Holcroft, Thomas, *The Adventures of Hugh Trevor*, ed. Seamus Deane (London: Oxford University Press, 1973).

Hume, David, *Essays, Moral and Political*, 2 vols (Edinburgh: A. Kincaid, 1741–2).

—, *A Treatise of Human Nature: A Critical Edition*, ed. David Fate Norton and Mary J. Norton (Oxford: Clarendon Press, 2007).

Hunt, Leigh, *Essays and Sketches by Leigh Hunt*, ed. R. Brimley Johnson (Oxford, 1906).
Inchbald, Elizabeth, *A Simple Story*, ed. J. M. S. Tompkins (London: Oxford University Press, 1967).
—, *Nature and Art*, ed. Shawn L. Maurer (London: Pickering & Chatto, 1997).
—, 'To the Artist', *The Artist*, No. XIV, Saturday, 13 June 1807.
Jewsbury, Maria Jane, *Phantasmagoria: Or, Sketches of Life and Literature*, vol. 1 (London: Hurst, Robinson and Co., 1825).
Johnson, Samuel, *The Works of Samuel Johnson, LL.D.: Together with His Life, and Notes on His Lives of the Poets*, ed. John Hawkins, 11 vols (Cambridge: Cambridge University Press, 2011).
—, 'On Studies' [originally untitled], *The Adventurer* 85 (28 August 1753): 85–90.
Kant, Immanuel, *Critique of the Power of Judgment*, ed. and trans. Paul Guyer (Cambridge: Cambridge University Press, 2000).
Locke, John, *An Essay Concerning Human Understanding*, 7th edn, 4 vols (London: printed for J. Churchill, at the Black-Swan in Pater-Noster-Row; and Samuel Manship, at the Ship in Cornhill, 1715).
—, *Posthumous Works of Mr. John Locke: Viz. I. Of the Conduct of the Understanding. II. An Examination of P. Malebranche's Opinion of Seeing All Things in God. III. A Discourse of Miracles. IV. Part of a Fourth Letter for Toleration. V. Memoirs Relating to the Life of Anthony First Earl of Shaftsbury. To Which Is Added, VI. His New Method of a Common-Place-Book, Written Originally in French, and Now Translated into English* (London: W.B. for A. and J. Churchill at the Black Swan in Pater-Noster-Row, 1706).
Malthus, Thomas Robert, *An Essay on the Principle of Population, as it affects the future improvement of society, with remarks on the speculations of Mr. Godwin, M. Condorcet, and other writers* (London: J. Johnson, 1798).
Mill, John Stuart, *The Spirit of the Age* (Chicago: University of Chicago Press, 1942).
Milton, John, *Complete Prose Works of John Milton*, ed. Ernest Sirluck, 8 vols (New Haven: Yale University Press, 1959).
Orton, Job, *Memoirs of the Life, Character and Writings of the Late Reverend Philip Doddridge, D.D. Of Northampton* (Salop: printed by J. Cotton and J. Eddowes; and sold by J. Buckland, in Pater-Noster-Row, London, 1766).
Palmer, Samuel, *A Defence of the Dissenters Education in Their Private Academies: In Answer to Mr. W–Y's Disingenuous and Unchristian Reflections upon 'Em. In a Letter to a Noble Lord* (London: A. Baldwin, 1703).

Price, Richard, *Observations on the Importance of the American Revolution, and the Means of Making It a Benefit to the World* (Cambridge: Cambridge University Press, 2013).

Priestley, Joseph, *Disquisitions Relating to Matter and Spirit. To Which Is Added, the History of the Philosophical Doctrine Concerning the Origin of the Soul, and the Nature of Matter; with Its Influence on Christianity, Especially with Respect to the Doctrine of the Pre-Existence of Christ* (London: J. Johnson, 1777).

—, *The Importance and Extent of Free Inquiry in Matters of Religion: A Sermon, Preached before the Congregations of the Old and New Meeting of Protestant Dissenters at Birmingham. November 5, 1785. To Which Are Added, Reflections on the Present State of Free Inquiry in This Country; and Animadversions on Some Passages in Mr. White's Sermons at the Bampton Lectures; Mr. Howes's Discourse on the Abuse of the Talent of Disputation in Religion; And, A Pamphlet, Intitled, 'Primitive Candour'* (Birmingham: printed by M. Swinney; for J. Johnson, no. 72. St. Paul's Churchyard, London, 1785).

—, *Miscellaneous Observations Relating to Education: More Especially as It Respects the Conduct of the Mind* (London: J. Johnson, 1778).

Reeve, Clara, *The Progress of Romance, through Times, Countries, and Manners* [. . .], vol. 2 (Colchester: Keymer, 1785).

Scott, Sir Walter, 'Review of Godwin's "Life of Chaucer"', *Edinburgh Review* 3 (January 1804): 437–52.

[Sharpe, Kirkpatrick C.], 'The Vision of Liberty: Written in the Manner of Spencer [sic]', *Anti-Jacobin Review and Magazine* 9.38 (August 1801): 515–20.

[Shelley, Percy Bysshe], 'Godwin's Mandeville', *The Examiner*, Iss. 522 (28 December 1817): 826–7.

Smith, Adam, *The Theory of Moral Sentiments*, ed. D. D. Raphael and A. L. Macfie (Oxford: Clarendon Press, 1976).

Smith, Charlotte, *Desmond. A Novel*, in *The Works of Charlotte Smith*, vol. 5, ed. Stuart Curran (London: Pickering & Chatto, 2005).

Stewart, Dugald, *The Collected Works of Dugald Stewart*, ed. Sir William Hamilton, 11 vols (London: Thoemmes Press, 1994).

Swift, Jonathan, *A Tale of a Tub: To which is added The Battle of the Books and the Mechanical Operation of the Spirit*, ed. A. C. Guthkelch and David Nichol Smith, 2nd edn (Oxford: Oxford University Press, 2014).

Thelwall, John, *The Tribune*, vol. 2 (London: Symonds, Ridgway, and Smith, 1796).

Watts, Isaac, *The Works of the Late Reverend and Learned Isaac Watts, D.D.* [. . .], 6 vols (London: printed for T. and T. Longman at the Ship, and J. Buckland at the Buck, in Pater-Noster-Row; J. Oswald at the Rose

and Crown in the Poultry; J. Waugh at the Turk's-Head in Lombard-Street; and J. Ward at the King's-Arms in Cornhill, 1753).
Wollstonecraft, Mary, *A Vindication of the Rights of Woman*, ed. Janet Todd (Oxford: Oxford University Press, 1994).
—, *Letters Written in Sweden, Norway, and Denmark*, in *The Works of Mary Wollstonecraft*, ed. Janet Todd and Marilyn Butler, vol 6 (London: Pickering and Chatto, 1989).
Wordsworth, William, *The Prose Works of William Wordsworth*, ed. W. J. B. Owen and Jane Worthington Smyser, 3 vols (Oxford: Clarendon, 1974).
Young, Edward, *The Complaint: or, Night-Thoughts on Life, Death, and Immortality* (London: R. Dodsley, 1742).

Secondary Sources

Allan, David, *Commonplace Books and Reading in Georgian England* (Cambridge: Cambridge University Press, 2010).
Altick, Richard, *Lives and Letters: The History of Literary Biography in England and America* (New York: Knopf, 1966).
Anderson, Emily, '"I Will Unfold a Tale!": Narrative, Epistemology, and "Caleb Williams"', *Eighteenth-Century Fiction* 22 (2009): 99–114.
Anderson, Robert, 'Godwin Disguised: Politics in the Juvenile Library', in *Godwinian Moments: From the Enlightenment to Romanticism*, ed. Robert Maniquis and Victoria Myers (Toronto: University of Toronto Press, 2011), pp. 125–46.
—, 'Godwin, Keats and Productive Leisure', *The Wordsworth Circle* 33.1 (2002): 10–13.
Ashley Smith, Joe W., *The Birth of Modern Education: The Contribution of the Dissenting Academies, 1660–1800* (London: Independent Press, 1954).
Avery, Gillian and Julia Briggs (eds), *Children and Their Books: A Celebration of the Work of Iona and Peter Opie* (Oxford: Clarendon, 1989).
Barbour, Judith, '"Obliged to Make This Sort of Deposit of Our Minds": William Godwin and the Sociable Contract of Writing', in *Romantic Sociability: Social Networks and Literary Culture in Britain, 1770–1840*, ed. Gillian Russell and Clara Tuite (Cambridge: Cambridge University Press, 2002), pp. 166–85.
Barrell, John, *The Spirit of Despotism: Invasions of Privacy in the 1790s* (Oxford: Oxford University Press, 2006).
Behrendt, Stephen, *Romanticism, Radicalism, and the Press* (Detroit: Wayne State University Press, 1997).

Bentley, David, *English Criminal Justice in the Nineteenth Century* (London: The Hambledon Press, 1998).
Berry, Christopher J., *The Idea of Commercial Society in the Scottish Enlightenment* (Edinburgh: Edinburgh University Press, 2013).
Binhammer, Katherine, 'The Persistence of Reading: Governing Female Novel-Reading in "Memoirs of Emma Courtney" and "Memoirs of Modern Philosophers"', *Eighteenth-Century Life* 27.2 (2003): 1–22.
Bour, Isabelle, 'Sensibility as Epistemology in "Caleb Williams", "Waverley", and "Frankenstein"', *Studies in English Literature, 1500–1900* 45 (2005): 813–27.
Bradley, Arthur, and Alan Rawes (eds), *Romantic Biography* (Aldershot; Ashgate: Routledge, 2003).
Brooks, Marilyn L., 'Hays/Godwin Correspondence 1794–1800', in *The Correspondence (1779–1843) of Mary Hays, British Novelist* (Lewiston, NY: Edwin Mellen Press, 2004), pp. 363–81.
Brown, Homer Obed, *Institutions of the English Novel from Defoe to Scott* (Philadelphia: University of Pennsylvania Press, 1997).
Burden, Mark, *A Biographical Dictionary of Tutors at the Dissenters' Private Academies, 1660–1729* (London: Dr Williams's Centre for Dissenting Studies, 2013).
Burke, Peter, *The Art of Conversation* (Cambridge: Polity, 1993).
Butler, Marilyn (ed.), *Burke, Paine, Godwin, and the Revolution Controversy* (Cambridge: Cambridge University Press, 1984).
—, *Jane Austen and the War of Ideas* (Oxford: Clarendon, 1988).
—, *Romantics, Rebels and Reactionaries: English Literature and its Background, 1760–1830* (Oxford: Oxford University Press, 1981).
Cafarelli, Annette Wheeler, *Prose in the Age of Poets: Romanticism and Biographical Narrative from Johnson to De Quincey* (Philadelphia: University of Pennsylvania Press, 1990).
Cambers, Andrew, *Godly Reading: Print, Manuscript and Puritanism in England, 1580–1720* (Cambridge: Cambridge University Press, 2011).
Carlson, Julia, *Romantic Marks and Measures: Wordsworth's Poetry in Fields of Print* (Philadelphia: University of Pennsylvania Press, 2016).
Carlson, Julie A., *England's First Family of Writers: Mary Wollstonecraft, William Godwin, Mary Shelley* (Baltimore: Johns Hopkins University Press, 2007).
Chandler, James, *England in 1819: The Politics of Literary Culture and the Case of Romantic Historicism* (Chicago: University of Chicago Press, 1998).
Clemit, Pamela, *The Godwinian Novel: The Rational Fictions of Godwin, Brockden Brown, Mary Shelley* (Oxford: Clarendon Press, 1993).

—, 'Godwin, Women, and "the Collision of Mind with Mind"', *Wordsworth Circle* 35.2 (2004): 72–6.
—, 'Godwin's Educational Theory: "The Enquirer"', *Enlightenment and Dissent* 12 (1993): 3–11.
—, 'Holding Proteus: William Godwin in His Letters', in *Repossessing the Romantic Past*, ed. Heather Glen and Paul Hamilton (Cambridge: Cambridge University Press, 2006), pp. 98–115.
—, 'Self-Analysis as Social Critique: The Autobiographical Writings of Godwin and Rousseau', *Romanticism* 11 (2005): 161–80.
Clemit, Pamela and Avner Offer, 'Godwin's Citations, 1783–2005: Highest Renown at the Pinnacle of Disfavor', *Nineteenth-Century Prose* 41 (2014): 27–52.
Colley, Linda, *Britons: Forging the Nation, 1707–1837* (New Haven: Yale University Press, 1992).
Connell, Philip, 'Bibliomania: Book Collecting, Cultural Politics, and the Rise of Literary Heritage in Romantic Britain', *Representations* 71 (2000): 24–47.
—, 'Death and the Author: Westminster Abbey and the Meanings of the Literary Monument', *Eighteenth-Century Studies* 38.4 (2005): 557–85.
—, *Romanticism, Economics and the Question of 'Culture'* (Oxford: Oxford University Press, 2001).
Copley, Stephen, 'Commerce, Conversation and Politeness in the Early Eighteenth-Century Periodical', *British Journal for Eighteenth-Century Studies* 18 (1995): 63–77.
Craske, Matthew, 'Westminster Abbey 1720–70: A Public Pantheon Built upon Private Interest', *Pantheons: Transformations of a Monumental Idea*, ed. Richard Wrigley and Matthew Craske (Aldershot: Ashgate, 2004), pp. 57–79.
Cummings, Brian, 'The Book as Symbol', in *The Oxford Companion to the Book*, ed. Michael F. Suarez and H. R. Woudhuysen (Oxford: Oxford University Press, 2010), pp. 63–5.
Davis, Arthur Paul, *Isaac Watts: His Life and Work* (London: Independent Press, 1948).
De Ritter, Richard, *Imagining Women Readers, 1789–1820: Well-Regulated Minds* (Manchester: Manchester University Press, 2015).
Debray, Régis, 'The Book as Symbolic Object', in *The Future of the Book*, ed. Geoffrey Nunberg (Berkeley and Los Angeles: University of California Press, 1996), pp. 139–52.
DeMaria, Robert, *Samuel Johnson and the Life of Reading* (Baltimore: Johns Hopkins University Press, 1997).
'Dissenting Academies Online', *The Dissenting Academies Project*, The Queen Mary Centre for Religion and Literature in English, Queen Mary

University of London, <www.qmulreligionandliterature.co.uk/research/the-dissenting-academies-project> (last accessed 29 September 2020).

'Dissenting Education and the Legacy of John Jennings, c.1720–c.1729 (Second Edition)', *The Dissenting Academies Project,* The Queen Mary Centre for Religion and Literature in English, Queen Mary University of London, 2011 <www.qmulreligionandliterature.co.uk/online-publications/dissenting-education> (last accessed 29 September 2020).

Downie, Alan, 'The English Novel at the End of the 1820s', *The Oxford Handbook of the Eighteenth-Century Novel* (Oxford: Oxford University Press, 2016).

Duncan, Ian, *Scott's Shadow: The Novel in Romantic Edinburgh* (Princeton: Princeton University Press, 2007).

Engell, James, *The Creative Imagination: Enlightenment to Romanticism* (Cambridge, MA: Harvard University Press, 1981).

Erikson, Lee, 'The Romantic-Era Book Trade', in *A Concise Companion to the Romantic Age*, ed. Jon Klancher (Oxford: Blackwell, 2009), pp. 212–31.

Esterhammer, Angela, 'Godwin's Suspicion of Speech Acts', *Studies in Romanticism* 39.4 (2000): 553–78.

Favret, Mary, *War at a Distance: Romanticism and the Making of Modern Wartime* (Princeton: Princeton University Press, 2010).

Ferris, Ina, *The Achievement of Literary Authority: Gender, History, and the Waverley Novels* (Ithaca: Cornell University Press, 1991).

—, 'Book Fancy: Bibliomania and the Literary Word', *Keats-Shelley Journal* 58 (2009): 33–52.

—, *Book-Men, Book Clubs, and the Romantic Literary Sphere* (Basingstoke: Palgrave Macmillan, 2015).

—, 'Introduction', *Romantic Circles Praxis Series*, Romantic Libraries issue, ed. Ina Ferris (University of Maryland, 2004) <https://www.rc.umd.edu/praxis/libraries/index.html> (last accessed 19 February 2019).

—, 'Transformations of the Novel – II', in *The Cambridge History of English Romantic Literature*, ed. James Chandler (Cambridge: Cambridge University Press, 2009), pp. 473–89.

Ferris, Ina and Paul Keen (eds), *Bookish Histories: Books, Literature, and Commercial Modernity, 1700–1900* (Basingstoke: Palgrave Macmillan, 2009).

Fielding, Penny, *Writing and Orality: Nationality, Culture, and Nineteenth-Century Scottish Fiction* (Oxford: Clarendon Press, 1996).

Flint, Christopher, *The Appearance of Print in Eighteenth-Century Fiction* (Cambridge: Cambridge University Press, 2011).

Flint, Kate, *The Woman Reader, 1837–1914* (Oxford: Clarendon, 1993).

Fulford, Tim, 'Millenarianism and the Study of Romanticism', in *Romanticism and Millenarianism*, ed. Tim Fulford (Basingstoke: Palgrave, 2002), pp. 1–22.

Gallagher, Catherine, 'The Romantics and the Political Economists', in *The Cambridge History of English Romantic Literature*, ed. James Chandler (Cambridge: Cambridge University Press, 2009), pp. 71–100.

Gallagher, Noelle, 'Don Quixote and the Sentimental Reader of History in the Works of William Godwin', in *Historical Writing in Britain, 1688–1830: Visions of History* (Basingstoke: Palgrave Macmillan, 2014), pp. 162–81.

Gamer, Michael, 'A Select Collection: Barbauld, Scott, and the Rise of the (Reprinted) Novel', in *Recognizing the Romantic Novel: New Histories of British Fiction, 1780–1830*, ed. Jillian Heydt-Stevenson and Charlotte Sussman (Liverpool: Liverpool University Press, 2008), pp. 155–91.

Gigante, Denise, *Life: Organic Form and Romanticism* (New Haven: Yale University Press, 2009).

—, *Taste: A Literary History* (New Haven: Yale University Press, 2005).

Gilmartin, Kevin, *Print Politics: The Press and Radical Opposition in Early Nineteenth-Century England* (Cambridge: Cambridge University Press, 1996).

Gladfelder, Hal, *Criminality and Narrative in Eighteenth-Century England: Beyond the Law* (Baltimore: Johns Hopkins University Press, 2001).

Goldstein, Amanda Jo, *Sweet Science: Romantic Materialism and the News Logics of Life* (Chicago: Chicago University Press, 2017).

Goodman, Kevis, *Georgic Modernity and British Romanticism: Poetry and the Mediation of History* (Cambridge: Cambridge University Press, 2004).

—, 'Reading Motion: Coleridge's "Free Spirit" and its Medical Background', *European Romantic Review* 26.3 (2015): 349–56.

Graham, Kenneth, W., *The Politics of Narrative: Ideology and Social Change in William Godwin's "Caleb Williams"* (New York: AMS Press, 1990).

—, *William Godwin Reviewed: A Reception History, 1783–1834* (New York: AMS Press, 2001).

Grenby, Matthew, *The Child Reader, 1700–1840* (Cambridge: Cambridge University Press, 2011).

Guillroy, John, 'Enlightening Mediation', in *This Is Enlightenment*, ed. Clifford Siskin and William Warner (Chicago: University of Chicago Press, 2010), pp. 37–63.

Gurton-Wachter, Lily, *Watchwords: Romanticism and the Poetics of Attention* (Stanford: Stanford University Press, 2016).

Haakonssen, Knud (ed.), *Enlightenment and Religion: Rational Dissent in Eighteenth-Century Britain* (Cambridge: Cambridge University Press, 1996).

Halsey, Katie, 'The Home Education of Girls in the Eighteenth-Century Novel: "the pernicious effects of an improper education"', *Oxford Review of Education* 41.4 (2015): 430–46.

Halsey, Katie and Jane Slinn (eds), *The Concept and Practice of Conversation in the Long Eighteenth Century, 1688–1848* (Newcastle: Cambridge Scholars Publishing, 2008).

Handler, Philip, 'James Mackintosh and Early Nineteenth-Century Criminal Law', *The Historical Journal* 58.3 (2015): 757–79.

Harkin, Maureen, 'Mackenzie's Man of Feeling: Embalming Sensibility', *ELH* 61.2 (1994): 317–40.

Hesse, Carla, 'Books in Time', in *The Future of the Book*, ed. Geoffrey Nunberg (Berkeley and Los Angeles: University of California Press, 1996), pp. 21–36.

Heydt-Stevenson, Jillian and Charlotte Sussman (eds), *Recognizing the Romantic Novel: New Histories of British Fiction, 1780–1830* (Liverpool: Liverpool University Press, 2008).

Heyer, Paul, *Communications and History: Theories of Media, Knowledge, and Civilization* (Westport, CT: Greenwood Press, 1988).

Huang, Daniel Patrick L., '"Private judgment" in the Anglican writings of John Henry Newman (1824–1945)' (doctoral dissertation, The Catholic University of America, 1996), *ProQuest Dissertations Publishing*.

Israel, Jonathan I., *Enlightenment Contested: Philosophy, Modernity, and the Emancipation of Man 1670–1752* (Oxford: Oxford University Press, 2006).

Jackson, Heather J., *Romantic Readers: The Evidence of Marginalia* (New Haven: Yale University Press, 2005).

—, 'What's Biography Got to Do with It?', *European Romantic Review* 22.3 (2011): 357–72.

James, Felicity, 'Romantic Readers', in *The Oxford Handbook to British Romanticism*, ed. David Duff (Oxford: Oxford University Press, 2018), pp. 478–94.

Janowitz, Anne, 'Amiable and Radical Sociability: Anna Barbauld's "free Familiar Conversation"', in *Romantic Sociability: Social Networks and Literary Culture in Britain, 1770–1840*, ed. Gillian Russell and Clara Tuite (Cambridge: Cambridge University Press, 2002), pp. 62–81.

Jarvis, Robin, *The Romantic Period: The Intellectual and Cultural Context of English Literature 1789–1830* (Harlow: Longman, 2004).

Johns, Adrian, *The Nature of the Book: Print and Knowledge in the Making* (Chicago: Chicago University Press, 1998).

Jones, Aled, *Powers of the Press: Newspapers, Power and the Public in Nineteenth-Century England* (Aldershot: Scolar Press, 1996).

Keen, Paul, *The Crisis of Literature in the 1790s: Print Culture and the Public Sphere* (Cambridge: Cambridge University Press, 1999).

Kinnell, Margaret, 'Childhood and Children's Literature: The Case of M. J. Godwin and Co., 1805–25', *Publishing History* 24 (1988): 77–99.

—, 'Sceptreless, Free, Uncircumscribed? Radicalism, Dissent and Early Children's Books', *British Journal of Educational Studies* 36 (1988): 49–71.

Klancher, Jon, 'Godwin and the Republican Romance: Genre, Politics, and Contingency in Cultural History', *Modern Language Quarterly* 56.2 (1995): 145–66.

—, 'Wild Bibliography: The Rise and Fall of Book History in Nineteenth-Century Britain', in *Bookish Histories: Books, Literature, and Commercial Modernity, 1700–1900*, ed. Ina Ferris and Paul Keen (Basingstoke: Palgrave Macmillan, 2009), pp. 19–40.

Leaver, Kristen, 'Pursuing Conversations: "Caleb Williams" and the Romantic Construction of the Reader', *Studies in Romanticism* 33 (1994): 589–610.

Locke, Don, *A Fantasy of Reason: The Life and Thought of William Godwin* (London: Routledge and Kegan Paul, 1980).

Lupton, Christina, *Knowing Books: The Consciousness of Mediation in Eighteenth-Century Britain* (Philadelphia: University of Pennsylvania Press, 2012).

—, *Reading and the Making of Time* (Baltimore: Johns Hopkins University Press, 2018).

Lynch, Deidre Shauna, *Loving Literature: A Cultural History* (Chicago: University of Chicago Press, 2015).

—, 'Transformations of the Novel – I', in *The Cambridge History of English Romantic Literature*, ed. James Chandler (Cambridge: Cambridge University Press, 2009), pp. 451–72.

McAllister, David, *Imagining the Dead in British Literature and Culture, 1790–1848* (Basingstoke: Palgrave Macmillan, 2018).

McCann, Andrew, *Cultural Politics in the 1790s: Literature, Radicalism and the Public Sphere* (Basingstoke: Palgrave, 1999).

—, 'William Godwin and the Pathological Public Sphere: Theorizing Communicative Action in the 1790s', *Prose Studies* 18.3 (1995): 199–222.

McCracken, David, 'Godwin's Literary Theory: The Alliance between Fiction and Political Philosophy', *Philological Quarterly* 49.1 (1970): 113–33.

McDowell, Paula, *The Invention of the Oral: Print Commerce and Fugitive Voices in Eighteenth-Century Britain* (Chicago: Chicago University Press, 2017).

—, 'Towards a Genealogy of "Print Culture" and "Oral Tradition"', in *The Broadview Reader in Book History*, ed. Michelle Levy and Tom Mole (Peterborough, ON: Broadview, 2015), pp. 395–415.

McGann, Jerome, *The Romantic Ideology: A Critical Investigation* (Chicago: Chicago University Press, 1985).

McGowen, Randall, 'The Image of Justice and Reform of the Criminal Law in Early Nineteenth-Century England', *Buffalo Law Review* 32 (1983): 89–125.

McKitterick, David, 'Introduction', *The Cambridge History of the Book in Britain: Vol VI, 1830–1914*, ed. David McKitterick (Cambridge: Cambridge University Press, 2010), pp. 1–74.

McLachlan, H., *English Education Under the Test Acts: Being the History of the Non-Conformist Academies 1662–1820* (Manchester: Manchester University Press, 1931).

McLane, Maureen N., *Balladeering, Minstrelsy, and the Making of British Romantic Poetry* (Cambridge: Cambridge University Press, 2008).

Manguel, Alberto, *The Traveler, the Tower, and the Worm: The Reader as Metaphor* (Philadelphia: University of Pennsylvania Press, 2013).

Maniquis, Robert and Victoria Myers (eds), *Godwinian Moments: From the Enlightenment to Romanticism* (Toronto: University of Toronto Press, 2011).

Manly, Susan, 'William Godwin's "School of Morality"', *The Wordsworth Circle* 43.3 (2012): 135–42.

Manning, Susan, 'Antiquarianism, Balladry and the Rehabilitation of Romance', in *The Cambridge History of English Romantic Literature*, ed. James Chandler (Cambridge: Cambridge University Press, 2009), pp. 45–70.

Marshall, Peter H., *William Godwin* (New Haven: Yale University Press, 1984).

Mee, John, *Conversable Worlds: Literature, Contention, and Community, 1762 to 1830* (Oxford: Oxford University Press, 2011).

—, '"The Press and Danger of the Crowd": Godwin, Thelwall, and the Counter-Public Sphere', in Maniquis, Robert, and Victoria Myers, eds., *Godwinian Moments: From the Enlightenment to Romanticism* (Toronto: University of Toronto Press, 2011), pp. 83–102.

—, *Print, Publicity and Radicalism in the 1790s: The Laurel of Liberty* (Cambridge: Cambridge University Press, 2016).

Miller, Peter N., '"Free Thinking" and "Freedom of Thought" in Eighteenth-Century Britain', *The Historical Journal* 36.3 (1993): 599–617.

Milnes, Timothy, *The Truth About Romanticism: Pragmatism and Idealism in Keats, Shelley, Coleridge* (Cambridge: Cambridge University Press, 2010).

—, 'Trusting Experiments: Sociability and Transcendence in the Familiar Essay', *Romantic Circles: Praxis Series*, 2017, <https://www.rc.umd.edu/praxis/prose/praxis.2016.prose.milnes.html> (last accessed 24 May 2018).

Monro, D. H., *Godwin's Moral Philosophy: an Interpretation of William Godwin* (London: Oxford University Press, 1953).

Monsam, Angela, 'Biography as Autopsy in William Godwin's "Memoirs of the Author of A Vindication of the Rights of Woman"', *Eighteenth Century Fiction* 21.1 (2008): 109–30.

Munby, A. N. L. (ed.), *Sale Catalogues of Libraries of Eminent Persons*, 12 vols (London: Mansell with Sotheby Parke Bernet Publications, 1971–4).

Myers, Victoria, 'William Godwin and the "Ars Rhetorica"', *Studies in Romanticism* 41.3 (2002): 415–44.

Odell, D. W., 'The Argument of Young's "Conjectures on Original Composition"', *Studies in Philology* 78.1 (1981): 87–106.

O'Shaughnessy, David, *William Godwin and the Theatre* (London: Pickering & Chatto, 2010).

Packham, Catherine, *Eighteenth-Century Vitalism: Bodies, Culture, Politics* (Basingstoke: Palgrave Macmillan, 2012).

Parker, Fred, *Scepticism and Literature: An Essay on Pope, Hume, Sterne, and Johnson* (Oxford: Oxford University Press, 2003).

Parker, Irene, *Dissenting Academies in England: Their Rise and Progress and Their Place among the Educational Systems of the Country* (Cambridge: Cambridge University Press, 1914).

Pasanek, Brad, *Metaphors of Mind: an Eighteenth-Century Dictionary* (Baltimore: Johns Hopkins University Press, 2015).

Passmore, John, *The Perfectibility of Man*, 3rd edn (Indianapolis: Liberty Fund, 2000).

Paul, C. Kegan, *William Godwin: His Friends and Contemporaries*, 2 vols (Boston: Roberts Brothers, 1876).

Pearson, Jacqueline, *Women's Reading in Britain, 1750–1835: A Dangerous Recreation* (Cambridge: Cambridge University Press, 1999).

Phillips, Mark Salber, *Society and Sentiment: Genres of Historical Writing in Britain, 1740–1820* (Princeton: Princeton University Press, 2000).

Philp, Mark, *Godwin's Political Justice* (London: Duckworth, 1986).

—, 'Godwin, Thelwall, and the Means of Progress', in *Godwinian Moments: From the Enlightenment to Romanticism*, ed. Robert Maniquis and Victoria Myers (Toronto: University of Toronto Press, 2011), pp. 59–82.

—, 'Godwin, William (1756–1836)', *Oxford Dictionary of National Biography* (Oxford University Press Online, 2004).

—, 'Rational Religion and Political Radicalism in the 1790's', *Enlightenment and Dissent* 4 (1985): 35–46.

—, *Reforming Ideas in Britain: Politics and Language in the Shadow of the French Revolution, 1789–1815* (Cambridge: Cambridge University Press, 2014).

Piper, Andrew, *Dreaming in Books: The Making of the Bibliographic Imagination in the Romantic Age* (Chicago: University of Chicago Press, 2009).

Pollin, Burton Ralph, *Education and Enlightenment in the Works of William Godwin* (New York: Las Americas, 1962).

Price, Leah, 'Reading: The State of the Discipline', *Book History* 7 (2004): 303–20.

Rajan, Tilottama, 'Framing the Corpus: Godwin's "Editing" of Wollstonecraft in 1798', *Studies in Romanticism* 39.4 (2000): 511–31.

—, *Romantic Narrative: Shelley, Hays, Godwin, Wollstonecraft* (Baltimore: Johns Hopkins University Press, 2010).

—, *The Supplement of Reading: Figures of Understanding in Romantic Theory and Practice* (Ithaca: Cornell University Press, 1990).

Raven, James, *The Business of Books: Booksellers and the English Book Trade, 1450–1850* (New Haven: Yale University Press, 2007).

Raven, James, Helen Small and Naomi Tadmor (eds), *The Practice and Representation of Reading in England* (Cambridge: Cambridge University Press, 1996).

Richardson, Alan, *British Romanticism and the Science of the Mind* (Cambridge: Cambridge University Press, 2001).

—, *Literature, Education and Romanticism: Reading as Social Practice, 1780–1832* (Cambridge: Cambridge University Press, 1994).

Rivers, Isabel (ed.), *Books and Their Readers in Eighteenth-Century England* (Leicester: Leicester University Press, 1982).

—, *The Defence of Truth through the Knowledge of Error: Philip Doddridge's Academy Lectures* (London: Dr Williams's Trust, 2003).

—, 'Doddridge, Philip (1702–1751)', *Oxford Dictionary of National Biography* (Oxford University Press Online, 2004).

—, *Reason, Grace, and Sentiment: A Study of the Language of Religion and Ethics in England, 1660–1780*, 2 vols (Cambridge: Cambridge University Press, 1991; 2000).

Rohrbach, Emily, *Modernity's Mist: British Romanticism and the Poetics of Anticipation* (New York: Forham University Press, 2016).

Rubery, Matthew, *The Novelty of Newspapers: Victorian Fiction after the Invention of the News* (Oxford: Oxford University Press, 2009).

Russell, Gillian and Clara Tuite (eds), *Romantic Sociability: Social Networks and Literary Culture in Britain, 1770–1840* (Cambridge: Cambridge University Press, 2002).

Ruston, Sharon, *Creating Romanticism: Case Studies in the Literature, Science and Medicine of the 1790s* (Basingstoke: Palgrave Macmillan, 2013).

Sachs, Jonathan, *The Poetics of Decline in British Romanticism* (Cambridge: Cambridge University Press, 2018).
—, *Romantic Antiquity: Rome in the British Imagination, 1789–1832* (Oxford: Oxford University Press, 2010).
St Clair, William, *The Godwins and the Shelleys: the Biography of a Family* (London: Faber, 1989).
—, *The Reading Nation in the Romantic Period* (Cambridge: Cambridge University Press, 2004).
—, 'William Godwin as Children's Bookseller', in *Children and Their Books: A Celebration of the Work of Iona and Peter Opie*, ed. Gillian Avery and Julia Briggs (Oxford: Clarendon, 1989), pp. 165–79.
Sambrook, James, *The Eighteenth Century: The Intellectual and Cultural Context of English Literature, 1700–1789* (London: Longman, 1986).
Schofield, Robert E., *Mechanism and Materialism: British Natural Philosophy in an Age of Reason* (Princeton: Princeton University Press, 1970).
Sell, Alan P. F., *Philosophy, Dissent and Nonconformity, 1689–1920* (Cambridge: James Clarke, 2004).
Siskin, Clifford, *The Work of Writing: Literature and Social Change in Britain, 1700–1830* (Baltimore: Johns Hopkins University Press, 1998).
Siskin, Clifford and William Warner (eds), *This Is Enlightenment* (Chicago: University of Chicago Press, 2010).
Solomonescu, Yasmin, *John Thelwall and the Materialist Imagination* (Basingstoke: Palgrave Macmillan, 2014).
Spadafora, David, *The Idea of Progress in Eighteenth-Century Britain* (New Haven: Yale University Press, 1990).
Suarez, Michael F., 'Introduction', *The Cambridge History of the Book in Britain: Vol V, 1695–1830*, ed. Michael F. Suarez and Michael F. Turner (Cambridge: Cambridge University Press, 2009), pp. 1–35.
Sullivan, Garrett A., '"A Story to Be Hastily Gobbled Up": "Caleb Williams" and Print Culture', *Studies in Romanticism* 32 (1993): 323–37.
Sweet, Rosemary, *Antiquaries: the Discovery of the Past in Eighteenth-Century Britain* (London: Hambledon and London, 2003).
Taylor, Barbara, *Mary Wollstonecraft and the Feminist Imagination* (Cambridge: Cambridge University Press, 2003).
Thomas, D. O., *The Honest Mind: the Thought and Work of Richard Price* (Oxford: Clarendon Press, 1977).
Thompson, Jon W., 'Personal and Bodily Identity: The Metaphysics of Resurrection in 17th Century Philosophy', PhD thesis (Kings College London, 2019).
Todd, Janet, *Sensibility: An Introduction* (London: Methuen, 1986).
Trumpener, Katie, *Bardic Nationalism: the Romantic Novel and the British Empire* (Princeton: Princeton University Press, 1997).

Turner, Mark, 'Periodical Time in the Nineteenth Century', *Media History* 8.2 (2002): 183–96.
—, 'Time, Periodicals, and Literary Studies', *Victorian Periodicals Review* 39.4 (2006): 309–16.
Tyson, Nancy Jane, *Eugene Aram: Literary History and Typology of the Scholar-Criminal* (Hamden, CT: Archon Books, 1983).
Valdez, Jessica, *Plotting the News in the Victorian Novel* (Edinburgh: Edinburgh University Press, 2020).
Valenza, Robin, *Literature, Language, and the Rise of the Intellectual Disciplines in Britain, 1680–1820* (Cambridge: Cambridge University Press, 2009).
Van Sant, Ann Jessie, *Eighteenth-Century Sensibility and the Novel: The Senses in Social Context* (Cambridge: Cambridge University Press, 1993).
Vincent, David, *Literacy and Popular Culture* (Cambridge: Cambridge University Press, 1993).
Warner, William, *Licensing Entertainment: the Elevation of Novel Reading in Britain, 1684–1750* (Berkeley: University of California Press, 1998).
Watts, Michael R., *The Dissenters: Vol. 1: From the Reformation to the French Revolution* (Oxford: Clarendon, 1978).
—, *The Dissenters: Vol. 2: The Expansion of Evangelical Nonconformity* (Oxford: Oxford University Press, 1995).
Weston, Rowland, 'History, Memory, and Moral Knowledge: William Godwin's "Essay on Sepulchres"', *The European Legacy* 14.6 (2009): 651–65.
Westover, Paul, *Necromanticism: Traveling to Meet the Dead, 1750–1860* (Basingstoke: Palgrave Macmillan, 2012).
—, 'William Godwin, Literary Tourism, and the Work of Necromanticism', *Studies in Romanticism* 48.2 (2009): 299–319.
Whale, John, *Imagination Under Pressure, 1789–1832: Aesthetics, Politics and Utility* (Cambridge: Cambridge University Press, 2000).
White, Daniel E., *Early Romanticism and Religious Dissent* (Cambridge: Cambridge University Press, 2006).
Whitehouse, Tessa, *The Textual Culture of English Protestant Dissent, 1720–1800* (Oxford: Oxford University Press, 2015).
Willey, Basil, *The Eighteenth Century Background: Studies on the Idea of Nature in the Thought of the Period* (London: Chatto & Windus, 1940).
Yarrington, Alison, 'Nelson the Citizen Hero: State and Public Patronage of Monumental Sculpture 1805–18', *Art History* 6.3 (September 1983): 315–29.
Yolton, John W., *Thinking Matter: Materialism in Eighteenth-Century Britain* (Oxford: Blackwell, 1983).

Index

Addison, Joseph, 127
affections, 62, 152, 159, 164, 172
animal vitality, 32
antiquarianism, 153–4
Aram, Eugene, 73
Aristotle, 65
attachment *see* affections
Austen, Jane, 37, 79

Bacon, Sir Francis, 128
Barbauld, Anna, 16, 60, 68
Bentley, Richard, 64, 68
Bible, 101–2
bibliomania, 4
biography, 149, 150–7, 172
Blackstone, Sir William, 71
book
  as medium, 17–18, 120–43, 148–76
  production, 15, 154–6
  trade, 3–4, 15, 63–4, 149, 154–5, 157, 167
  see also reading
Brooks, Marilyn, 50
Browne, Sir Thomas, 18, 149, 164–6
Bulwer-Lytton, Edward, 64, 73
Bunyan, John, 111
Burke, Edmund, 11, 95, 139, 161, 170

candour, 67, 129, 137
capital punishment, 72

Carlisle, Anthony, 33
Carlson, Julie, 157
Carlyle, Thomas, 6, 133, 176
causation, 29–32, 35
censorship, 97, 130, 134–5, 166
Chaucer, Geoffrey, 152–7
childhood, 85–6, 97–8, 102–3
Clemit, Pamela, 46
Colburn, Henry, 64, 68
Coleridge, Samuel Taylor, 64, 141, 167
commerce, intellectual, 126–9
commonplace books, 93
communications technology *see* media technology
Condorcet, 13, 172–3
confession, 45, 67–8, 75–6, 111
Connell, Philip, 161
Constant, Benjamin, 131
conversation, 100, 120–30, 132, 133, 136–8, 169–70
criminal justice, 16, 69–78
Cudworth, Ralph, 28

death, 18, 148–76
Defoe, Daniel, 45, 64, 76
determinism *see* necessity
discipline, 16–17, 84–112, 123
dissent, religious, 5, 8–9, 13, 15–16, 59, 66, 67–8, 84–112, 121, 129, 136–9, 167

dissenting academies, 67, 87–8, 136, 171
Ditton, Humphrey, 28
Doddridge, Philip, 16, 84, 87, 88–91, 92, 94–5, 96, 107, 108, 110, 136
drama, 67, 100, 104
Duff, William, 102–3

Edgeworth, Maria, 98
education, 16–17, 84–112, 125, 134
empiricism, 30, 32, 34–5, 141
  figurative, 34–6, 45–6
ephemeral print, 130–1; see also newspapers
epistemology, 17, 28, 84–5, 127, 138–9, 159
epistolary communication, 131–2
epistolary fiction, 45, 50, 76
essay form, 86–7
Esterhammer, Angela, 120
ethics, 16, 60–80, 100, 129, 151

Ferris, Ina, 3, 60, 68
figuration, 35
Foxe's Book of Martyrs, 42–3
'free enquiry', 87–9, 94, 102, 136–7
freedom, 85, 94
French Revolution, 12

Gagging Acts, 97, 134–5
gender convention, 48, 51, 76, 152
Gerrald, Joseph, 59, 69
Gigante, Denise, 93
Godwin, William
  diary, 105, 108
  letters, 15, 60, 86, 154–6, 163, 174; see also epistolary communication

WORKS
'Account of the Seminary That Will Be Opened [. . .] at Epsom', 96
Cloudesley: A Tale, 16, 64–7, 69, 74
'Considerations on Lord Grenville's and Mr Pitt's Bills', 12, 97, 123, 134–6
Deloraine, 16, 59–60, 69–80, 99
Enquiry Concerning Political Justice, 9, 10, 14, 15, 17, 27–36, 38, 39, 59, 62, 72–4, 97, 111, 119–25, 127, 129, 130, 135, 140–1, 142, 143, 158, 161, 172
'Essay on Sepulchres', 18, 148–9, 157–68, 171–3, 175
Fleetwood: or, The New Man of Feeling, 16, 41, 58–9, 66, 68–9, 75, 79, 133–4
'Letter of Advice to a Young American', 86, 100–1, 106
Life of Geoffrey Chaucer, 133, 152–7, 172
Mandeville: A Tale of the Seventeenth Century in England, 15, 41–7, 76, 101, 164
Memoirs of the Author of A Vindication of the Rights of Woman, 14, 151–3, 164, 172
'Of History and Romance', 61–4, 69, 74, 151, 154
Of Population, 12, 158
'Of Religion', 101, 166
'Of Scepticism', 9, 140
'Of the Length of the Life of Man', 15
'Reply to the Attacks of Dr. Parr', 10, 12, 62, 158
St Leon: A Tale of the Sixteenth Century, 41, 46, 62, 99, 164

Sketches of History in Six Sermons, 62
The Enquirer, 1, 17, 38, 61, 85–7, 96–100, 102–6, 109, 120, 124–5, 126, 127, 128
The Genius of Christianity Unveiled, 2, 14, 166
The Herald of Literature, 14
Things As They Are; or, The Adventures of Caleb Williams, 14, 15, 37–41, 45–7, 49, 50, 58, 59, 60, 66, 69, 74, 76, 77, 78, 120, 131, 136, 164
Thoughts on Man, His Nature, Productions, and Discoveries, 2, 10, 13, 17, 36–7, 86, 103–4, 106–7, 109–11, 120, 125–7, 142–3, 149–50, 173–5
'Untitled [Essay on Death]', 18, 149, 168–73
Goldstein, Amanda, 35
Goodman, Kevis, 5
Gothic fiction, 41, 45, 75
government *see* institutions
gradualism, 12, 134–6, 143
Guillroy, John, 5

Hardy, Thomas, 48
Hartley, David, 33
Hays, Mary, 16, 48–52
Hazlitt, William, 9, 16, 60, 68, 162
Helvétius, Claude Adrien, 33–4
historiography, 10, 61–3, 65, 153–4
Holcroft, Thomas, 48, 52, 67, 73, 157
Horne Tooke, John, 137
Hoxton Academy, 8, 34, 61, 87, 95–6

Hume, David, 16, 17, 26, 31–2, 34–6, 121, 127, 128
Hunt, Leigh, 161

imagination, 13, 31, 37, 99, 120, 129, 142, 160
Inchbald, Elizabeth, 48, 51, 64
institutions, 27, 97, 129–30
Israel, Jonathan, 7

'Jacobin' writers, 16, 48, 52, 73
Jennings, John, 16, 84, 87, 88–9, 91, 136
Jewsbury, Maria Jane, 4
Johns, Adrian, 6, 84, 150
Johnson, Joseph, 47, 157
Johnson, Samuel, 17, 95, 121, 128, 134
journalism, 69, 74; *see also* newspapers
Juvenile Library, 15, 86

Kant, Immanuel, 31
Keats, John, 141
Kippis, Andrew, 95
Klancher, Jon, 45

Lackington, James, 48
language, 5, 96, 102, 131, 137
law, 72–3; *see also* criminal justice
leisure, 104
Lennox, Charlotte, 37
letters *see* epistolary communication
libraries, 4, 89, 132–4, 168
literacy, 3, 4
Locke, John, 16, 25, 26, 32, 34, 86
London Corresponding Society, 39–40, 59, 123, 139
Lupton, Christina, 3, 120
Lynch, Diedre, 75

McDowell, Paula, 3
Mackenzie, Henry, 64
Malthus, Thomas Robert, 6, 12, 18, 149, 158, 168, 173
Martin, Marmaduke, 86, 109
materialism, 16, 25–52, 159
media consciousness, 3
media history, 6, 13, 18, 150, 172–3
media technology, 2–3, 18, 119–43
mediation, 5, 11, 79, 119–43
Mee, Jon, 129
Mettrie, Julien Offray de La, 29
Mill, J. S., 176
millenarianism, 5, 13, 28
Milnes, Timothy, 141
Milton, John, 13, 89, 97, 100, 124, 156, 161, 166–7, 168
mind, 10, 16, 29–37, 60–1, 66–7, 73–4, 84–5, 87, 90, 95, 111, 150–1, 153, 157–9; *see also* private judgement; thought

Napoleonic Wars, 148, 154, 161–2
narration, 45–6, 66, 75–8
nationhood, 161–2
necessity, 28–31, 40–4, 48–51
Newgate novels, 72, 74
newspapers, 74–5, 78, 130–1
Newton, Isaac, 32
Nicholson, William, 33
novel form, 2, 16, 52, 58–80

orality, 3, 4, 123, 125–6, 130, 135, 139; *see also* conversation
'original genius', 102–3
Orton, Job, 90

Paine, Thomas, 12, 157
Palmer, Samuel, 89
Parker, Fred, 127
Pasanek, Brad, 34

Peel, Sir Robert, 72
Percy, Thomas, 154
perfectibility, 8–15, 18, 45, 63–4, 66–7, 72–3, 79, 128, 137, 140, 148–76
Phillips, Richard, 154–7, 163, 174
philosophes, 29, 33
Piper, Andrew, 7, 150
Place, Francis, 48
Planta, Joseph, 132
Price, Leah, 18
Price, Richard, 88, 94, 95, 96, 105
Priestley, Joseph, 16, 26, 33, 98, 99, 137
printing press, 4, 13, 14, 135, 172–3, 176
private judgement, 9, 10–11, 16, 25–52, 60, 67–8, 72, 76, 88, 92, 96, 100, 102, 108
progressivism, 2, 6, 13, 18, 28, 64, 96, 120, 142, 148–76, 166, 175; *see also* perfectibility

quixotism, 37, 38, 47

Radcliffe, Ann, 45, 64
radicalism, 120, 121, 123–4, 134–5, 139–40
rational dissent *see* dissent, religious
reading
　advice, 4, 16–17, 84–112, 129
　eating metaphor, 58–9, 92–3, 105–6
　practice, 4, 52, 58–9, 79, 84–112, 175
Reeve, Clara, 58
reform, 10–11, 16, 39–40, 44, 47–52, 59–61, 67, 97, 121, 123, 134–5, 139–41, 143, 150–2, 157, 164, 175

Reid, Thomas, 28
republicanism, 40, 129, 161
resurrection, 18, 153, 164–6
Ritson, Joseph, 154
Rivers, Isabel, 89, 101

Sachs, Jonathan, 48, 52, 107, 149
Sandemanianism, 88
Savage, Samuel Morton, 95
scepticism, 9, 35, 101, 127
Scott, Sir Walter, 64, 79, 153–4
sensibility, 59, 67
sentiment, 9, 59, 61–3, 134, 160
Shakespeare, William, 81n, 161
Shelley, Mary, 75, 164
Shelley, Percy Bysshe, 44, 84, 86, 100–1, 109, 141
Siskin, Clifford and William Warner, 4
Smith, Adam, 61
Smith, Charlotte, 67
social class, 47, 51, 162
Solomonescu, Yasmin, 31
Southey, Robert, 159
stadial history, 6, 14, 28; *see also* progressivism
Standard Novels series, 64, 68
Stewart, Dugald, 14, 18, 142, 149, 172–3
Swift, Jonathan, 167–8
sympathy, 61, 99–100, 129–30, 151

Taylor, Barbara, 27
temporality, 6, 77, 103–4, 107, 120–43, 148–50, 172–6

theatre *see* drama
Thelwall, John, 17, 33, 40, 48, 119, 121, 135
Thompson, Jon W., 165
Thomson, James, 100
thought, 15–16, 26–37, 159–60; *see also* mind
Todd, Janet, 62
Trumpener, Katie, 60
truth, 11, 17, 35, 119–21, 125, 134–43, 167, 175
Turner, Mark, 130–1

Valenza, Robin, 127

Warner, William, 60; *see also* Siskin, Clifford and William Warner
Watts, Isaac, 16, 17, 25, 84, 86, 87, 91–5, 96, 101, 102, 104, 105, 107–8, 109, 110–11, 121, 137–8
Wedgwood, Thomas, 131–2
Wesley, John, 89–90
Weston, Rowland, 62
White, Daniel, 62
Whitehouse, Tessa, 88
Wollstonecroft, Mary, 13, 27, 48, 51–2, 164, 172
women's education, 51–2
Wordsworth, William, 64, 159

Yolton, John, 29
Young, Edward, 55n, 102

EU representative:
Easy Access System Europe
Mustamäe tee 50, 10621 Tallinn, Estonia
Gpsr.requests@easproject.com

www.ingramcontent.com/pod-product-compliance
Lightning Source LLC
Chambersburg PA
CBHW070816250426
43671CB00037B/2517